The Many Ways
Jews Loved

ALSO BY CONSTANCE HARRIS

The Way Jews Lived: Five Hundred Years of Printed Words and Images (McFarland, 2009)

Portraiture in Prints (McFarland, 1987)

The Many Ways Jews Loved

A History from Printed Words and Images

CONSTANCE HARRIS

Foreword by TODD M. ENDELMAN

McFarland & Company, Inc., Publishers
Jefferson, North Carolina

All images unless otherwise credited are taken from public domain sources.

Library of Congress Cataloguing-in-Publication Data

Names: Harris, Constance, author.
Title: The many ways Jews loved : a history from printed words and images / Constance Harris ; foreword by Todd M. Edelman.
Description: Jefferson, North Carolina : McFarland & Company, Inc. Publishers, 2020. | Includes bibliographical references and index.
Identifiers: LCCN 2020019140 | ISBN 9781476678184 (paperback : acid free paper) ∞
ISBN 9781476638218 (ebook)
Subjects: LCSH: Love in literature. | Jewish literature—History and criticism. | Rabbinical literature—History and criticism.
Classification: LCC PN842 .H37 2020 | DDC 809/.88924—dc23
LC record available at https://lccn.loc.gov/2020019140

British Library cataloguing data are available
ISBN (print) 978-1-4766-7818-4
ISBN (ebook) 978-1-4766-3821-8

© 2020 Constance Harris. All rights reserved

No part of this book may be reproduced or transmitted in any form or by any means, electronic or mechanical, including photocopying or recording, or by any information storage and retrieval system, without permission in writing from the publisher.

Front cover images © 2020 Shutterstock

Printed in the United States of America

*McFarland & Company, Inc., Publishers
Box 611, Jefferson, North Carolina 28640
www.mcfarlandpub.com*

To Ruth and Steve,
for your unbounded love

Acknowledgments

Books don't get written by themselves or by a single author. Especially this one, which is a collective enterprise and a gift of friendship. In gratitude and pleasure, I am happy to share complicity with the following individuals who gave generously of their time and efforts: Rabbi-Dr. Louis Finkelman of Michigan, who was my first redactor; Ken Blady, for his indefatigable editing and rare scholarship; Martha Conway, Director of Special Collections Research Center at the University of Michigan Library, who graciously provided access to the Judaic material under her supervision; Elliot Gertel, the Irving M. Hermelin Curator of Judaica and Senior Associate Librarian at the Frankel Center for Judaic Studies; William Gosling, University of Michigan Librarian Emeritus; Stephen Harris, infinitely patient computer maven; Judaica book dealer Eric Chaim Klein, for providing fascinating books; Rabbi Jay LeVine, my Midrash "*rebbe*" at Temple Isaiah in Lafayette, California; Melissa Levine, Director, Copyright Officer at the University of Michigan Library; Dr. Deborah Lipstadt, Dorot Professor of Modern Jewish History and Holocaust Studies at Emory University in Georgia; Howard Lupovitch, Associate Professor of History and Director of the Cohn-Haddow Center for Judaic Studies at Wayne State University, Detroit; Peter Rosmarin, who polished the manuscript. I am especially grateful to Dr. Todd Endelmann, William Haber Professor of Modern Jewish History at the University of Michigan, who graciously wrote the Foreword.

I am very grateful to my editor at McFarland, David Alff, who produced the book in your hand.

Table of Contents

Acknowledgments — vi
Foreword by Todd M. Endelman — 1
Introduction — 3

Part I—The Way Jews Loved Each Other

1. Overview Over Time — 6
2. Marriage: Good, Better and Not So Good — 18
3. The Bible In and Out of Love — 32
4. The Family: More Questions Than Answers — 52
5. The Golden Middle Ages — 71
6. Midrash and Magic — 81
7. The Many Languages of Love — 93
8. Age of Reason—Challenge of Tradition — 104
9. Chasing Modernity — 119
10. Tracing Modernity — 132
11. How God Coped with Sex — 150

Part II—The Way Jews Loved Tradition

12. Essen un Fressen — 164
13. Artisanship and Crafts — 179
14. Laughing at Love — 193

Glossary — 201
Selected Bibliography — 203
Index — 205

Foreword
by Todd M. Endelman

The most important Jewish historian of the twentieth century, Salo W. Baron, described the work of the most important Jewish historian of the nineteenth century, Heinrich Graetz, as a history of suffering and scholarship (*Leidens-und Gelehrten-geschichte*). By this, Baron meant that Graetz saw the history of the Jewish people as primarily a history of the persecutions they had endured and of the books their intellectual elite had written. Baron believed that the stage of Jewish history was much broader and that Graetz's emphases distorted its richness and complexity. In the last half-century, academic Jewish historians have overwhelmingly endorsed Baron's critique of Graetz. Although some continue to conflate the history of Jewish thought with the history of the Jewish people, few reduce the sweep of Jewish history to a seemingly unbroken chain of expulsions, massacres, confiscations, and the like. Outside the academy, however, Graetz's belief in the centrality of suffering in Jewish history is alive and well. Both the undergraduates whom I have taught and the adults to whom I have lectured unthinkingly accept Graetz's lachrymose view of the Jewish past (even if they have never heard of Graetz). It is firmly embedded in the way they imagine and recall the history of their people. The horror of the Holocaust and its preeminent place in Jewish consciousness and political discourse since the 1970s have cemented the hold of this lachrymose view.

Constance Harris's approach to the history of Jewish culture and civilization breaks with this conventional outlook. While not denying the reality of persecution, her newest book shows that the Jewish past is much more than a record of scholarship and victimhood. In her reading of the past, Jews were flesh-and-blood human beings who experienced both pain and pleasure. Theirs was a world that was more complex and richer in emotional experiences than popularly believed. She reminds us that, like their neighbors, they loved and lusted as well as studied Torah—and that they continue to do so today. (If they had not, after all, they would have disappeared long ago.) Her wide-ranging survey of the ways Jews loved moves back and forth through the centuries. It brings into view biblical and rabbinic stories about sexual attraction and the threats that such attraction can at times pose. It reviews how Jewish law functions both to encourage and to regulate sexual interaction. It includes generous selections from the frankly sensuous love poetry of medieval Spanish Jewry, including passages whose occasional homoeroticism is striking. She even follows the encounter between Jewish humor and Jewish sexuality.

What emerges from Harris's study is the diversity of Jewish attitudes towards love and sexuality. What was acceptable in medieval Spain is not acceptable in the ultra-Orthodox enclaves of modern Brooklyn. If so, which is the more authentic Judaism? Which Judaism has remained truer or closer to the eternal truths of Torah? The mix of sources on which Harris draws suggests the inappropriateness of this question. Different communities at different times have each crafted their own distinctive outlook. Those writers and speakers who claim that their version of Judaism is timeless, unchanging, and impervious to outside influence might want to rethink their assumption after considering the various ways in which Jews thought about love and sexuality over the centuries. From this perspective, it is ironic that the attitudes of the contemporary ultra–Orthodox (the *Haredim*) toward sexuality and the relations between men and women more closely resemble those of fundamentalist Christians than they do of Jews from earlier periods in Jewish history. Still, as Harris emphasizes, there seems to have been one thread in Jewish thinking that remained constant almost everywhere and at all times. Unlike Christianity, Judaism never celebrated celibacy. It always recognized the reality and the power of the sexual drive. Rather than trying to ignore or suppress it, Judaism sought to incorporate its expression into a divinely sanctioned legal system (*halakhah*). It accepted what was, in effect, impossible to deny—try as some religious systems did. It sanctified and harnessed (or civilized) sexuality—an approach that Sigmund Freud would certainly have endorsed.

This book is not, I should point out, didactic or cautionary in nature. It does not endorse one outlook on sexuality or another. Nor does it make the claim that one century's view of correct sexual behavior represents a more "authentic" Jewish position (pun intended) than another's. It is open-minded and exploratory in character. Above all, it seeks to acquaint readers with the abundance and multiplicity of texts that speak to the omnipresence of love and sexuality in Jewish history.

—Todd M. Endelman

Todd M. Endelman is professor emeritus of history and Judaic studies at the University of Michigan. His specialty is the history of British Jews in the modern period and what it has in common with other Western Jewish communities.

Introduction

"Steve, I've finished the book *The Way Jews Lived*. What can I do with the rest of my life?"
"Write another book."

Well, this book is different. It is not about conventional Jewish history or traditional "truths." It does not attempt to "prove" or "disprove" the psychological or religious foundations of human relationships. It does not argue whether the Scriptures are an eternal covenant between God and the Hebrew people or a compilation of mythical legends. It does not ask if the universally worshipped God is real or a cognitive aberration, nor does it address the issue of a perfect God in an imperfect world.

Many questions are proposed; few answers are certain. Do the ancient rabbinical texts justify the idea of God's love for a small class of chosen people, as many stories and poems suggest? Do these narratives convey standards of morality that are no longer normative or relevant? Does love derive from God's benevolence, or is it controlled by heightened emotions and needs? Does God's love create blessing and veneration or chaos and confusion? We are meant to love, but not to understand. There are other questions:

What is love between Man and Man? The great Jewish songwriters thought they knew: Irving Berlin asked, "How deep is the ocean? How high is the sky?" Yip Harburg suggested that love wants to "croon" and "laugh like a loon" with "that old devil moon in your eyes." But those are not the ways most Jews loved. They loved with passion and conflict; sometimes they loved with tenderness and caring (or didn't).

What is love between Man and God? The great Jewish prophets thought they knew: Man's first priority is God, to be loved with all his being. Is that it? Do the ancient rabbinical texts warrant nothing else? We shall see.

The limited objective of this work is to explore the distinctive ways in which Jews connected with God, broke with one another, or pursued what passed for loving-kindness as they chased the blurred subjects of love and happiness. It asks whether sacred and secular topics involve single or multiple layers of meaning and why they often appear to defy interpretation. It roams through the magical filter of Biblical tales, classical *Midrashim*, and borrowed superstitions and objects. (Italicized words are defined in the glossary.) It connects the utopian past to the familiar present in life-cycle events, as Jews celebrated festivity, drowned care, faced mortality, explored sex, polished off shocking novels, ate humble and exotic foods, laughed at jokes when there was little else to laugh at, and patiently dealt with the slings and arrows of disorder. Bundled into a multinational potpourri of fun and friction, fantasy and fright, these stories reflect the harmony or alienation between Jews whose eccentricities, strengths, and imperfections are still sources of interest and entertainment. Over time and place, their lives and lore—traced through historical artistic and literary images, social satire, and native wit—filled the gaps between the seen and unknown, between giving and receiving, between meaning and mission, between daylight and dream. Their prejudices or judgments guided and regulated much of their behavior or misbehavior in the endless kaleidoscope of contention and love between Man and Man, and Man and God.

It is at this point that our narrative begins, with each entry recalling a moment in the way Jews loved.

The book is divided into two parts: Part I discusses the many way Jews loved each other (or didn't); Part II discusses the way Jews love their traditions, including Jewish food, artifacts and humor.

Part I

The Many Ways Jews Loved Each Other

1

Overview Over Time

Love, they say, makes the world go 'round. Freely given or withheld, love has been analyzed and illustrated as drama and mystery by skilled artisans and wordsmiths of every race and nationality. Its bickerings and brokerings, successes and failures, have been diagnosed by the world's earliest known creators and storytellers. But they were not the first.

God was the first.

Genesis tells us that at the beginning of time God formed man after His own likeness, extracting from the void a wide range of emotions—zeal, anger, regret, and love. Unseen but known, He emerges from the Torah as a distinct personality with human strengths and weaknesses, sometimes good, sometimes not so good. He is candidly proud: "I form the light and create darkness. I make peace and create evil. I, the Lord, do all these things" (Isaiah 45:7). He is stern as well as indulgent: "I will be generous to whom I will be generous, giving man the option to choose love over hostility" (Proverbs 16:16). "I will be gracious to whom I will be gracious, I will have compassion to whom I will have compassion" (Exodus 33:19). Above all, He is needy: He wants to be loved and feared with all of man's heart and soul, rewarding devotion with length of days (Deuteronomy 6:5; 10:12).

Fundamental to His being is His uniqueness (Deuteronomy 6:4). (Yet, what can we make of Genesis 1–26: Let *Us* make man?) Never before did any cult or religion insist that man submit to a single ethical god, second to none. Never before had an all-powerful God demanded that mankind do His will—to "know" as well as to love Him (Exodus 20–23). But although underived and undivided, He was aware that love could not be commanded. He tried to earn it by offering man a garden in which to dwell in beauty, a wife to bring him joy and companionship, descendants to be a light among nations. He promised eternal life, although He warned that disobedience would bring retribution and penalty (Deuteronomy 28:15–68; 32:35).

By and large, His conditions were not heeded. What He demanded was too hard, too abstract, and too ambiguous for His simple creatures to translate into action. The best they could do over time was to rely on His goodness with resolution and uncertainty. Through *tikkun olam,* they would forge a model society with good deeds and loving relationships. And while they strove to love God, they trusted that they, too, were worthy of merit and approbation.

Through *hiddur mitzvah,* they expressed their love in aesthetic forms that glorified their Maker by embellishing His ritual objects with spiritual content (Exodus 15:2). Jews were, however, relative latecomers to artisanship: the Second Commandment, banning the making or reverencing of graven images, precluded pictorial likenesses. It has been assumed that fear of paganism, as expressed in idol worship, was its motive rather than any intrinsic objection to esthetic works (Exodus 20:4–5; Deuteronomy 5:8). Qualms that pagan beauty would supplant Biblical purity were real; the power of images was believed to suppress the voice of God. Artistic development was further curtailed because, as an adjunct to the permissible pleasures of life, the emphasis on man's creation of the perishable undermined and demeaned God's creation of the eternal. However, it was largely through visual forms—together with the legends, myths, and fables that tied love to daily living—that many Jews first became familiar with and devoted to the traditions, languages, and cultures expressed in the Bible. Certainly, this brief overview of their social and political histories, along with significant bits and pieces of their lifestyles and interests, cannot adequately evoke the drama, achievements, and tragedies of Jewish memory. But we will try.

Our narrative begins, recalling the ways Jews loved—or were loved.

Or didn't.

Or weren't.

As credible theology or as religious narrative, the Bible represents God's law to Moses, and, through later regulations and commentaries, connects morality to divinity (Leviticus 19). But it is more than dogma: it is literature, the history of the Jewish people. It introduces a wide variety of players; from the humblest to the most arrogant, its diverse cast has hardly been superseded. As an account of the world's first lovers, it declares that Adam and Eve shared a sexual relationship (and perhaps an emotional attachment), made free choices, and learned that they were responsible for their actions. As a code of civil and spiritual ideals, it affects and influences much of humankind's behavior. As a psychological tool, it deals with people's imperfections, sufferings, and successes. As a testament of God's infinite patience with their transgressions, it chronicles Him as distressed but steadfast. As the record of His personal love for any of His human partners, the Bible is strangely silent.

Yet Jews believed that God cared, that humans count, that their record has ethical and historical integrity, and that it should be told in spite of inconsistencies and incompatibilities. They believed that God was ever-present with His people, appointing prophets to comfort them in times of trouble as well as to navigate questions of theology and morality. When relentlessly pursued or threatened with extinction, Jews turned for emotional support to the leaders who exhorted them to preserve their faith and lent authority to their rituals. They mourned with them during the destruction of the First Temple and the Babylonian exile (586 BCE). They celebrated when the Persian king, Cyrus the Great (c. 600–529 BCE), permitted their return to Jerusalem and the establishment of the Second Temple (538 BCE).

But neither the Holy City of Jerusalem nor the Holy Temple sufficed to turn the Jews away from the sophisticated Greek standards of life, language, and religion, and the peril of its blandishments. The Syrian-Greek King, Antiochus IV (215–164 BCE), may not have understood that pious Jews were prepared to lead rebellions under the leadership of Mattathias and his five sons. The revolt succeeded under one of the sons, Judah the Maccabee, who regained control of Jerusalem. The Temple was purified, restored to its pristine condition, and rededicated in 165 BCE. According to legend, a single surviving oil candle burned for eight days, a supernatural event commemorated yearly by lighting a nine-branched *menorah* on each of the succeeding nights of the Hanukkah festivities. Celebrants spin four-sided tops with the Hebrew acronym "a great miracle happened there" ("here" in Israel), sing "I have a little *dreidel*," gorge on *latkes* (Ashkenazim), or *sufganiyot* (Sephardim), deliver necessities for the poor, and give presents to children who already have more than they need and less than they want.

Three unsuccessful and disastrous wars between Romans and Jews resulted in the defeat of major Eastern Mediterranean Jewish populations. The first uprising lasted from 66 to 73 CE, during which the Roman general Titus (39–81 CE) conquered Jerusalem, demolished the Sanctuary and destroyed the stone Masada fortifications—symbol of the Jewish peoples' determination to be free in their own land. A monumental arch depicting the sack of Jerusalem, the capture of Jewish prisoners, and the Temple's *menorah* still stands in Rome. The second conflict, the Kitos War (115–117 CE), annihilated vast Jewish communities in Cyprus and Alexandria. Then there was the catastrophic uprising culminating in the defeat of the commander Simon Bar Kokhba (132–136 CE), which destroyed the last hope for Jewish autonomy in an independent state. Emperor Hadrian (117–138 CE) prohibited and then burned the Torah, raising a statue to Jupiter at the former Temple site.

The Emperor Constantine (272–337) converted his lands to Christianity following the Council of Nicaea in 332, strengthening the Roman Empire, but weakening the position of the Jews. Charlemagne the Great (742–814), and his son, Louis the Pious (778–840), protected Jews, treating them as useful and valuable citizens during the early medieval period. Some of the later popes were more or less humane. Gregory I (590–604) opposed violence, although he demanded conversion of Jews; Calixtus II (1119–1124) protected Jews from thefts of property and conversion pressures; Innocent III (1161–1216) compelled them to wear distinguishing badges.

Jews were used to debilitating restrictions. They had accommodated to them over long centuries, particularly in Central and Northern Italy. Venice was the first city in Europe to demand compulsory separation between Christian and Jew, the first city in Europe to establish a locked ghetto. In 1516, Pope Paul IV (1476–1559) decreed that "Jews must live together" behind bricked-up windows and high walls on a small island that had been the site of an old copper foundry. Two gates, each opened in the morning and closed at midnight, were monitored by Christians paid by Jews. Two boats patrolled the island at night to prevent inmates from swimming to shore.

Still, the Inquisition never took hold in Venice. In spite of crowded, inadequately ventilated, and filthy conditions, the ghetto promoted Jewish cultural life and the return of a stricter orthodoxy, minimizing the lure of conversion. Christians regularly came to the area to admire its five magnificent synagogues, to patronize Jewish banks, to consult Jewish doctors, and to shop for second-hand goods, spices, fabrics, and jewelry.

The Roman Catholic Church accused Jews (at least partially true) of encouraging the Protestant Reformation. It promised retribution—and it kept that promise in 1553 when Pope Paul announced that it "ill befits" him to suffer the calumnies of the Talmud: wagonloads of Jewish books went up in flames on the Sabbath day of Rosh Hashanah. Two years later, he unleashed his *Cum Nimis Absurdum*, ordaining that "it was absurd and utterly inconvenient to allow Jews, who through their own fault were condemned by God to eternal slavery..." to live among God-fearing Christians.

∽ ∽ ∽

Opposed and oppressed by rapacious monarchs in Poland and Hungary and ecclesiastics in England, France and the German principalities, Jews were chased from one hostile place to another, fleeing to lands where religious and economic restraints were less burdensome. When flight was not an option—in 1096 during the First Crusade's effort to

1. Overview Over Time

Enclosed in 1516, the first Jewish quarter in which Jews were forced to live in special and separate quarters. Postcard with a reproduction of artwork of the Venetian Ghetto. Etching, 1516. By D. Curiel (University of Michigan Library, Special Collections Research Center).

recover Jerusalem from the Muslims, or in 1298 during the Rindfleisch pogroms (the first large-scale persecution in Germany)—they endured slaughter and horrific violence. Yet, for a time in the early Middle Ages, when finance and trade encouraged interaction among Christians, Muslims, and Jews, all sides cultivated the Jewish traders and bankers whose mercantile expertise was a strong political asset in their favor. But when Western nations developed their own financial skills, Jews were no longer needed. Jewish debts were disowned, and the property of Jews was stolen. Some 16,000 Jewish Englishmen were expelled from their homes in 1290. France followed in 1306, closing down *yeshivot* and initiating massacres. In Germany, Jews were hounded with charges of host desecration, blood libels, and erotic lust for pigs and their excrement. When the mid-fourteenth-century Black Death plague destroyed a third of Europe's population, blame was laid upon the Jews, although few of them were spared in its path.

As Professor Salo Baron reminds us, however, not all of Jewish history is lachrymose. During the so-called Golden Age of Spain (950–1150), Jewish poets riotously shared their appetite for friendship, drinking, and idealized love. Solomon ben Isaac, known as Rashi (1040–1105), offered his *Commentary on the Tractates of the Babylonian Talmud,* the standard explanations and clear interpretations of rabbinic literature. Throughout Western Europe, Jewish doctors, translators, philosophers, financiers, historians, and dramatists, as well as highly respected rabbis, contributed to the intellectual and emotional climate. Moses Maimonides (1135–1204), in his *Guide for the Perplexed* (1190), attempted to reconcile rationalism and dogma but was unable to resolve the conflict between religious and secular life.

Observant rabbis opposed his ventures into speculative philosophy as much as some rigid Catholics did.

When Catholic homogeneity in Spain and Portugal was established in 1492 and 1497, Sephardi Jews were forced to choose between abandoning their heritage and exile from the countries in which they had lived for centuries. Some converted sincerely, some posed as *conversos* or New Christians, and some lived secretly as observant Jews in Holland and North Africa and Bordeaux, where they were permitted to settle (as Christians). The Inquisition emptied the Iberian Peninsula of a large number of its most valued merchants and scholars. Cut off from organized religious influences, most melted into the local culture and were lost to Judaism.

The good news was that during the fourteenth to seventeenth centuries of the Italian Renaissance, there was a serious reconsideration of Jewish studies and a revival of classical literature and art. Much of this was owed to the Medici popes who protected the Jewish community, respected its scholarship and social achievements, and encouraged its printing presses. Jews immediately became proficient in the new art of dissemination of information and misinformation while educating and entertaining themselves with published love stories, poetry, songs, and almost forgotten prayers.

In 1517, Martin Luther (1483–1546) and other radical anti–Catholic reformers splintered Western Christendom. Turning his attention to Jews three years later, Luther's *Sermon von dem Wucher (Sermon on Usury)* focused unpleasantly on money-lending Jews. He had originally opposed their persecution in his 1523 book, *Das Jesus Christus Ein Geborener Jud Sei (That Jesus Christ Was Born a Jew)*, hoping they would convert to the "true faith." They didn't. Twenty years later, bitterly disappointed by their intransigence, Luther published *Von den Juden und Iren Lugen (Concerning the Jews and Their Lies)*, a treatise in which he urged his followers to burn synagogues, homes, and cherished books. Many took the hint, producing salacious texts and images demeaning the Jewish experience, revealing how little they understood—or how much they intentionally misunderstood—Jewish values. Hitler later adopted Luther's writings to rationalize genocide.

Jewish values and existence were threatened again by the atrocities of Ukrainian and Southern Russian Cossacks and peasants led by Bogdan Chmielnicki (1648–1655). Impoverished Jews were persecuted for collecting—not imposing—taxes for absentee magnates who leased privileges to the Jewish managers of their estates. Survivors fled westward, eventually establishing thriving communities in Galician Poland, Hungary, Romania, Slovakia and Carpato-Rus. Expectations that either civilian or divine intervention would lead to the amelioration of their afflictions were sadly unrealistic.

Was it possible that a Jewish messiah or reformer would accelerate the process? The notion was seized upon by eager Jews who anxiously awaited a descendant of King David in the person of God's messenger. Messiahs had regularly appeared in Jewish history (the most famous being Jesus of Nazareth). The most notorious was Shabbtai Zvi (1626–1676), a 39-year-old mentally unstable "redeemer." He mobilized thousands of impassioned adherents from all classes of Jews who believed in his mission to bring about the millennium and liberate Jerusalem from Ottoman rule. Among his idiosyncrasies were unions with multiple young women, marriage to a prostitute named Sarah, and, reportedly, to a Torah scroll as well. His demand that Jews return to Palestine from all parts of the world led many idealistic and credulous Jews to abandon their businesses, trudge off to Jerusalem, acknowledge him as the messiah, and attempt to force the Ottoman sultan to abdicate in his favor. Instead, he was charged with treason and stowed in a commodious jail in Istanbul to consider his sins. Offered the choice between conversion and death, he opted for the former. The anguish that most Jewish communities experienced towards his defection accelerated Jewish apostasy as well as the formation of schismatic sects throughout Europe.

Dismayed by what he perceived as Jewish spiritual disintegration following the Shabbtai Zvi debacle, Israel ben Eliezer (1700–1760), known as *Baal Shem Tov (Master of the Good Name)*, launched the *Hasidic* movement whose disciples, however poor or ignorant, might achieve communion with God by fulfilling His commandments through mystic song, joyful prayer, and ecstatic practices. His opponents (*misnagdin*), under the leadership of Rabbi Elijah ben Shlomo Zalman, the Vilna Gaon (1720–1797), attacked Hasidism, believing that the sect was a threat to rabbinic power, among other means by de-emphasizing Talmudic learning, introducing innovations into the liturgy, reciting prayers after the designated hours, and ritually slaughtering animals with specially honed knives rather than with ordinary sharpened blades.

Existing differences or points of view led the way to the Jewish Enlightenment or *Haskalah*. The movement, which lasted from the mid-eighteenth century to the last quarter of the nineteenth century, advanced slowly but deliberately across Europe, adopting Western social, literary, and artistic conventions. A nationalistic, as well as a scientific, spirit attempted to reconcile rabbinic learning with modern ideals and diverse religious opinions while looking for rational proofs of God's existence and the immortality of the soul. Led by Moses Mendelssohn (1729–1786), who linked Judaism to humanistic or ethical values, the *maskilim*, or proponents of the *Haskalah*, were open to some renovation and change, as well as insisting upon intellectual autonomy and the separation of church and state. Scientific progress, they believed, would benefit not only the Jews but also the surrounding communities in which they lived and worked. Traditionalists argued that Mendelssohn had led to assimilation and secular culture, thereby losing much of Jewish identity. Fueled by the rise of political anti-Semitism in the 1880s, the Zionist movement began to displace the goals of *Haskalah* while searching for programs to strengthen Jewish solidarity and aspirations for a national Jewish homeland.

Shabbtai Tzvi (1626–1676), leader of the largest messianic movement in Jewish history in 1665. This is probably the only portrait done from life (Joods Historisch Museum, Amsterdam).

Leading the argument for modification of traditional expression, Rabbi Abraham Geiger (1810–1874) proposed to reform or reconstitute Judaism by offering a system to accord with current beliefs stripped of most ritual practices and perceived outmoded rituals but retaining basic social verities. Straddling both radical reformism and divine law, Rabbi Zacharias Frankel (1801–1875) posited Conservative Judaism, a compromise denomination embracing "the integrity of Judaism simultaneously with progress" driven by community choice but remaining traditionally observant. Rabbi Samson Raphael Hirsch (1808–1888) disagreed. In his view, only a Modern or Neo-Orthodox Judaism could ameliorate some of the stringent objections to participation in secular life, while clinging to the "indwelling spirit of Torah." Finally, a strict or meticulous *Haredi* Orthodoxy rejected secular culture as well as Conservative and Reform movements, prohibiting any changes or anything "new," raising the question, "We know what they are against, but what are they for?"

Moses Mendelssohn (1729–1786), German Enlightenment philosopher and religious leader of German Jewry (University of Michigan Library, Special Collections Research Center).

Devotees of *Hasidism, Haskalah*, Reformism, Conservatism, Orthodoxy, Modern-Orthodoxy, and *Haredism* chose up sides, ready to do battle for their own perceptions of Jewish cultural identity, acknowledging that, like it or not, religious pluralism is entrenched and here to stay.

∼ ∼ ∼

England had prospered during the Enlightenment primary due to its comparatively tolerant property-owning middle class as well as the improved health care that raised the birth rate and lowered the death rate. Still, civic enfranchisement, economic latitude, and problematic marital laws challenged the courts, including perplexing royal questions. Henry VIII (1491–1547) hoped that an Italian rabbi might provide him with Biblical justification for annulling his legal contract to Catherine of Aragon in order to marry Anne Boleyn. Perhaps the king had been aware that a copy of the Talmudic tractate on divorce rested on a shelf in the royal library. Rabbi Rafael Paglione, under papal pressure, refused the request.

By the end of the eighteenth century, the English population had almost doubled. The budding Industrial Revolution, with all its energy and technical power, had, nevertheless, created withering poverty in London's East End, where small numbers of Sephardic and German immigrants had settled. After almost four hundred years of exclusion, Jews were returning in considerable numbers—although full emancipation was delayed until 1871. Discrimination alternated with tolerance and hope because relative freedoms depended on the whims of local authorities. Jews were still legally barred from holding civil, military, or other offices, or becoming members of Parliament without taking the Christian oath of office. However, for England's native-born Jews, many equitable arrangements already existed: they were citizens; they could live with few restrictions and work mostly where or how they chose; and they were exempt from some taxes. Not exempt, however, from aggressive conversion organizations.

Things were different in France. In 1789, after generations of corruption and an intransigent Church, a bloody rebellion initiated a Reign of Terror. Religious institutions were not immune—churches and synagogues were as willfully vandalized as landed estates. Despite having been granted full citizenship under the terms of the Revolution in 1791, Jews nevertheless were urged to suppress their peoplehood and discard their traditional distinctiveness. The French military officer Count Stanislas de Clermont-Tonnerre (1747-1792) declared, "To Jews as individuals, everything; to Jews as a nation, nothing.... There must be no nation within the Nation." He believed the Jews would be amenable to assimilation—and up to a point they were. Otherwise, they faced expulsion.

By the early nineteenth century, Napoleon Bonaparte (1769–1821), having established himself as dictator of much of Europe, began a friendly, albeit cynical, relationship with its Jews, gaining their favor by ordering the removal of the walled ghettos of Europe. He needed their money and sought their enlistment in his armies, both of which contributed to his successful military campaigns. Once those objectives were achieved, however, he rescinded many of the rights he had earlier extended.

Anti-Semitism, drowsing but hardly asleep, was reignited in the venom that convulsed France in 1894, during which Alfred Dreyfus (1859–1935), the only Jewish military officer on the General Staff, was falsely accused of supplying confidential documents to the hated German enemies. Theodor Herzl (1860–1904), an assimilated Viennese Jewish journalist who was horrified that *all* Jews were being condemned, declared that the trial was the turning point of his life. When the trumped-up charges led to Dreyfus's conviction, public disgrace, and exile to Devil's Island, Herzl dedicated the rest of his life to the idea of establishing a Zionist state where Jews might reorganize themselves as a nation of their own, an objective he boldly declared in his tract *Der Judenstaat* (*The Jewish State*, 1896).

Alfred Dreyfus, the sole Jewish military officer in the general staff, was falsely accused of supplying confidential documents to the Germans.

Those interests were furthered in 1917 when chemist Chaim

"The Traitor. The Degradation of Alfred Dreyfus 1859-1935," cover of *Le Petit Journal*, 13 January 1895. Oil on canvas, 1895. By Henri Meyer.

Weizmann (1874–1952), British Parliamentarian Viscount Herbert Samuel (1870–1963), and other sympathetic community leaders prioritized the effort. British Foreign Secretary Arthur Balfour (1848–1930) facilitated the establishment in Palestine of *a* (but not *the*) national home for the Jewish people. In 1922 Britain accepted a mandate to wrest the land of Israel from Ottoman control, with the area west of the Jordan River becoming known as Palestine and the land east of the Jordan River, as Transjordan. No sooner was the ink dry on the document than a military expedition was unleashed against the populace, steamrolled by the small but violent Arab army. Nevertheless, Herzl's dream was no longer a wish or aspiration but a reality.

There was a renaissance in Jewish secular letters and literature when Hebrew printing returned to Palestine with Israel Bak (1792–1874). Hebrew was adapted to the needs of everyday language with the publication of *Complete Dictionary of Ancient and Modern Hebrew* (begun in 1904, completed in 1959) by Eliezer Ben-Yehuda (1858–1922). Russian writers Asher Ginsberg (pen name Ahad ha-Am) (1856–1927), Hayim Nahman Bialik (1873–1934), Boris Schatz (1867–1932) and others fueled its cultural development, as did Technion University in Haifa in 1924 and Hebrew University a year later in Jerusalem.

The state of Jews in Russia was exemplified in a statement by Peter the Great (1682–1725), who reportedly said that he pitied any Jew who lived in his lands. By 1880, perhaps half of Eastern European Jews were confined to the Pale of Settlement, an area in Russia larger than France. Synagogues were forbidden near churches, Hebrew books were heavily censored, and crippling taxes were imposed. The assassination of Czar Alexander II in 1881 led to anti-Semitic pogroms because, during intervals of Westernization and increased tolerance to Jews during his reign, the czar had canceled some onerous anti-Jewish law, much to the displeasure of his countrymen. Alexander III (1845–1894) reacted to his father's relative liberalism by limiting Jewish residency rights and placing quotas on enrollment of Jews in schools and professions. His political adviser, Konstantin Pobedonostev (1827–1907), was quoted as predicting that by 1894 "one-third of Russia's Jews would starve to death, one-third would emigrate, and one-third would convert to Russian Orthodoxy." He was not far off. The first two forecasts were consistent with fact; stiff-necked Jewish resistance precluded the last.

The old order was fast crumbling. The moderates that still existed were losing power. The inevitable progress of the Industrial Revolution exacerbated tensions between rich and poor. The focus on class struggle provided the motive for Jewish-born but converted Karl Marx (1818–1883) and Friedrich Engels (1820–1895) to publish *The Communist Manifesto* in 1848. The document paved the way for Vladimir Lenin (1870–1924) and the 1917 Bolshevik Revolution to direct hostility against religion in general and Judaism in particular. World peace had been thought to be almost inevitable. It thus came as a tremendous shock when a European conflagration erupted in 1914, followed three years later by America's participation in the war.

By the tail end of the nineteenth century, Germany had entered a period of quasi-liberalism. Nevertheless, anti-Semitism had never been dormant. Following its defeat in World War I, Germany experienced the effects of the Weimar Constitution and the rise of fascism—and the German people were saddled with unrealistic post-war reparations, penalties with which they could not cope, penalties which were beyond their power to pay. The humiliation of loss encouraged fanatic right-wing parties to blame the economic and military disaster on "Jewish power." Genetic theories were floated and based on national and inherited mental and physical disabilities. Extremism and violence uprooted and destroyed millions of Jews and others. Admiral Alfred von Tirpitz (1849–1930) wrote in his memoirs, "Since we need hatred for our self-esteem, we will instill it into the heart of every German and we will let it flame on every mountain top of our Fatherland."

Military and industrial elements took control. Severe economic and political disturbances led to the onset of the 1929 financial depression. With about one-third of Germans unemployed or in dire straits, the panic and lawlessness were blamed on the "pacifist traitors," i.e., Communist Jews. The relatively weak 1933 National Socialist Party was submerged under an authoritative leader (Fuhrer). Adolf Hitler (1889–1945) took the country from a constitutional republic to total dictatorship in just a few months, enabling him to undertake the extermination of Jews his party perceived as guilty. A popular marching song expressed the Party's sentiments in chilling lines:

> Crush the skull of the Jewish pack
> And then the future is ours and won;
> Proud waves the flag in the wind
> When swords with Jewish blood will run.

Extermination orders went out. Millions of Jews and other "misfits" were tortured and starved in Germany's indiscriminate Final Solution, a genocide that could not have succeeded without citizen support.

The world once more undertook self-destruction. Great Britain and France belatedly declared war after the German invasion of Poland in 1939. Thanks to the added military strength of the United States, a severe Russian winter, and Allied invasions from 1942 to 1945, the Nazi victories were finally checked. By then, death camps and crematoria had already martyred most of Europe's Jewish population. In the blithe hope that prejudice and evil might be laid to rest, the atrocities of the Holocaust brought twenty-six countries together in 1945 as The United Nations. No surprise. It wasn't long before mutual distrust generated a great divide between Western democracy and Eastern European totalitarianism.

For the vast numbers of Eastern European Jews who had sought entry to the New World, America was the New Hope. But as more and more arrived, they were resented more and more. The welcome mat was withdrawn: the Johnson-Reed Act of 1924 established quotas targeting Jews, Slavs and Southern Italian Catholics. The earlier liberalism was fast disappearing.

On May 14, 1948, Israel declared itself a sovereign state—the euphoria tempered by successive battles for acceptance and security. Although the United Nations' General Assembly voted to partition Palestine into Arab and Jewish states with the implied intention of resolving mutual hostility, peace negotiations failed time after time as both sides continued to struggle for identity in different and antagonistic directions. When a coalition of five Arab states attacked Israel in 1967, the Six-Day War erupted between Israel and the neighboring states of Egypt and Jordan. Israel took the offensive, captured East Jerusalem, and annexed the area in a move that has still not been internationally recognized. The Yom Kippur surprise attack in 1973, on the holiest day in the Jewish calendar, coordinated Arab policies aimed at regaining the territories lost in 1967. After fearful destruction on both sides, Israel emerged as a major force in the Middle East. The peace process brokered by the Camp David Accords in 1978 offered political gains for Egypt and Israel, severe losses for Syria, and the first recognition of Israel by an Arab country. In 1994, the Nobel Prize was awarded to the Palestinian political leader, Yassar Arafat (1929–2004), Israeli statesman, Shimon Perez (1923–2016), and Prime Minister Yitzhak Rabin (1922–1995) "for their efforts to create peace."

On the domestic front, worrisome economic and social problems, unsettled by the 1950 Law of Return, highlighted Israel's need to integrate and resolve relationships between European and non-Ashkenazi Jews as well as to placate political ideologies of the Left and Right. The melting pot of civil fellowship afforded little assurance of uniting immigrants of different cultures and religions in political compromise to form an integrated society.

In 1980, Egypt and Israel exchanged ambassadors. Egypt accepted Israel's "right to exist" and renounced terrorism. Could amity be close behind? Well, no. Demands for a halt to settlement activity in the West Bank and Gaza were consistently renewed. Jerusalem was recognized as the capital of Israel by the American president, Donald Trump (b. 1946), in the final days of 2017. The United States embassy was moved to Jerusalem in 2018. Can amity and peace be far behind?

Were the old dreams unrealistic? Not at all. Despite the challenges—border disputes, settlements, terrorism, and social, political, and ethnic divides—Israel remains committed to a restructured tomorrow, moving the country forward into the twenty-first century and beyond. History is long. There still is time to extract hope from fear, time to jump from the fire back into the frying pan, time for love to make the world go 'round.

God had promised peace and demanded humanity.

If not now, when?

We are waiting.

2

Marriage: Good, Better and Not So Good

When a Roman lady asked Jose ben Halafta what God had been doing since He led the Exodus from Egypt, the rabbi answered that He had been arranging marriages and that it was harder work than dividing the Red Sea (Bereshit Rabba 65:4). Yet, nowhere in the Jewish experience has joy been more evident than in the coupling of husband and wife. Weddings were always festive occasions, a time for gathering family and friends. Genesis (29:22) tells us that Laban threw a grand party for Jacob and his brides, no doubt prepared by the best caterer and the most popular musicians in Nahor. The celebration lasted a whole week, during which period a good time was had by all—although bigamous unions may not have been what God had in mind when He designed Jacob's relationships.

But let us begin with the love lives of the Bible's earliest heroes. Tradition relates that, for many years, Abraham's heart had been devoted to Sarah, who surpassed all other women in beauty and worthy deeds. However, what had begun as a monogamous relationship turned sour after she gave him her maid, Hagar, to carry the child she could not bear. Abraham soon discovered that it was difficult to please competing women. When he apparently ignored Hagar's and Ishmael's offensive behavior towards his wife, Sarah jealously accused him of emotional distance (Genesis Rabba XIV). Caught in a difficult equation, he retired from the marital battlefield, telling Sarah to do as she pleased with the proud and arrogant duo (Genesis 16:6). Given that choice, she cast out both.

We next meet Abraham's niece, the beautiful and virginal Rebecca. Because Abraham wanted his son to marry among his own people, he delegated his servant to find a suitable mate for 40-year-old Isaac from within his own family (Genesis 24:57–58). Rebecca willingly accepted her unknown and unseen groom. Asked if she would go, the plucky girl said, "I will go." Along the way, she met Isaac by accident—an accident ordained on high. He brought her to Sarah's tent—and *then* he loved her—possibly more as a replacement for his mother than for himself. However, once they settled in, Rebecca conceived twins, Esau and Jacob. They were destined to be contending rivals, Jacob the bearer of tradition, and Esau, according to some interpreters, a man of low and evil inclinations.

Rebecca hastily arranged for Jacob to take flight after he tricked his brother out of his birthright and his father out of a blessing. Jacob escaped, finding a wife at the home of his uncle Laban and his cousin Rachel. After taking one look at the lovely girl, he impulsively kissed her and wept, believing that he had found true love (Genesis 29). He was so enamored that he purchased her from her father for fourteen years of hard labor. Jacob definitely

2. Marriage: Good, Better and Not So Good

was a one-woman man. Or so he thought. He unknowingly became a bigamist when her sister, Leah, was foisted on him on his wedding night after his first seven years of servitude. Jacob was trapped in marriages that were not morally fulfilling, even though they had been planned from above.

Yes, God had been busy, although perhaps not entirely pleased with what He had wrought. No doubt, He realized by now that suitable or appropriate mates were difficult to come by. If they were close at hand, they could be troublesome; if not troublesome, they could be eyesores. Unsure how to proceed, God called on the Mishneh—the authoritative code of Scriptures—to enlarge chances for marital bliss by setting aside Tisha B'Av and Yom Kippur afternoons for young girls to put a flower in their hair, dance in the vineyards, and catch the eye of an eligible bachelor (Taanit 26b). If that did not yield satisfactory results, He enlisted the aid of a professional *shadchan*, or matchmaker, to seek out partners, supervise betrothals, appease parents, soothe tempers, and negotiate finances. Theirs were once honorable and even sacred callings. During perilous times when Jews were forcibly moved from place to place, the ubiquitous *shadchan* followed along, always checking out eligible clients. Romantic love was not on his mind. Economics and *yichus* were. Of course, it was hoped that the prospective groom was Torah-learned, handsome, healthy, and of a kindly disposition. (Hope springs eternal.) But as community stability lessened the need to be here, there, and everywhere, the *shadchan* became a caricature held in mild contempt as a local busybody and chatterbox, exaggerating or concealing relevant information. Although his role has since waned, he may still be called upon—especially among the Orthodox—when spouses are in short supply, or if families present difficult challenges. (His current great rival is social media or online dating, where lovers now seek their own partners or whatever.)

Once the *shadchan's* task is accomplished and the modest fee collected, it is incumbent on the bride to visit the *mikvah*, a pool of running water that serves for spiritual—not physical—cleansing. It is through this ceremony that she is "reborn," her previous sins absolved, her religious beliefs heightened and elevated. The formality, fundamental to Jewish observance, is obligatory for women to renew the procedure monthly after their menses, as well as after childbirth, before physical intimacy can be renewed (Leviticus 18:19). The laws of family purity, *niddah*, are as binding as fast days or the restraints on eating certain foods during Passover. According to Maimonides (1135–1204), physician to sultans and nobility, Orthodox Judaism accepts the tenet that it is the

Traditional portrait of Maimonides (1135–1204), Rabbinic authority, philosopher and physician. From Ugolinus' *Thesaurus Antiquitatum Sacrarum*, Venice, 1744.

sexual ordinance—along with rules pertaining to *kashrut*—that gives the Jewish community its uniqueness.

Although customs and traditions differ among Jewish people, the primacy of marriage is among their shared beliefs. Broadly understood, marriage is sensuous between the young, tender between the elderly, but sinful when proscribed by *Halachah,* the rabbinic interpretation of Biblical law. Above all, it is practical: first build a house, then plant a vineyard, and after that, marry (Sotah 44a; Deuteronomy 20:5). God waits eagerly for men to take wives, channeling eroticism within the bounds of Torah law, forgiving wrongdoings when they marry (and sometimes when they don't) (Kiddushin 29b, Yebamoth 66b). The idea that the Sabbath is personified as a bride indicates that God, as a groom, seeks close ties with His creation (Mekhilta 19:17). Having taken His own counsel in an inspired moment at Sinai, He betrothed Himself to Israel: "As a bridegroom rejoicing over a bride, so shall I rejoice over you" (Isaiah 62:5). The prophet Hosea's marital vows are recalled at many weddings since: "I will betroth you to Me with righteousness, justice, and fidelity, and you will know God" (2:19, 20). Perhaps a chorus of angels sang *Lecha Dodi* to His mystical spouse as she was greeted with blessings and praise.

While neither love nor pledges are Biblically defined, procreating is. "Be fruitful and multiply" ranks as the first commandment after creation and shares with companionship the chief purpose of marriage. It was the transmission of this religious obligation that secured the promise to the Jewish people that their children would be the guarantors of renewal. But procreating is not the only imperative. Judaism exalts connubial love within *halachic* bounds. It recognizes the need to rejoice in the body as well as to elevate the mind. "Were it not for the sexual urge, no man would build a house, marry, or rear children" (Genesis Rabbah 9.7). The conjugal obligation, *onah,* mandates sex for mutual needs and gratification.

Judaism does not regard marriage as a civil contract or a supernatural sacrament, as does Christianity, which recognizes the union as between Christ and Church. Judaism does not idealize celibacy, regard sexual desire as an admission of human frailty, or teach that it was intended only for breeding, as did St. Paul, who asserted that marriage was at best a reluctant alternative to abstinence: "It is not good for a man to touch a woman. Nevertheless, in order to avoid fornication, let every man have his own wife and every woman her own husband.... I say this as a concession ... for it is better to marry than to burn" (1 Corinthians 7: 1–9). (There are some who say he took all the fun out of sex.)

The Babylonian rabbi Abba Areka (Rav) had alternate views: "A man will have a demerit in his record on Judgment Day for everything he beheld with his eyes and declined to enjoy." Added the tenth-century philosopher Saadiah Gaon, "There cannot be anything ugly about sex since God's holy people in the Bible engaged in it with His approval." Exodus (21:10) stipulates that every wife, holy or not, is entitled to sexual fulfillment, good food, and proper clothing, none of which may be ignored or withheld by her husband. On the other hand, she is considered undutiful if she refuses his advances for a period of twelve months, unless, as Maimonides humanely adds, she finds him offensive: "A woman should not be urged to have sexual relations with a person whom she finds repulsive. It is forbidden while either is intoxicated or sluggish or in mourning, nor when the wife is asleep, or incapable of defending herself, but only with her consent, and if both have not argued during the day, and are in a happy mood at night." The twelfth-century Talmudist Ravad (Rabbi Avrohom ben David of Provencal) stipulated that "the sexual frequency ordained by the sages should correspond to women's desires."

Added Rashi, Friday night, the holiest time of the week, is the best time for "delight, rest, and physical satisfaction."

All of which brings us to a closer look at the definitions and discords of love. In Jewish terms, love is most commonly expressed as *ahavah* and *yichud*. The former is explicit in Deuteronomy (6:5) with the *Shema* command to love God with all one's heart, soul, and strength; while we are told to love justice, the stranger, and one's neighbor, nowhere is the husband commanded to love his wife. Nevertheless, husbands were cautioned to treat their wives with kindness and forbearance, for God counts their tears.

Ahava speaks to an emotional or deeply felt reciprocal connection—*she lo t'luyah ba davar*—a bond that is simply there, basic to life. Although the term generally refers to non-romantic or erotic relationships, it includes love between friends such as David and Jonathan (1 Samuel 1:26; 18:1–3) and between parents and children (Genesis 22:12; 25:28; 37:3). Nevertheless, its intimate tone is usually understood as a celebration between marital partners. Men are exhorted to marry the daughter of a scholar and to "find your happiness with the wife whom you love ... for that is your portion in life." (Ecclesiastes 9:9). Happiness originated when God introduced Woman, in Genesis 2:18, because "it is not good for man to be alone." Man and wife became one flesh, one soul, sharing respect and risk in separate but commingled lives. The Book of Proverbs advises that a dinner of herbs where two are joined is better than one with a fatted calf when one is alone (15:17).

In addition to *ahavah*, *yichud* is perceived as privacy or seclusion, the couple close and alone in a Torah-centered home, denoted as the House of Israel. Originally designated as a suitable or proper time to consummate the marriage, *yichud* has evolved as a symbolic, rather than an actual, observance of intimacy or sexual union. Intended to arouse the bride with gentleness and appropriate words, it speaks of incorporating ethical and religious values, recognized as the ultimate expression of affection, especially during the years when the sexual component begins to fade. Rabbi Elijah, the eighteenth-century Gaon of Vilna, cautioned that youth's charms are deceptive and illusive, that youthful beauty without sensitivity lacks merit.

Jeremiah had prophesized that physical love between man and woman would evoke the "the voice of joy and the voice of gladness" (33:11). Happy couples, sanctified by religious commitment, were dedicated to the basic elements of morality and spirituality that mandated legal, economic, and social guarantees in order to ensure the cohesion and transmission of tribal history. The second-century Palestinian sage Rabbi Akiva assigned great value to marital harmony and woman's dignity, yet he sympathized with unfortunate husbands saddled with homely wives (Gittin 90a). He took a pragmatic position on *niddah*, declaring that even when a wife is forbidden to her husband, she should make herself pleasing with cosmetics and jewelry (Shabbath 64b). In a male-dominated world, he stressed reciprocity in loving relationships: "neither man without woman nor woman without man nor both of them without the spirit of God"—the perfect threefold combination (Bereshit Rabbah 22.2). Akiva was a revolutionary in his time, cautiously extending *halachic* rulings, always seeking and defending practices "unknown even to Moses" (Menachos 29 a-b).

Maimonides, on the other hand, perceived love more as an intellectual or ascetic experience, less as a sexual or physical response to emotional needs. In his twelfth-century *Guide for the Perplexed*, much like St. Paul, he recommended abstinence in sexual relations, raising spiritual perfection above carnal desire (Book III Chapter XLIX). Although intercourse with one's wife is a sacred duty, he wrote, the husband should not always be with his spouse, like a rooster (Mishneh Torah 40b). He advised restraint for those whose devotion to Torah exceeded biological urges, "but if they are overcome by desire, they must marry" (Hilkhot Ishot 16). The Midrash refutes abstinence under normal conditions, the ideal relationship remaining companionable as well as sensual (Bereshit Rabbah 34, 35.1).

Once the couple is married and ready to establish a home and assume their mutual responsibilities and pleasures, they resort to centuries-old *minhaggim*. These differed in various places. Sephardi rituals often called for elaborate presentations with opportunities for female friends and relatives to enjoy delicacies. After the bride's father accepted a satisfactory mate for his daughter, he gave a dowry to his prospective son-in-law. Brides painted their hands and face with red henna to ward off evil spirits, sprinkled themselves with rice water, and plaited their hair with colorful flowers. Couples chose distinctive wedding garments, a white silk suit for him, a lavishly jeweled gown and parasol for her. They exchanged gifts—perhaps an embroidered skullcap and *wimple* for him, an engagement ring for her. Families looked forward to displaying the loot from family and friends in trousseau rooms—*kiddish* cups, belts, decorated chains, prayer books, jewelry caskets, and silver objects. Popular items also included spoons and dishes engraved with the monogamous turtledove that, we learn, remains faithful to his mate throughout his life. With the acceptance of a ring before appropriate witnesses, loving couples consent to adhere to prescribed marital stipulations and to assume their duties. Personally designed wedding rings only came into fashion in the seventh or eighth century, although elaborate, community-owned examples representing the Temple were frequently lent for the ceremony. Whatever the type, because the circlet symbolized the cycle of life as well as a perfect form in nature, it was hoped that the union would become (reasonably) perfect as well. The bride sat high on a raised chair, her head and face covered with a heavy veil; the groom recited the blessings and promised to support her with appropriate clothes and to provide appropriate conjugal rights. With the ceremony and a week's festivities concluded, flaming lamps and fireworks signifying the light of Torah guided the entry to their new home where they remained indoors for a week to escape the wiles of lurking evil spirits. A dish

Traditional portrait of Rabbi Akiva (50–135 CE). He contributed extensively to the Mishnah and to the Midrash after the destruction of the Second Temple. 16th century illustration. Anonymous.

of sweet rice near their bed guaranteed a sweet life, and perhaps love—for a couple that had just barely met.

Ashkenazi wedding custom differs; families that originate from France and Germany have their own traditions. As Jews dispersed from Israel and Babylon to Europe and North Africa, each group developed its own rules. Ashkenazi couples often fast on their wedding day. They may not have met for a week or two before the wedding. Ashkenazi grooms may veil the bride before she walks down the aisle. However, many of these customs are fading as intermarriage renders them obsolete.

The Hebrew term for the first half of the marriage ceremony, *kiddushin*, is hardly mentioned in the Bible. The word, which first appears in the Mishneh, translates as "sanctification," the sacred ceremony. Its basic requirements include mutual consent and mental competence. Once these conditions have been met, the *kiddushin* or *erusin* changes the couple's status, introduces the *shtar tena'im*, a timetable that specifies the date of the marriage and outlines the monetary penalties for withdrawing from the arrangements. Although the couple is legally married during the betrothal, the marriage is yet to be consummated.

The second element of the ceremony, *nissu'in*, originally took place under the *chuppa* or wedding canopy about a year later. But by the twelfth century, the parts were necessarily combined because Jews never knew where or in what circumstances they would find themselves, because two separate *simchas* were more than most families could afford, and because it was difficult to keep the lovers apart. *Nissu'in* authorizes sexual union as the groom "takes" the bride and acknowledges the *ketubbah* or marriage contract through *kinyan sudar*—a handkerchief or scarf held at its corners by the couple in order to avoid physical contact. He then presents his bride with a small object or *perutah*, the smallest local currency, and finally places a ring on the forefinger of her right hand. Women were thus "acquired" either by money, legal document, or cohabitation (Kiddishin 1:1). While this terminology has connotations of subjugation or servitude, Jewish law does not imply ownership, but rather empathy and compatibility between husband and wife. It is clear that women were not arbitrarily bought and sold. Rebecca was the prototype or model for willing consent.

The *ketubbah* was unknown in Biblical times. It probably did not exist until the period of the Babylonian exile and the destruction of the Temple in 586 BCE, although there is evidence from papyri of simple marriage documents as early as 440 BCE when Jews established colonies in Egypt. Although its terms were not fixed, an entire section of the Talmud is devoted to it, curbing lenient opportunities for divorce. The bride's rights and the husband's duties are spelled out to protect the interests of widowed or divorced women, as well as to designate certain obligations incumbent on the groom, such as guaranteeing a standard of living "according to the universal custom," sexual fulfillment, medical care, and protection from abandonment. Appropriate verses were often added:

> And I will betroth you forever;
> I will betroth you with righteousness and justice, love, and mercy
> And I will betroth you with faithfulness… [Hosea 2:21]

Sixteenth-century and later *ketubbot*, especially in Sephardic Italy, were lavishly covered with flowers, birds, grapevines, nudes, Biblical and mythological patterns, all symbolizing marital happiness—and the family's wealth. When Jews did not have the means or the opportunity to indulge in fine artistry, the document could be written on whatever paper was available. During the mid-nineteenth century, when Persian Jews were forcibly converted to Islam, their marriage contracts, ostensibly conforming to Muslim tradition, were secretly designed as exuberantly colored Hebrew booklets.

The *chuppa* represents the bridal chamber in the couple's new home, a sacred space open on all sides, as was Abraham's when he welcomed three unexpected guests (Genesis 18:2). Or, it may derive from the Book of Ruth: "Spread your robe over your handmaiden" (3:9). It is first mentioned in *Ha-Manhig* by Abraham ibn Yarchi in the second half of the twelfth century but came into Ashkenazi usage by the sixteenth century when it was described by Moses Isserles as the symbol of a happy union (*Shulchan Aruch Eben ha-Ezer 55:1*).

With the acceptance of the ring before appropriate witnesses, the loving couple consents to adhere to the various marital stipulations and to assume their duties. Traditional wedding services conclude with cups of wine and the recitation of seven blessings. Finally, with the admonition, "Let the bridegroom go forth from his chamber and the bride from her *chuppa*," the rabbi blesses the loving couple and conveys the fond wishes of the parties. Wedding guests shout congratulations—*siman tov, mazal tov*. Rejoicing follows for as long as the guests can dance, eat, drink, and be merry (or for as long as the family is willing to go into debt). Not every loving couple was loving. Many endured loneliness, disappointment, infidelity, and insecurity. No one ever had a partner who pleased all his or her needs. A woodcut in the 1526 Prague Haggadah has a husband pointing to his wife with one hand while holding a plate of unpleasant herbs in the other.

Ecclesiastes sadly notes that women who cause suffering and pain are "more bitter than death" (7:26). (He might have included men who cause suffering and pain—unless such "unworthies" didn't exist.) Even King Solomon acknowledged negative moments. "*Better to live on the top of a house than inside it with a nagging wife*," he wrote in Proverbs (21:9). "*She is like dripping water. How can you keep her quiet? Have you ever tried to stop the wind or hold a handful of soil?*" No one was better qualified to complain about the hazards of matrimony than the world's greatest connoisseur.

Maimonides advised grooms to "*honor their wives more than themselves, and love her more than they love themselves, and constantly seek to benefit her according to his means; he should not unduly exert his authority, but should speak gently with her; he should be neither sad nor irritable.*" In turn, she was encouraged to participate in community and religious activities, maintain the home in keeping with *shalom bayit*, feed her family, and raise their children in agreement with social and spiritual norms. According to tradition, the first marital year is set aside to connect in intimacy. Grooms are exempt from some ordinary tasks and obligations as well as from military duty and business affairs in order to devote themselves to their wives (Deuteronomy 24:5). Brides undertake the laws of *niddah*. The new family looks forward to childbearing, representing perpetuity through its descendants.

When France annexed Algiers shortly after 1830, the French artist Eugene Delacroix accompanied a diplomatic mission there. He developed an interest in Sephardic Jewish affairs, recording wedding images as they were described to him by a Jewish guide, Abraham ben Chimol. His 1833 etching, *Algerian Jewess*, displays a richly clothed bride with her maid. Delacroix was not present himself since young women were traditionally isolated, but memories of his visit lingered a few years later when he painted *The Jewish Wedding in Morocco*, featuring a young couple descending from their apartment to a courtyard to enjoy the performance of a sultry dancer. Although dancing before the bride is considered a *mitzvah*, the painting aroused considerable European opprobrium with its suggestion of easygoing abandon. Nevertheless, postcards of exotic North African weddings were collected by tourists titillated either by the last word in loose living, oriental splendor, or both.

A 1716 engraving by Paul Kirchner, *The Wedding*, features a Nuremberg groom hurling a glass against a marriage stone imbedded in a synagogue wall—an alternative to crushing it with his foot. The tradition is generally understood to recall the destructions of the Jerusalem Temples in 586 BCE and 70 CE. Alternatively, it might suggest that love, like glass, is vulnerable; like glass, love is destroyed when reasonable precautions are neglected. Whatever its origin, the custom probably dates from legends that loud noises frighten away lingering demons. The Talmud in Berekhot tells of a rabbi who broke a beautiful glass at his son's wedding because the guests were celebrating with too much gusto. The noise sobered them up.

As guild restrictions relaxed, barriers against Jewish artists began to fall. Moritz Daniel Oppenheim (1800–1882) became the first professing Jewish artist to be widely acclaimed, the first to step outside of the Jewish ghetto to build an eminent career based on Jewish integration into modern life, the first to portray Jews as members of a dignified, enlightened tradition "worthy" of emancipation. From his *Scenes of Traditional Jewish Life* (1861), *The Wedding* illustrates a tastefully dressed couple covered with a *tallit (prayer shawl)* ready to pass muster with the best of the upper crusts. Maurycy Gottlieb (1856–1879) picked up Oppenheim's intimate style in his *Jews at Prayer on the Day of Atonement* (1878), which included a self-portrait at age twenty-two and an image of his fiancée who, it was said, broke his heart when she called off their engagement.

In the Eastern world, which remained somewhat cut off from the West, marriage customs were distinctive or often unique. In addition to the *mikvah*, preparatory ceremonies for the Mizrachi bride included outlining her eyes with black kohl to ward off evil spirits. If her family could afford the extravagance, she was clothed in sumptuous outfits lavishly adorned with precious jewels. Grooms dressed in fine silk shirts and trousers, embroidered skullcaps and turbans. Because they were viewed as alien, colorful, or disappearing, oriental Jewish marriages were exhaustively reported in the Western press; in the remote Libyan coastal town of Tripoli, Jews traditionally married exclusively among themselves. The bride was brought to the synagogue heavily veiled, women friends sang praises to her and her bridegroom, and children clapped hands and stuffed themselves with goodies.

No artist ever seemed to tire of loving couples. In 1903, the first internationally important Jewish painter, the Dutchman Jozef Israels (1824–1911), depicted a bride and groom surrounded by a *minyan* of ten men in *A Jewish Wedding*. Issachar Ber Ryback (1897–1935) adopted his native Russian folk style in his 1917 *Wedding in a Village*, in which the *chuppa* served as a symbol of revitalized Jewish life. The mid-twentieth-century *Wedding Dance*, a woodcut by Albert Abramovitz (1879–1963), likewise tells a happy story in picturesque detail where the festivities include song and dance. Lithographed sheet music, too, was always available at the piano for somebody's sister to bang out the noisy strains of *Choson Kale Mazel Tov (Joy to the Groom and Bride)*, first published in 1909 and noisily echoed ever since.

Many weddings were held out of doors, under the stars, stressing the concept of spiritual oneness between nature and the house of God. When the neo–Orthodox rabbi Samson Raphael Hirsch (1808–1888) performed the ceremony in a synagogue, he was charged with aping Christian practices. Nevertheless, when an 1881 wood engraving threw the spotlight

The image portrays a Turkish couple getting married and is taken from Van Lennep's portfolio. Lithograph, 1862. By Charles Parsons (University of Michigan Library, Special Collections Research Center).

on the wedding of Leopold Rothschild and his cousin, Marie Peruga, inside London's Central Synagogue, the occasion was declared significant enough to settle the issue of location. The celebration brought out England's bluest blood, including the Prince of Wales, who presented the couple with a silver ewer and basin. Wedding images never fell out of vogue, particularly if the bride was beautiful, and the groom, sinfully rich.

∼ ∼ ∼

Most marriage traditions remained integral to the Jewish Enlightenment or *Haskalah* period that spanned the mid-eighteenth century to the last quarter of the nineteenth and the beginning of the twentieth. Although some institutional values were challenged in what were considered irrelevant religious ordinances, and some secular precepts outside

The Wedding of Lionel's Son Leopold to Mlle. Marie Peruga. **The Prince of Wales attended the wedding. Engraving, 1881. From** *The Graphic.*

entrenched standards were promoted, an effort was made to retain basic Jewish identity and spiritual principles. Reform Judaism abbreviated or neglected some ceremonial laws and rites "according to the spirit of the times" but closely followed wedding ceremonial usage.

The modern era encompasses enormous social, political, economic, intellectual, and religious ideas radically different from what Jews had known. Secularist and universalistic theories challenged ideologies of being Jewish in the modern world, of God's existence, of the notion of a chosen people indifferent or averse to Jewish status or identity, of inbred religious and moral codes. The very question of Judaism's continued existence was linked to the world's reaction to virulent anti-Semitism. Millions of immigrants, fleeing poverty and worse, experienced an acute sense of culture shock as they adjusted to new concerns of mixed marriages, easy divorces, and falling birth rates. The stress of two world wars within twenty years, together with a painful economic slump and the harrowing genocide that swept over Europe, raised doubts that cherished traditions could—or would—survive the devastation, whether folks could—or would—pick up their lives and continue to marry and to bear children.

A dramatic post-war episode exemplifies courage and persistence as when British warships, freed from combat duties, rounded up evacuee vessels attempting to reach sanctuary in Palestine. More than fifty thousand refugees were dumped into barbed-wire camps in Cyprus. The artist, Moshe Bernstein (1920–2006), himself a prisoner, illustrated their three-year incarceration when neither food and water nor other amenities were readily available. Among the twenty-seven prints of Bernstein's *The Exiles in Cyprus* (1947) is one illustrating a traditional Jewish wedding under the steely eyes of watchtower police looming over the ceremony.

Since the declaration of the State of Israel in 1948, there are no marriage options for Israeli couples outside of Orthodoxy. If they wish to circumvent the rabbis, they go elsewhere to tie the knot. Cyprus has become the delegated place where authorities first offer a brief story of its heroic role in permitting Jewish prisoners a haven during painful British harassment before providing fast legal marriages without the presence of clerics to invoke God or His mandates. Relatively cheap flights from Tel Aviv, abundant hotels, and sunny weather are great inducements to avoid pre-marital classes, costly celebrations, and the chance to say "I do" without weeping in-laws. Visibly sober unmarried pairs of permissible age are eligible; first or second cousins are not. Same-sex or other types of partners may find nearby offices to document them legally. Couples kiss and the honeymoon begins, all in less than six minutes.

Others, hoping to avoid aggravation, turn to the unromantic Internet for wedding plans. Tech resources offer personalized invitations and online reviews of moonlit or sun-drenched locations. Faceless websites make decisions easier and manage venues, vendors, caterers, photographers, musicians, registries, and locate coordinators who customize wedding cakes, table decorations, and seating and eating arrangements. Add wedding rings and wedding clothes and underestimated budgets. It is enough to encourage elopements to Cyprus.

Israel had unique problems as a relatively new country. It geared up for unknown political adventures and economic gambles to build an upstart state in the land its settlers never forgot. Everyone worked to clear the ground, grow food, build homes and businesses, develop industries, and organize social services, communal life, culture, and fun and games. Writers and artists pitched in, cheering or comforting young people with happy/sad stories and pictures, including love images and wedding scenes. Samy Briss (1930–) borrowed the floating images of Marc Chagall (1887–1985) but made them over in his own highly stylized screen print *Flight of the Beloved*: as lovers soar over home and synagogue, their arms impossibly intertwined, their hands and feet missing fingers and toes, they are oblivious to normal anatomy. A fanciful flight by Michael Muchnik (1952–) conjures up a cloud-born illusion in *The Ring and the Rose*, in which the bounties of nature unfold into a New Jerusalem. *The Wedding* by Ben Avram (1941–) is full of joy and harmony, despite incessant rumblings as to the security of the country. A dash of humor permits David Schneuer (1905–1988) to cast an uneasy artistic eye on the *First Meeting* between a privileged gentleman and a more-than-willing lady.

2. Marriage: Good, Better and Not So Good

Love was not limited to the rich and handsome or the young in thrall to sexual urgencies. The close relationship between mother and child is certainly qualitatively different from all other emotional connections, as Hagar exemplifies in her fierce love for her helpless son Ishmael (Genesis 21:15). A quiet image of mother and child is shown in the Joel Ballin etching below. Naomi takes on the role of mother to her daughter-in-law, Ruth, and grandmother to Ruth's son, Obed (Ruth 1:4). In addition, we meet friendship-love between David and Jonathan (1Samuel 18:1), as well as sibling-love between Absolam and Tamar (2Samuel 20). Warm personal relationships are, then and now, critical to feelings of sensibility and responsiveness, as well, perhaps, to spiritual wholeness and sound psychological development.

Love and marriage for those far along in years are sanctioned by God Himself. The early twentieth-century Russian Jewish artist Anatoli Kaplan (1902–1980) linked his *Golden Wedding* to a sentimental Yiddish song by the poet Mark Warshavski (1848–1907):

Mother and Child. Etching, 1830. By Joe Ballin.

> It is fifty years ago today
> Since they walked together along life's way,
> They grew old together, look at them, see.
> Eighty he and seventy she.
>
> God blessed them with honor, wealth and long life,
> They have never known quarreling and strife,
> She is his darling, her sweetheart is he,
> Eighty he and seventy she...

But while love often came, sadly it often went. Separation and divorce became part of the equation.

Rabbinic literature quotes a man who observed, "When love was strong, we could have made our bed on the edge of a sword. Now that our love has grown weak, a bed of sixty cubits is not large enough for us" (Sanhedrin. 7a). Ecclesiastes (3:1) tells us, "For everything there is a season ... a time to plant and a time to uproot ... a time for embracing and a time to refrain from embracing." Shammai, a leading first-century rabbi, decreed that a man has grounds for divorce only for serious transgressions such as unchastity (Talmud Ketubbot 16b-17a), while the school of Hillel generously permitted divorce when relationships were irreconcilably frustrated or thwarted—but not if she "spoiled his dish." According to the final Mishneh in Tractate *Gitten* (90a), Judaism does not rule that divorce is a sin or that marriage is indissoluble. The *ketubbah* permits a properly conducted procedure when love or expectations of happiness turn to heartache (Ketubbot 5:10). Maimonides frees woman—"she is not a captive." Malachi warns that God rejects offerings from the man who deals treacherously with his wife (2:13–16).

Neither the Bible nor the Talmud suggests lenient methods to separate from an unhappy marriage. The husband must prove that he has cause, such as finding an "unseemly or unclean" problem, if his wife has diseases of which he was unaware, if she has been barren for ten years, if she dresses or acts immodestly, or if she berates him. He is constrained from divorce if she is unwilling or if he has falsely accused her of premarital sex or adultery. Tradition stipulates that a wife cannot be divorced except of her free will and consent unless she is guilty of adultery. While the husband may unilaterally initiate divorce proceedings, a wife may obtain relief or release if she has been badly or physically mistreated, if he is impotent, or if he has loathsome diseases or defects that prevent normal sexual cohabitation.

Only a formal *sefer keritut,* or *get* given by the husband in the presence of witnesses and the sanction of a *Beth Din,* can dissolve the marital status. Serious problems continue to challenge women. If her spouse refuses a divorce or has remained absent for a long period of time, or evidence is lacking that he is still alive, she remains an *agunah,* chained to him for life. Rabbinic interpretations—which attempt to protect the wife's interests, to soften or mediate divorce laws—narrowly define "physical defects or obnoxious behavior." Credible reasons, such as an invalid or incestuous marriage, may enable wives to terminate the relationship.

Rabbinic courts also oversee levirate marriages: because of high rates of mortality, and in order to ensure the lineage of the deceased and to keep property rights within each family, childless widows may marry their late husband's brother (Deuteronomy 25:5–10). At a time when widowhood was belittled or humiliating, levirate marriage was regarded as a compassionate solution. However, because such arrangements might be construed as incest, the Bible in Deuteronomy (15:7) offers an alternative—should the brother-in-law refuse to cooperate, the *halitzah* ceremony releases the widow and enables her to remarry

(25:7–10). In this procedure, originally meant as a public chastisement, the widow removes and spits into the unwilling gentleman's shoe while reciting, "So shall be done to the man who will not perpetuate his brother's house." The unbinding of the shoe symbolizes the wife's rights over the property of her late husband, while the public disgrace is intended to force him to observe the obligation. The ancient ceremony is illustrated in the Italian rabbi Leone da Modena's *History of Jewish Rites* (1637). The process had also been examined in four engraved panels by Johann Christian Georg Bodenshatz (1717–1797).

Vexing religious, familial, and social ties regularly call for unique approaches. Some authorities maintain that marriage and divorce are civil acts requiring only secular arrangements. Some liberal authorities accept "elastic" adjustments within modified rules. Orthodoxy, operating within *Halachah*, usually requires rabbinic supervision and pre-marital agreements to temper legal issues. Uniting disparate values under one canopy is still a legislative dream away.

Is it? Marriage in the twenty-first century may invalidate those assumptions or prompt irrelevance. Fewer adults overall, Jewish or otherwise, are tying the knot, many deciding to live together, legally or otherwise, and to raise children in or out of wedlock. The socioeconomic status of unemployed men and women in falling labor markets, the widespread use of factory automation which reduces the pool of well-paid jobs, the increasing populations with criminal drug or alcohol abuse records, and the number of individuals able to support themselves without partners all affect the supply or need of acceptable spouses. Delaying or avoiding marriage for career enhancement and the use of readily available birth control methods, together with higher incomes for college-educated people, tend to lessen the desire for traditional arrangements.

It is also certain that today's uncertain Jews are living in a delicate balance between a secular, me-first world and *tikkun olam*—repairing lives in spiritual harmony and discipline. In the face of unhappy statistics, the need to be bound to one another remains the transcendent ideal of love and marriage—good, better, and not so good.

∽ ∽ ∽

Adam's Diary by Mark Twain, 1893: "*After all these years, I see that I was mistaken about Eve in the beginning; it is better to live outside the Garden with her than inside without her. At first, I thought she talked too much; but now I should be sorry to have that voice fall silent and pass out of my life. Blessed be the tree that brought us together and taught me to know the goodness of her heart and the sweetness of her spirit!*"

Adam discovered that his own marriage consisted of coming home day after day to Eve, but he never asked God why He created marriage as an enchanting bubble, a fleeting, often painful, moment loosened from real time. Although he never got a proper reply, his descendants have labored over that question ever since. Having brought the God of Love into an open forum, they demanded an answer: "Why do You allow broken hearts and unhappy marriages? Don't You care that we suffer?"

God referred them to Job and took the Fifth.

3

The Bible In and Out of Love

    Once upon a time in the sleepy village of Iloveyou, a young woman and man came together to be united in holy matrimony. As they stood before the pious rabbi, they were shy, they were nervous, and they were hungry, having fasted all day to atone for past sins. The bride wore a white dress stitched lovingly by her younger sister; on her head rested gifts from the groom—a simple cap and a veil modestly covering her face. If her spouse was Sephardic, he might have worn brightly colored clothes. Or he might have donned a white *kittel* or gown, as did many Ashkenazim; it would inevitably be his shroud—having come from dust, to dust he would return. But, for now, his thoughts turned eagerly to his bride and future joy. And they lived happily ever after.

    Not so fast.

    It all began long before they met. The Bible tells us that God labored for six days, calling into existence a harmonious "world without end," a bright and starry heaven, and a motley variety of animal life. The Maker, having organized the neighborhood to His satisfaction, was ready to undertake His prime goal of creation—a rational and just being in His own image and likeness. Molded from the dust of the ground and with the Divine breath of life in his nostrils, Man was a fusion of lowly soil and soaring spirit. As the prototype of future lines of descent, he was gifted with an awareness of God, the capacity for imagination and innovation, and the ability to make moral choices. He was directed to be fruitful and multiply and to subdue and have dominion over the animal kingdom and the earth. His special kinship with God, separate from and above animals, implied dignity in his own right and in his own sphere of activity. He would dwell in a utopian garden east of Eden and cultivate plants that look beautiful and taste good. And yet, his appetite was limited. Eating from the tree that imparts knowledge of good and evil was forbidden on pain of death (Genesis 2:17). He was unconcerned because he had no conscious understanding that death is the extinction of life.

    But never mind, God will compensate Adam with a lover and companion because he is alone and therefore incomplete. God knows the feeling, since He Himself is lonely, lacking partners (other than angels). But He will yield to Adam: behold Eve. He notices that she is different from anything he has yet encountered. He is unaware that she was taken from his rib—bone of his bone, flesh of his flesh, to be a partner in his life and intimacy, to make him whole in monogamous unity (Genesis 2:18–23). Unity, perhaps, although the Hebrew word *k'negdo* suggests contending forces among harmony, conflict, and desire. She may have believed that she transcended him, having emerged from living tissue, rather than

3. The Bible In and Out of Love

lowly dust. Through her fitness for procreation and replenishing the earth, she emerges as the mother of all mankind. An independent woman, she wasn't formed from Adam's head, lest she should prove headstrong; nor from his eye, lest she be a flirt; nor from his ear, lest she should be meddlesome; nor from his mouth, lest she be a gossip; nor from his heart, lest she be jealous; nor from his hand, lest she be grasping; nor from his foot, lest she be a vagabond (Genesis Rabbah 18:2).

The couple's fateful assignation offers no clues to their past circumstances, if any. There were no family issues to resolve, no tensions to sort out between the familiar and the forbidden, nor any of the human problems that will plague their progeny. But God is satisfied. Having rested on the seventh day of his work, he blessed the Sabbath and pronounced His efforts "very good."

Disaster followed. Heedless of God's mandates of the permissible and the forbidden, and swayed by guile and seduction, Eve allowed the serpent, prompted by envy and his own lust, to induce her husband to sin (Sotah 9b). After sharing the fruit of the knowledge of

Adam and Eve. Etching, 1502. By Albrecht Dürer. Note the snake curled around the tree, handing Eve the fruit.

good and evil, along with a splash of sexual desire, they understood they were naked and were ashamed. They did not die as threatened but instinctively knew that punishment was inevitable. Adam blamed his wife, and she blamed the serpent—and by implication, God Himself—from whom they were now estranged. God blamed both, although, in their defense, they had had no previous life experiences and only a few instructions on how to keep out of trouble. Having eaten from the tree of knowledge, they had not learned much. Or had they? They knew that the possibility of their eternal existence threatened God. And so, before they could sample the Tree of Life, He drove them from a known land of enchantment to an unfamiliar environment where they would struggle in adversity, work the land for subsistence and assure the continuity of the human family (Genesis 3:20). Civilization had arrived.

No longer innocent and no longer childlike, mortal beings would wrestle with right and wrong—and with obedience and repentance. The love that had existed in a perfect world could not survive in an imperfect one. It was not that God's original mission had

The Expulsion from Paradise. Engraving, 1529. By Lucas van Leyden (Rijksmuseum, Amsterdam).

failed, but rather that love would have to be relearned in each generation. But all was not lost. The power to learn and change, to exercise free will and determine moral choices, would endure. Over time, humans would strive to repair their relationship with God, seeking justice tempered with mercy. They would cleave to each other and give life to rising generations. And they would learn to love as well as to cleave.

Because the arts were believed to engender moral responsibility, the Second Commandment forbidding the making of images was soon overlooked. Biblical stories became a resource for almost every craftsman who put ink to paper, paint to canvas, chisel to stone. For those who wished to study the human form but were constrained by prevailing notions of modesty, the Scriptures provided ample opportunities to portray sexual (mis)conduct or sensuality in ways that would have been unacceptable were they not associated with Biblical texts. Artists drew the first couple in glorious or homely undress, offering a variety of classical, Renaissance, and prurient images. Masaccio's 1427 fresco depicted nude Adam and Eve bidding an anguished farewell to their former home. Dürer portrayed the famous pair in 1507. Michelangelo immortalized them in 1511 in the Vatican's Sistine Chapel, Titian painted them in 1570, and Rembrandt etched them in an atmospheric setting in 1638.

Among Jewish artists, Chaim Shahor posed a wayward Adam and Eve representing atonement and redemption in the 1526 Prague Haggadah. Jozef Israels (1824–1911) painted the sinful couple in 1902, bringing the saga into the twentieth century. In 1922, Reuven Rubin (1893–1974) melded Eastern European folk themes with a Zionist ideology in *The God Seekers*—a traditional scholar is deposed by a reborn Jew, strong and independent, who will regenerate and reclaim the land. Abel Pann (1883–1963) followed in 1923 with Adam and Eve wandering in the Garden of Eden, in a lush Art Nouveau setting, united with nature in purity and innocence. Marc Chagall (1886–1985) depicted *Paradise* and *Expulsion from Eden* (1967), exploiting the transgressions of the first parents who paid a high price for sexual awakening and a system of values.

In an epiphany that transitioned history from polytheism to monotheism, God, having dealt with our begetters as best He could, appeared unbidden to seventy-five-year-old Abram (later Abraham), whose story was touched upon in Chapter 2. God commanded him to leave his familiar home in Chaldea with his wife, Sarai (later Sarah), and his nephew Lot and to travel to an unknown land. There he would father a great nation to be dedicated to the one true God. Without seeking an explanation or reason, but simply obeying the Voice, they arrived in Canaan in the midst of a crop failure, moving south to Egypt and adequate food (Genesis 12:1–7).

It was widely known that Pharaoh had an eye for the ladies. Sarah, "a fair woman to look upon," was immediately whisked off to his harem. Because Abraham feared he would be killed if it was known that she was his wife, he urged her to say that she was his sister, letting her go without protest, aware that the lie imperiled her life. Didn't he realize that if she was cloistered among royal concubines, there could be no Israelite descendants? (We are not privy to her reaction.) When God informed Pharaoh of the situation, he angrily threw them out along with their accumulated animals, servants, and precious silver and gold (Genesis 12:11–20). Abraham was now very rich, having conveniently neglected to return the booty (Genesis 13:2). The incident was repeated when they moved on to Gerar, where King Abimelech likewise cast longing eyes on Sarah, installing her in his palace. Having dreamed that God protected her virtue, Abimelech took the hint and sent them on their way, again with ill-gotten possessions (none of which were returned). No doubt he was glad to see them go since the Lord had afflicted his household as long as they remained. Abraham apparently was a slow learner. According to the Midrash, he attempted the same trick once more to avoid paying the tax collectors when they arrived in Egypt. This time he packed his wife in a locked chest beneath a pile of blankets. It didn't work. As soon as the clumsy plot was discovered, they were unceremoniously rushed out.

In Abraham's defense, however, it must be noted that he had no way of knowing whether God had the ability or the wish to protect him, or even if He controlled forces in lands that had their own gods. Abraham had misunderstood—or had never been told—that love, or at least protection, was due to one's mate. While the thirteenth-century Talmudist Nachmanides (Ramban) charged Abraham with a great sin for placing Sarah in grave danger, he recognized that the Bible gives us no absolute heroes or models of virtue, only imperfect humans.

The plot thickens. Sarah was free but unhappy. She was barren. In tune with the prevailing custom, she gave her handmaiden to Abraham in hopes of having a son through a third party, but became understandably jealous when Ishmael was conceived. In her frustration, she blamed Abraham when Hagar, no longer submissive, became proud and scornful. Abraham, at this point indifferent and unfeeling, threw up his hands, removing himself from the fracas and telling Sarah to do with her as she pleased (Genesis 16:1–6). Was she justified in treating Hagar so harshly that the girl fled their home? Did she sin, as Nachmanides suggested, earning Hagar comfort from the "Angel of the Lord" (Genesis 16:11)? The situation was "very grievous" in Abraham's eyes, although he apparently was unconcerned that the meager allotment of bread and water (portioned out by Sarah?) would soon result in their starvation. Did Sarah create a rift in their relationship by insisting that Abraham expel Hagar and their son (Genesis 21: 9–21)?

God negotiated a truce. Sarah would conceive Isaac, designated Abraham's true heir; Hagar's son, Ishmael, would father a great nation (Genesis 21:8–19). Both boys, as well as Abraham's entire household, were duly circumcised in the covenant *brit milah*, the religious duty incumbent on male Jews that bound God to future generations.

Abraham was deeply attached to Sarah, Hagar, and Ishmael, but the Bible reserves the first mention of "love" for Isaac, "your son whom you love." Abraham was informed that he loves his son; he apparently did not instinctively sense or internalize the concept. When God tested his faith by instructing him to offer Isaac as a burnt offering, didn't it occur to Him that the promise "in Isaac shall your seed be called" could not be fulfilled if Isaac were to be destroyed (Genesis 21:12)? Nevertheless, satisfied that God was as good as His word, father and son walked together for three whole days, father laying the split wood on his son's back, carrying the fire and a knife himself. But where is the ram? He could only explain to his perhaps terrified, but passive, son that God would provide what was needed for the sacrifice. The Talmud says that Isaac was 37 years old at the time of his binding (*Akedah*). Once he realized that he was the intended offering, he avoided confrontation, but never again spoke with his father. Abraham returned alone to his servants (Genesis 22:19). The Biblical lesson taught man's willing submission and obedience to a higher law, but it has been a difficult ethical and moral legacy for mankind to absorb and accept.

Rabbis tell us maddeningly little about God's responses to His children's personal dilemmas. Had God planned to sacrifice Isaac without Sarah's knowledge? (Rashi comments that her soul flew from her and she died on hearing the news.) Did Abraham challenge God over Isaac as he did in the story of Sodom and Gomorrah (Genesis 18:20)? Did he understand why God was willing to negotiate the lives of unknown inhabitants of sinful cities but appeared unwilling to save His own beloved son? Did he look back and protest anything? Did he regret anything? God no longer kept in touch with him after a final blessing and arrangements for a bride for Isaac.

Abraham and Sarah were not together when she died; he purchased a burial site for her in the Cave of Machpelah. After a suitable period of mourning, he remarried. With his new wife, Keturah (Hagar?), he fathered six sons, none of whom were recognized as his true heirs (Genesis 25:1). Keturah might have been very young; perhaps love had come to soften his final days. Isaac and Ishmael buried their father next to Sarah. Was Ishmael at all concerned about where his own mother would be buried? Ishmael's family settled in villages near Egypt, and Isaac's family, in the Negev desert. Perhaps the brothers never met again.

It is Isaac and Rebecca, also introduced in Chapter 2, who are remembered as the first pair for whom amorous love is expressed. Abraham had sent his servant, Eliezer, to find a wife for his son among his own kindred in Nahor rather than from the heathen land of Canaan. As Eliezer carefully looked over a group of young women who had come to draw well water, he prayed for divine guidance to find a suitable bride with proper *yichus*. He sealed his choice when Rebecca, virginal, attentive to animals, and, of course, beautiful and kind, offered him a drink as well as refreshment for his camels. After her brother Laban

Rebecca greets Abraham's servant to provide water for the camels, proving she is worthy to be Isaac's bride. Engraving, 1851.

observed that appropriate gifts of a nose ring and bracelets had been proffered, and, no doubt intrigued by Eliezer's favorable report of the intended groom, he extended an invitation for food and a place to rest. Her family's permission for the match duly confirmed, they cleared the plan with Rebecca herself (Genesis 24:58). Perhaps they knew she wished to leave her father's foreign idols behind. Perhaps they knew she had her own mind and thought it best to consult her. "Will you go with this man?" And she said, "I will go."

God, who could produce a coincidence at a moment's notice, had arranged for Isaac to take a stroll in the field one balmy evening. He looked up, and —lo! — there was Rebecca descending from her camel. "Who is this man walking towards me?" she asked. It was instant attraction. He took her to his mother's tent, after which she became his wife—and *then* he loved her. While their romance may have been a delightful idyll, the congeniality and trust they shared were only achieved over time. Rebecca became worthy of taking Sarah's place when Isaac found comfort in her love (Genesis 24).

Like his father, Isaac followed God's command to dwell in the land of Gerar. Like his father, Isaac misrepresented his wife as his sister. But when the local king spotted the couple embracing in no brotherly-sisterly manner, perhaps he remembered his own youthful days and tactfully looked away. God, too, had also observed Isaac's enthusiasm and, perhaps in fatherly affection, decided to let bygones be bygones.

We can never know the ways of the Lord.

Rebecca remained childless for many years. Isaac turned to a merciful God who responded to their prayers. But the birth of their twins was marked by unfortunate partiality. Isaac loved Esau; Rebecca favored Jacob (Genesis 25:28). They were unsound role models for their children, who lived out much of their lives in deceit and antagonism. Which led to predictable troubles. Twice Esau disobeyed his parents, first by marrying outside the clan, and then compounded the offense by taking Ishmael's daughter as an additional wife. Twice Jacob cheated his brother, first by bartering some lentil stew for Esau's birthright, and then by deceiving his father in order to receive a blessing to which he was not entitled.

But when Jacob and Esau met years later, the qualities that had once defined their moral failures had undergone a transformation. Esau had conquered his murderous grudge, magnanimously forgave, and graciously renounced ownership of his due: "I have enough, my brother, let what you have remain yours." Jacob offered gifts and perhaps a blessing but declined Esau's invitation to visit him in Seir, perhaps in repentance or guilt. (Despite later *Midrashic* efforts to present Esau as crude or uncouth in order to raise Jacob's significance, in the long run, he exhibited a higher behavior. Perhaps Jacob was the more tragic figure.)

The Bible follows Rebecca's life story longer than that of any other woman, although its narrative style omits gossipy details. The text never mentions whether she and her husband shared the normal intimacies of daily life. If they did not complete each other emotionally, they did supply what each needed—she was a savvy and determined woman able to manipulate events; he was a loyal, compliant, and monogamous partner. He did not take a concubine as did his father or would his sons. Perhaps he didn't want to risk life with another woman as headstrong as Rebecca.

Of all the lovers we shall meet in our travels through the Bible, the most ardent and patient were Jacob and Rachel, who appeared in the last chapter. Unlike his grandfather Abraham, who delegated a servant to choose a wife for Isaac, Jacob required no matchmaker. His first sight of Rachel was all the inspiration he needed to lift a heavy stone from the well, a feat too difficult for the combined efforts of the local shepherds. Then he kissed her and sealed his fate (Genesis 29:10–11). Jacob asked his uncle Laban for her hand, agreeing to a seven-year work contract—years that seemed "but a few days, for the love he had for her." Alas, his uncle tricked him into marrying Rachel's older sister, Leah. Although he complained bitterly—"What have you done to me—why have you trapped me?"—he was on morally weak ground, having previously hoaxed Esau and deceived his father as well. But he accepted another seven years' work for Rachel, loving her more than Leah. For Leah, the knowledge was painful; it was not until her son Reuben was born that she wistfully noted, "Now my husband will love me" (Genesis 29:18–30). Unhappily, he didn't (Genesis 39:32). She still felt unloved after Simeon was born. Believing that three would be her lucky number, she trusted that Jacob would finally become attached to her through their son Levi (Genesis 29:31–34). Let us hope he did.

Throughout these early stories, the Bible is concerned with the problems caused by polygamy, infertility, and sexual anxiety. Rachel not only hated sharing her husband but also was resentful and distraught because she was childless—"Give me children else I die!"

Jacob snapped, "Am I in God's stead, who has withheld the fruit of your womb?" (Genesis 30:1–2). Nevertheless, he "entreated the Lord" to give them a child. Which He did—after first providing him with a household of sons and a daughter courtesy of Leah and handmaids Bilhah and Zilpah.

But the rivalry between the sisters had not ended. Jacob was helpless in their hands. He slept where and with whom he was told. When Rachel requested aphrodisiac mandrakes from Leah in return for permitting Jacob to sleep with her, Leah informed him that she had "hired" him to lie with her that night. Ever accommodating, he did. After the births of their fifth and sixth children, Leah felt entitled to dwell with him in a permanent home (along with their daughter, Dinah) as his primary wife (Genesis 30:1–21).

But God had not forgotten Rachel. When her turn came to share Jacob's bed, He finally answered her prayers: she conceived and bore Joseph. But her happiness did not last. Jacob, having decided to separate from Laban and return to Canaan, packed up his family and set off for a new life in the land of his fathers. Along the way, Rachel gave birth to her second son, naming him Oni, son of my mourning—for in giving him life she died. Jacob renamed him Benjamin—son of my right hand. He had fathered a child as an old man. Jacob buried Rachel in Bethlehem where, Jeremiah tells us, she still weeps for her children (Genesis 35:16–20; Jeremiah 31:14). If the Bible is silent at Jacob's grief in losing the love of his youth, perhaps he found comfort in God's promise that their progeny would fill the world, through the partnership of both his wives generating the Twelve Tribes of Israel.

The narrative had enormous appeal, fostering many illustrations of the three-way marriage, although most feature his connection to Rachel as the ultimate symbol of idealized love. A fifteenth-century French manuscript depicts an anxious Jacob torn between Rachel's discontent and Leah's self-content. Nineteenth-century painters offered graceful images of the Biblical couple: *The Meeting of Rachel and Jacob* by William Dyce (1806–1864), *Jacob Sees Rachel at the Well* by Sidney A. Weston, and an anonymous engraving, *Jacob's First Sight of Rachel*.

But before the Bible turned loose of Jacob's family, it turned to the lurid story of Leah's daughter Dinah (Genesis 34). Times had changed since the days when Rebecca and Rachel were able to walk safely and unmolested to water their flocks, to engage in conversation with an unknown man, to accept a kiss from a total stranger, and to invite mysterious visitors to meet their families. When Dinah ventured out to visit some local girls, she was brutalized by Shechem, a Canaanite prince of the land. Jacob had not protected her from local practices: a girl alone might be viewed as a temptress who demanded sexual pleasure.

Rape was a common enough event, but what was less common was that the prince fell in love with his victim, offered marriage, a generous settlement, and whatever else her family demanded. However, the suggestion of intermarriage between Israelite and pagan was perhaps even more abhorrent to her family than the rape.

Jacob did not rage when he learned what had happened to his daughter. He "held his peace" until his sons returned from the fields. Unlike their patient father, they were greatly distressed and instantly decided on a terrible revenge. First, they accepted the circumcision of the entire male population, then pretended to accept Shechem's offer of marriage. Operations accomplished, two of the brothers, Simeon and Levi, swooped down on the recovering men and slaughtered them, one and all. The other brothers soon followed—and woe to the area, for all was plundered, and widows and children, abducted. Did the punishment fit the crime? Deuteronomy 19:11–13 says yes. "Do to him as he schemed to do his fellow … life for life, eye for eye." (This law was never implemented in the Bible to justify personal animosities. It always required a hearing before a civil authority.)

Jacob rebuked the violent murderers. He had given his word that his people would forgive the offense and remain at peace. Because his children repudiated his oath, defying the prevailing honor system, he cursed them on his deathbed—but not until then. Although he claimed moral ascendancy in this situation, he had been, like a coward, fearful for his life at the hands of neighboring villagers. God absented Himself from the story. Perhaps He was so disappointed with Jacob's servile performance and the brothers' deceit and violence that He elected to wash His hands of the whole sordid mess.

Joseph and Potiphar's Wife. Etching, 1634. By Rembrandt van Rijn.

3. The Bible In and Out of Love

Having dealt with sexual assault and wanton murder, the Bible now explored the troubling implications of seduction. Iniquity took a turn in the story of Joseph and Potiphar's wife (Genesis 39:1). Jacob's favored son, Joseph, had been sold by his brothers to some Bedouins, who, in turn, sold him to one of Pharaoh's officers, who then installed him as a trusted supervisor of his household. The handsome fellow caught the eye of the boss's wife—and ran for his life. Vindictive as only a spurned woman can be, she seized his cloak as he fled and accused him of attempted rape. Potiphar might have known of his wife's amorous peccadillos, for he imprisoned the young man rather than disposing of him otherwise, as was the custom. Fortunately, Pharaoh recognized the Hand of God in endowing Joseph with the skill to interpret dreams and foretell the future and released him from jail, granting him authority over the entire kingdom. Joseph's rule was crowned with success—a metaphor for Israel's eventual triumph over the military power of Egypt (Genesis 41).

Unfortunately, we do not learn what befell Potiphar's erring wife.

We do know that Joseph's rectitude and integrity were depicted in a manuscript page from the Wenceslaus Psalter (1250). Paintings by Renaissance artists Guido Reni and Jacopo Tintoretto show Joseph as a model of chaste behavior against an importunate lady's advances—a lesson for young men to beware of lovesick women. Rembrandt painted *Joseph Accused by Potiphar's Wife* as she brazenly fabricated the charges for which Dante sentenced her to Hell. When the eighteenth-century poet William Congreve revealed that Heaven has no rage like love turned to hatred, nor hell a fury like a woman scorned, he may have had Mrs. Potiphar in mind.

Genesis ends with the death of Joseph. As the story unfolds in Exodus, a new pharaoh, forgetful of the hero in whom dwelt the spirit of God, and fearful of the Israelites' growing numbers and strength, ordered them crushed with hard labor, slavery, and the deaths of their newborn boys (Exodus 1:22). Had his daughter not rescued one such infant and raised him as her own, Moses surely would have drowned in the basket his mother placed at the edge of a river. Following the infamous royal decree, some prospective parents questioned the mandate to be "fruitful and fulfill the Law." Some chose abstention over love. A 1609

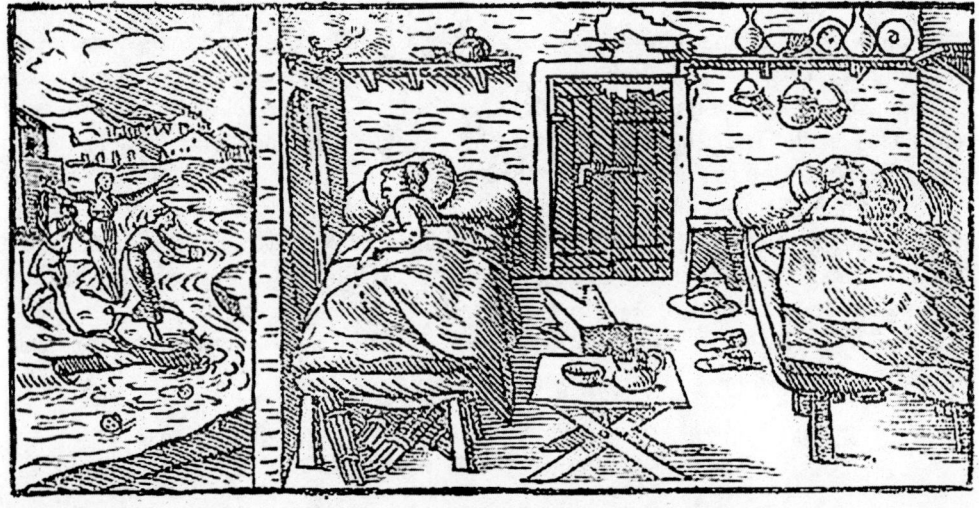

"Egyptian" Bedroom, depicting a couple sleeping apart to avoid having a child that would be killed by the Egyptians. Woodcut, 1609. *Venetian Haggadah.*

Venetian Haggadah allows a peek into an Egyptian bedroom where a couple sleep apart so as not to conceive children destined to perish.

As the new pharaoh had forgotten Joseph, so had the wandering Israelites forgotten the painfully learned lessons that God had decreed. They had been doing evil in His sight, worshipping local gods, straying from the righteous path. Moses was now old and tired; he had done what he could. Now he explained that Joshua would soon replace him. Moses knew the time had come for the people to recognize a different kind of leader, one who would further expand Israel's mission and advance its charge. He hoped that God would permit him to see the land that had been the end purpose of forty desert years. Although he was denied his final wish, God rewarded him with the consolation that the nation would grow and succeed. That, too, was love.

But love does not last forever. The question now was who would deliver them from the enemies who were sure to turn up? Fast forward to the Book of Judges, where we meet the nominee, who, unfortunately, had none of the qualifications for leadership either by birth or by experience. What he had was God.

And they had man-mountain Samson. God had chosen him to deliver Israel from the Philistines. He was an unlikely candidate to fulfill that task. Samson had married a destructive Philistine wife, was liable to a fierceness of temper, and was weak in discretion but strong in unchecked libido—all of which culminated in cruelty, mutilation, and violent death (Judges 16). Along the way, he found trouble—leonine as well as human. He single-handedly killed thirty men, set fire to three hundred foxes in order to burn Philistine food supplies, destroyed a host of Philistine invaders "hip and thigh" and a thousand more with the jawbone of an ass. He must have had some redeeming qualities, however, as God granted him leadership of Israel for twenty years. There he lived among prostitutes until he fell disastrously in love. Mighty as he was, he was no match for the smoldering allure of Delilah, who was bribed to betray him and to discover the source of his power. He was a naïve man—unable to know that the Philistines were plotting his murder, unable to tell love from obsession or common sense from folly. And so he revealed that as a Nazirite, a sect especially devoted to God, he must never cut his hair (Judges 16:17). Delilah handed that information to Philistine soldiers, who captured him and gouged out his eyes. Once his seven locks were shorn, he was lost—lost to love, lost to freedom, lost to prowess, lost to eyesight, but not lost to God, from whom he derived divine intercession. Samson asked to be taken from prison to a Philistine temple, where he placed himself between its supporting pillars. He repented and asked God to restore his strength—and "down came the temple on the rulers and all who were in it" (Judges 16: 28–30).

The story of Samson was told and retold over the centuries with plays, novels, poems, paintings and musical interpretations. John Milton's 1652 sonnet *"On His Blindness"* and his 1671 drama *Samson Agonistes* recalled the poet's own blindness. In the sonnet he drew a distinction between his own affliction—for which he demanded justice: "Doth God exact day-labor, light denied?"—and that of the idealized Biblical hero whose troubles were endured in stoic submission:

> "Who best bear His mild yoke, they serve Him best;
> His state is kingly; thousands at His bidding speed..."

When Samson was depicted by the fifteenth-century Master E.S. and the sixteenth- and seventeenth-century painters Lucas Cranach the Elder, Rembrandt and Rubens, among others, he was variously portrayed as a flawed Israelite, a mythological Hercules, a military

Delilah shearing the hair off Samson so that he loses his strength, while soldiers look on. Engraving, 1575. By Crispijn van den Broeck (British Museum).

folk hero, a symbol of Protestant conflict against Catholic Rome, or a prefiguration of Jesus. His legacy, however, remains one of personal liability and sin—woman against man, man against himself, man against divinity. But Samson is ultimately a love story—the wanton love of the libertine, the importunate love for women, and the ultimate love for God.

But let us turn to a happier book—the uplifting relationships between the widowed Israelite Naomi and her widowed Moabite daughters-in-law, Ruth and Orpah. Because of a famine in Moab, Naomi decided to return to her former home in Bethlehem, where food was more accessible. Although Orpah tearfully went back to her people, Ruth was determined to remain with Naomi, "For where you go, I will follow; your people will be my people, and your God, my God" (Ruth 1:16). Once they had resettled, Naomi became aware that her wealthy kinsman, Boaz, had noticed Ruth as she hungrily foraged (and perhaps sang) for scraps of barley. John Keats, in his 1819 *Ode to a Nightingale,* likened her voice to that of a bird:

> Perhaps the self-same song that found a path through the sad heart of Ruth, when, sick for home, she stood in tears amid the alien corn…

Perhaps Boaz, too, heard her and was delighted by the melody. He instructed his people to protect her and drop extra handfuls of wheat among the sheaves for her to gather. He hoped that she would remain with him and "not go to glean in another field." The attraction being mutual, she followed Naomi's sensible plan (for Naomi, and a like-minded God, had already orchestrated the whole scenario): "Wash and perfume yourself and put on your best clothes.…" And further—"when he lies down, uncover his feet" (understood as a euphemism for the penis). Ask him to spread the corner of his garment over you (perceived as a marriage proposal), as God spread the corner of His garment over the Jewish people (Ezekiel 16:8).

Naomi reminded Boaz that, according to Levirate law, he had the moral obligation, as a close relative, to redeem the family's land and to raise Ruth's children in the name of her late husband (Deuteronomy 25:25). Boaz immediately agreed, charmed and flattered that Ruth hadn't opted for a younger man, and claimed her when her nearer kinsman declined the honor. Of course, they married. (Although Nehemiah and Ezra objected to ethnic intermarriage, the union between sworn enemies—Moabites and Israelites—was later offered as a model for religious tolerance.) Ruth became a faithful member of the Jewish people, exemplifying the ideal of the righteous convert who willingly accepts the requirements of Jewish law. And so, love triumphed—a happy marriage, mutual devotion between the women, and the eventual arrival of Ruth's great-grandson, King David, the hero of the Jewish nation.

It may be safe to report that the most affecting Biblical love story is that of Elkanah, a righteous man, and his wives, Hannah and Peninnah. Once again we read, as in the stories of Sarah and Rachel, that God "shut up the womb" of the favored wife, who suffered from the barbs of an insolent rival. After ten years of childlessness, Hannah urged Elkanah to take Peninnah, who indeed turned out to be fertile. While Peninnah and her children received adequate portions of Elkanah's wealth, the childless Hannah received double portions. It was not enough to compensate her for a longed-for son. Hannah became bitter, unable to eat or withhold her tears. Elkanah's consoling words have become timeless expressions of love: "Hannah, why do you weep? Why can't you eat? Why is your heart so grieved? Am I

Boaz sleeping on the threshing floor while Ruth sleeps next to him. Naomi is shown in the background. Engraving, 1585. Anonymous.

not better to you than ten sons?" Like her foremothers, she ultimately was the beneficiary of God's blessing: her son, Samuel, was destined to be a prophet of the Lord and a great leader in Israel.

Prophet and leader though he was, Samuel could not check Israel's demand for a king. Although wise to the pitfalls of monarchy, he chose Saul, upon whom the spirit of God had descended. It is through Saul's erratic history that we are introduced to the Bible's most difficult and ambitious individual. David rose from shepherd boy to hero-king of Israel. A gifted harpist and singer, he was God's successful warrior over Goliath, the man who delivered two hundred Philistine foreskins as a bride price for Saul's daughter Michal, and a loving friend of Jonathan. He became the deadly enemy of the jealous Saul when the town's ladies turned out to sing, dance, and herald the young hero: "Saul has slain thousands, David tens of thousands" (1Samuel: 18: 6,7). Furious and fearful that David was after his kingdom, Saul twice attempted his death. David, however, spared him more than once, although he rightly suspected that Saul married him to Michal under the assumption that she would betray him to the enemy. Their marriage had been a political connection for him, a breathless romance for her. David didn't recognize or care that she was in love with him, saving him from her father's wrath as he escaped from her window. She didn't recognize that he would prove indifferent and ungrateful. He took off without so much of a thank-you or good-bye. If she expected to hear from him soon, she was bitterly disappointed. It was years before they would meet again (1Samuel 18–19).

Saul never gave up his jealousy of David, becoming more and more unhinged and intent on murder as he realized that God was with David, but had departed from himself. Jonathan warned David to flee, but could only watch as David and his six hundred ragtag followers became rebel outlaws, exacting supplies wherever they could. Eventually, they arrived at the home of Abigail and Nabal, wealthy owners of sheep and goats (1Samuel 25). Nabal refused him support and food. Abigail secretly gave him the necessaries. When Nabal discovered that she had deceived him, he had a stroke and dropped dead. Not a bad thing, for he was a drunken boor and a selfish scoundrel.

Meantime, Abigail had been subtly flirting with the handsome warrior who was never indifferent to a beautiful woman. He appreciated her efforts on his behalf. He appreciated her eagerness to join him in marriage. (Had he already forgotten Michal and the law against adultery?) She asked him to remember her in the days of his prosperity, and when the time came, he did. He must have cared for her in more than was typically his style, for when she was taken captive by the dreaded Amalekites, he rescued her—in addition to adding a couple of additional wives (1Samuel 30:18–31).

But his love life could not stay the relentless wars against the Philistines. Saul, mortally wounded in the skirmishes, refused to be taken prisoner and committed suicide by falling on his sword. So ended the life of the troubled king who died along with his son, Jonathan. David was distraught at the loss of his worst enemy and best friend:

> The beauty of Israel is slain in the high places!
> How the mighty have fallen in the midst of battle....
> I am devastated for you, my brother Jonathan,
> You have been very dear to me.
> Your love was wonderful,
> Surpassing the love of women. [2 Samuel 1:17]

God was by now habituated to David's highs and lows: his conquest of Jerusalem and reign over Israel, his recovery of the Ark of the Covenant, his collection of concubines and wives, and his flouting of several of the Commandments (not all: at least he didn't engrave images). Nevertheless, to legitimize his kingship, David wanted the royal princess Michal back, and she did indeed return. Knowing him too well, she watched in highborn contempt as he danced half-naked around the captured Ark. "How glorious was the king today" she flung at him, "shamelessly uncovering himself before the maids of his servants!" Unperturbed, he shot back, "I will be even more undignified than this, and as for the maidservants, by them will I be honored!" Their barren marriage was over (2 Samuel 6:14–23).

God's loving relationship with David was not over. The prophet Nathan had assured him that he could do "all that is in your heart for the Lord is with you." He also told him to build a house for God to dwell in, in return for which Israel would be safe from her enemies (2 Samuel 7:3–11). In the end, David was a lucky man: a flawed figure and a national hero. With all his faults and weaknesses (and there were more to come), he managed to keep the

King David standing on the balcony of his palace admiring Bathsheba as his old servant approaches her. Engraving, 1710. By Halma Scheits.

hearts of his wives, his subjects, and God, who credited him with authoring many of the immortal Psalms and four hundred poems (2 Samuel).

God had blessed David not only with excess but also with tolerance. "When he does wrong, I will punish him … but I will never remove my mercy for him" (2 Samuel 7:14–15). But along with mercy, God, who had been patiently bearing with mankind's moral infirmities for as long as He could remember, was surely startled as the anointed king of united Israel and Judah ogled the lovely Bathsheba at her bath when he should have been with his troops in battle. She was tantalizing; he was lustful. One thing led to another, and soon she was pregnant. Unfortunately, she was already the wife of Uriah, a soldier in his army. David hastily arranged for Uriah's death so that the child would be known as Uriah's.

What he didn't reckon with was that God knew it was not (Talmud Bavli, Shab. 56a). God was not pleased. He sent the prophet Nathan to chastise David with a parable about the sin of a rich man who had many flocks but, having no pity, took the only lamb of his poor neighbor. David was furious. Nathan pointed his finger—"You are that man!" (2 Samuel 12:7). Said God, "I will raise up evil against you out of your own house and give your wives to your neighbors, for what you did was deceitful." Acknowledged David: "I have sinned." His child did not survive. God put away his sin.

But God was not quite through with David or his family. His children, Absalom, Amnon, and their sister Tamar, shaped a harrowing story of unbridled desire, incest, rape, revenge, and death (2 Samuel 4–19). "I am in love with Tamar," wailed Amnon, morning after morning. His friend Jonadab offered to help. "When your father visits you pretend that you are too sick to eat; ask him to send Tamar to your house to feed you. Dismiss the servants and you will soon have your way." As Potiphar's wife had taken hold of Joseph, so did Amnon take hold of Tamar. "Come lie with me, sister." And he forced her and lay with her, ignoring her pleas. "Such things should not be done in Israel!" she cried. "Where can I take my shame?" His love turned to loathing. He put her out of his house, aware that rape and incest were tantamount to banishment and aloneness: she would be unable to find a husband. Her father professed anger but did what Jacob had done before him to avenge Dinah. Nothing. Another strike against David. Absalom took her in, and, when the opportunity came, had Amnon killed.

David had to face his accumulated sins. He paid the consequences of power and abuse: he was accessory to a crime against his daughter, which led to murder, to the loss of his and Bathsheba's first child, and to his son Absalom's rebellion and savage end. For the first time in David's life, he was helpless. He had lost control over his children. Neither wealth nor his army could undo disgrace or bring back the son he had loved unwisely: "My son, my son Absalom! If only I had died instead of you! O Absalom, my son, my son!"

The Bible makes it plain that transgression of the Law is evil—king or prince, all are subject to its code of morals and ethics. Lust cannot masquerade as love. Egocentric behavior, misplaced authority, and irresponsibility must be paid for with stunning intensity. "When we sow the wind," said Hosea, "we reap the whirlwind" (Hosea 8:7). Yet, despite David's guilt, and perhaps because he had comforted Bathsheba after the loss of their child, he achieved redemption, later fathering Solomon, who succeeded him as king.

David was now old and fading. The wives and concubines were gone. Infatuation and libido were exhausted, and the years of indiscretion had exacted their price. In spite of warm blankets, he was cold and numb. God could not bear to let him die this way, a faded thing of the past. He sent Abishag, a beautiful young virgin, to his bed so that her ministrations might renew his strength. It was too late, even for God (1 Kings: 1–4). Bathsheba remained his life partner, having forged a torrid relationship into a mature love. At the end, she and Nathan manipulated to confer kingship on Solomon—who promptly eliminated rival candidates to his throne.

A host of artistic possibilities were elicited from this captivating story, producing a generous supply of Bathsheba's shapely charms—the thirteenth-century *Saint Louis Psalter*, Peter Paul Rubens's seventeenth-century *Bathsheba at the Fountain*, and Rembrandt's nude image of the lady reading a letter from David, one in which her melancholy attitude introduces a psychological rather than a sensual element. A twentieth-century lithograph by the Israeli artist Reuven Rubin offered still another version of unadorned beauty, a work in which the prurient eye of David inspects her from above.

We meet a very different style of queen in Esther, the Jewish winner of a beauty pageant ordered by the Persian King Ahasuerus. As his bride, she spent time in the royal harem between summonses to the royal bed—and was forbidden to seek him otherwise. When her cousin Mordechai warned her of a plot to assassinate the king, the incident was noted in the royal record book. Ultimately, the warning rescued the king's Jewish subjects. When Esther, who had kept her Jewish identity hidden, learned that Haman, the evil chief of state, planned to exterminate the Jews of the Persian Empire, Mordechai convinced her to notify the king of the proposed genocide.

Although panicked by the need to approach him, Esther risked the confrontation, counting on his love. Providentially, he held out his scepter, heart in hand, offering. "Whatever you request, up to half my kingdom" (Esther 5:1–3). Esther, "beautiful as the morning

Esther beseeching the king to save the Jews of Persia. Engraving, 1767. By R. Strange, after Guercino (Wellcome Images).

star," having divulged her Jewish heritage and Haman's duplicity, handed down to posterity a legacy of courage and integrity, and, from a modern perspective, a will to Jewish nationalism and identity. The *Book of Esther* is a love story with a happy ending—unique and very welcome in the Biblical writings. It is commemorated each year by the reading the Esther Scroll or *Megillah* and in the Purim carnival that celebrates Mordechai's honors, records Haman's destruction, and proclaims the victory of the Jews over Persian insurgents.

On Purim, Jews put on funny hats, wink at suggestive behavior, and host festive food and wine parties. But they also remember to send gifts to each other and provide presents for the poor. Children, outfitted as Mordechai and Esther, parade around the neighborhood offering pastries in the shape of Haman's tri-cornered hat; they are also encouraged to boo loudly or spin a noisy *grogger* whenever his name is mentioned during the reading of the *Megillah*. Jewish adults, traditionally abstemious, are encouraged to get so happily drunk that they cannot distinguish between villain and hero (B. Megillah 7b). (Strangely, the reading never mentions God. He is present, nevertheless, choosing to act from the shadows.)

The love story of Esther and the king, depicted in a third-century painting in the Dura-Europos synagogue, shows the royal couple enthroned while Mordechai proudly rides by on Haman's elegant white horse. A thirteenth-century French illumination shows the queen pleading for the lives of her people. In Germany, some two hundred years later, Konrad Witz painted a gracious Ahasuerus granting her appeal. Almost every Renaissance and seventeenth-century artist depicted the story—from Botticelli to Veronese in Italy, from Rubens to Rembrandt in the Netherlands. Young lovers dancing the night away at Purim balls appear in nineteenth-century prints as masked revelers (concealed, as was the invisible God).

Shir haShirim (Song of Songs) stands alone in erotic literature. Known as the *Song of Solomon*, the poem speaks frankly of the physical desires of the "dark but lovely" Shulamite woman—as well as of the sexual prowess of a king who was more or less faithful to three hundred wives and seven hundred concubines. The amorous partners speak with mutual eagerness, apparently unconcerned with spiritual or religious matters. Like the Purim story, it makes no mention of God.

The *Song* underscores woman's traditional role, working in the vineyard, "Go and follow the flock; find pasture for your goats close to the shepherds' tents." (1:8). Recited during the Passover *Seder,* it addresses the beauties of nature: "The winter is past; the rain is over and gone; the flowers appear on the earth.… The mountains and hills burst into song" (2:11). Read as a bawdy manual of explicit sexual appetite (7:3), it has had devoted followers among Freudian scholars and pubescent boys: "He kisses me with the kisses of his mouth…. By night on my bed I sought him" (1:2). As a group of sublime love poems, it has led artists, composers, and writers to explore the many ways of a man with a maid: "My beloved is mine and I am his" (6:3). During the second century CE, Rabbi Akiva successfully defended the *Song*—the "holy of holies"—as worthy of inclusion in the Bible. Depicting the love between God and Israel, the allegorical relationship is spiritual, certainly not literal, and certainly not carnal. Those of his colleagues who held it to be a collection of profane amatory poems apparently lost the debate.

The Jewish twelfth-century poet Judah Halevi remembered it in his own love songs, as did virtually every songsmith that discovered untapped meaning within its lines. The *Song* found expression in Byzantine miniatures, inspired Edmund Spenser's *Marriage Ode—Epithalamium* (1595), and influenced John Milton's description of Paradise (1667–1674). Heinrich Heine, in his *Salomon* (1851), includes the poem *Du bist wie eine blume* ("You are like a lovely flower"). Nineteenth- and twentieth-century European Jewish artists Simeon Solomon and Marc Chagall, the American illustrator Saul Raskin, as well as Israelis Shraga Weill and Ze'ev Rabban, have all derived amorous images from the *Song*.

Turning from ecstatic lovers, we discover a troubled God in yet another metaphor that mirrors His love affair with Israel. Although the Northern Kingdom had indulged in moral laxity and polytheism and had broken the Covenant, God would not renounce His bond or destroy the ones He had chosen: "How can I give you up, how surrender you, O Israel?" He urged the prophet Hosea to marry the whore Gomer, an ungodly wife for a righteous man. As did ungodly Israel, Gomer flaunted vows, took one rival of Hosea's after another in physical and spiritual adultery, deserted her children, and risked everything to a decadent future, unable or unwilling to recognize the consequences of sin and corruption. But God and Hosea offered love in spite of disappointment, in spite of perversion and apostasy. Hosea believed that love would lead Gomer to a virtuous and pious life and would not abandon her. God threatened but did not give up, promising that the Covenant would be fulfilled when Israel would once again declare, "Thou art my God." Although love had gone awry, the unfaithful people would surely tremble before the great Judge, seek forgiveness and entreat His mercy. Then Israel, like Gomer, "will sing as in the days of her youth" (Hosea 11:8–11).

While these stories have enchanted readers across the centuries, other Biblical episodes focused on the desperation or violence pursued by women: Salomon de Bray and Artemisia Gentileschi were among the many artists who depicted female warriors as defenders of the Jewish people. When necessary, heroic women used their sexual talents to challenge authority. In a patriarchal society, they played strong roles, managing their personal lives as well as manipulating political events. Denied real power, they resorted to cunning tactics, discovering tactful and cautious methods to circumvent male authority. All are remembered among the stalwarts who will again redeem Israel with love in the days of the Messiah.

Judith was a model heroine who, with the power of God, rescued Judea from the marauding soldiers of Holofernes. Calling on her considerable charms, she set out to destroy the great general who was plotting to ravage Jerusalem. He invited her to a sumptuous dinner, hopefully to be followed by a sexual dalliance, but, after tossing off one drink too many, he fell into a drunken stupor. Then she and her maidservant cut off his head. It was a bloody mess but legitimate revenge for the deaths and destruction wreaked by his invading armies. Following the loss of their leader, the Assyrians disbanded. Her history is not included in the official Hebrew canon (but does appear in the Catholic and Eastern Orthodox Bibles). Judith was a deeply religious woman, exhorting the frightened townspeople to have faith even as they feared that God had deserted them. His methods, she explained, are inscrutable and beyond comprehension. Her story, celebrating freedom and Jewish sovereignty, has been connected to the holiday of Chanukah when the Temple in Jerusalem was rededicated following the defilement of its altars to Greek gods.

Judith appeared in Chaim Shahor's woodcut border in the 1526 Prague Haggadah where she holds an avenging sword. Michelangelo incorporated the horrifying event in the Sistine Chapel, c. 1508. Donatello, Botticelli, and Giorgione also were drawn to the grisly tale. The Baroque artist Artemisia Gentileschi, having herself been raped by one of her father's friends, specialized in paintings of female victims conquering belligerent or combative males. In 1901, Gustav Klimt turned out a melodramatic image that simmers with heat. Mozart and Vivaldi based compositions on the story; Dante and Chaucer added leaven to her epic adventures.

God, who had all along been trying to cope with evil, now delegated the prophet and leader Deborah to mount fierce resistance against the Canaanite army and its commander, Sisera, the lone survivor of the defeated forces against Israel's victorious armies. After twenty years of Canaanite oppression, God thought it was time to send a strong woman, together with Barak, a great general, to rescue His people. They achieved resounding success, with Sisera fleeing to the neighboring tent of Jael, hoping that she would be sympathetic to his cause. She was not. She killed him as he slept, swinging the deathblow with a hammer that drove a spike through his head. Grateful to God, Deborah (first taking personal credit for the victory, and only belatedly paying tribute to Jael) burst into song: "Village life had ceased until I, Deborah, arose, a loving mother in Israel."

The Bible teaches that love, sweeter than honey, is what makes life worthwhile. We have picked and chosen from love's totality—opting for the better, forgoing the worst. And so, as it turns out, love in its various and inconsistent ways, remains a grand enigma—exasperating, capricious, scandalous, illogical, ill-omened, and cruel—but also compassionate, glowing, generous, tender, and blessed.

4

The Family: More Questions Than Answers

The Talmud cautions us to be prepared to answer three questions when we appear before our Creator: "Were we ethical in business? Did we set aside time to study the Torah? And, did we raise a family?" (Shabbat 31). Judaism recognizes that it is through the family that tradition of "a holy nation" (Exodus 19:6) can best be maintained and transmitted to successive generations. *Shalom Bayit* echoes the values of peace and harmony in the home through adherence to the 613 Biblical and Talmudic rules and practices. Detailed instructions govern the household, conceived as a social agency as well as a spiritual unit, its quality and merit resting on personal responsibility as well as on wider kinship and partnership (Eruvin 3a).

The Jewish family begins in Genesis, functioning to satisfy the basic needs of sex, economic survival, and group and cultural identification. Its nuclear structure typically revolves around a man, a woman, and their offspring in a common residence tied by marriage, blood or adoption, reciprocal obligations, and accepted restrictions. It allows for alternative arrangements: polygamy and concubinage were permitted in Biblical times; adultery was forbidden as knowledge of paternity was crucial to knowledge of ancestral descent. Homosexual relationships between men were outlawed; lesbians were shamed but not legally victimized. Seduction or rape involved severe penalties. Fornication with animals was an abomination, and a miscreant was severely punished. Incestuous and other sexual relations between consanguineous partners were spelled out and prohibited (Leviticus 18, 20). (As mentioned before, Abraham was married to his half-sister, Sarah [Genesis 20:12]; the Bible ignored the situation. And when Tamar, daughter of King David, was raped by her half-brother Amnon [2 Samuel 13:13], her father did nothing.)

Divorce is barely mentioned, although it was accepted in ancient Israel. Where true love was hardly anticipated, perhaps it was not an issue. However, laws did restrict men from remarrying their wives and required them to write a *get* (Deuteronomy 24:1–4). Divorced women, unfortunately, were generally left in a sad state, sent back to their father's home, covered with disgrace and humiliation, often forced to leave children behind. In cases of divorce by mutual consent, other issues arose—impotence, barrenness, physical defects, or just plain disgust; unsatisfied parties could appeal to the *bet din* or law court.

Marriage with pagan peoples was viewed as destroying the integrity and survival of the Jewish nation, yet it must have been fairly common given there are Biblical injunctions against it: "Thy daughter thou shalt not give to someone who serves other gods, nor take his daughter unto thy son" (Deuteronomy 7:3-4). The prohibition was echoed by Malachi: "An abomination has been committed, for Judah has married the daughter of a foreign god" (2:11). To avoid the possibility of his son's marriage to a local girl, Abraham sent Eliezer to find a wife for Isaac from among his own people, but he couldn't prevent Esau's marriage to Canaanite women. A generation later, Isaac and Rebecca sent Jacob to his uncle Laban for the same reason (unaware that Laban was an idolater, information we only learn when Rachel took off with her father's gods). Because there were no Hebrew girls in his neighborhood, Moses married Zipporah, the daughter of a pagan priest—who happily acknowledged the Jewish God. Ezra, returning from Babylonia to Jerusalem in 458 BCE, ordered the Jews of Palestine to divorce their non-Jewish wives.

To keep families intact, each member had a function and a clearly defined role. The father was the authoritative and religious head of the household. He exhorted his children to remember the Exodus from Egypt and the day at Mount Horeb. He charged his children to love God and to perform charitable acts and good deeds (Deuteronomy 4:10). Honor and obedience in the *bet av*, the father's house, was expected. His home was a miniature temple—*mikdash me'at*—the educational center for worship and ceremonies, more sanctified than the synagogue or school. Over time, it boasted *mezuzot*, treasured prayer books, festive Sabbath and holiday appointments, and certainly a box for distributions to the poor.

Fathers oversaw the needs of their children as long as they were minors and chose or approved their daughters' spouses from selected families with *yichus*—purity of descent and worthy pedigrees. They earned a *mitzvah* by providing their girls with dowries and suitable adornments so that men would pursue them. Fathers circumcised their sons and redeemed the firstborn in the *pidyon ha-ben* ceremony. They supervised their education, beginning as soon as the child learned to speak, observe *mitzvoth*, and recite prayers. At five, his boys were introduced to the Torah; at ten, they began the study of Mishnah; at thirteen, they were considered adults and could be called to the Torah. Religious responsibility was reckoned with the onset of puberty, defined as the appearance of two pubic hairs.

Fathers tried to find a trade or profession to keep their sons honest and honorable, to provide them with sustenance (including swimming lessons), and to assure their independent way through life (Kiddushin 29a). Nor did the father's obligations stop there: he was told to spend less than his means on food, up to his means on clothes, but beyond his means on his family because they were dependent on him (Hullin 84b). Nor was that all. According to the second-century CE Rabbi Akiva, fathers bestowed the gifts of strength, wealth, wisdom, and longevity to their sons. Although fathers did their best to encourage their children's education and natural abilities and were expected to be sympathetic and benevolent, they were firm in their upbringing (Deuteronomy 8:5). Proverbs (13:24) explains, "He who spares the rod hates his son, but he who loves him disciplines him promptly." Nevertheless, the Talmudic tractate Bava Batra (21a) counsels that an obstinate child should not be struck with anything more than a shoelace, while Maimonides' in Mishneh Torah (Hilchot Mamrim 6:8) exhorts him to forgive his children and to close his eyes to small faults; as God loves Israel, a father loves his children and will not fail them (Deuteronomy 31:6; Hosea 11:3-4). Fathers were warned against showing favoritism in order to prevent resentment or rebellion (Sukkah 46b). (Unfortunately, they didn't have good Biblical role models or understand the hazards of partiality.)

And women? In a patriarchal society, they were subordinate to men and were expected to honor and defer to their husbands. In practice, however, they often exerted the stronger influence in ritual and family affairs (not always openly). Many were engaged in business, contributing financially as caretakers, midwives, weavers, and professional mourners. And yet, women were not always described favorably. Some rabbis characterized them as lazy. Others were less charitable, identifying them as deceitful, jealous, gluttonous, vain, and susceptible to the occult and witchcraft. True, the Talmud likens the Torah to women, identifying them as the conveyors and sustainers of life (Kiddushin 30b), but it also mentions that some talked too much and too often: "Of the measures of speech which came down to the world, women took nine" (Kiddushin 49b). Yossei, the son of Yochanan of Jerusalem, warned men not to engage in excessive conversation with women—even with their own wives—as this causes evil to himself, negligence in the study of Torah, and ends in suffering and remorse (Pirkei Avot, 1:5). Various medieval Passover *haggadot* depict husbands covering a wife's head with horseradish leaves or pointing to their well beloveds while reciting "this bitter herb"—a reminder that bitterness includes marriage as well as vegetables.

God was more forgiving. The Babylonian Talmud suggests it was the merit and righteousness of women that brought about the Exodus from Egypt; they are honored at the Seder with the four cups of wine representing the four roads of spiritual renewal (Sota 11b). And more. It was the midwives who risked their lives to spare Hebrew infants. It was Moses' sister who ensured his safety until Pharaoh's daughter took him in. When Moses at Mount Sinai spoke to the "House of Jacob," Rashi explained that Exodus 19:3 referred to women as God's "special treasures." Women were additionally singled out for approval because, unlike men, they had refused to contribute gold and jewelry for the Golden Calf, donating their precious objects solely for the beautification of the sanctuary. And what better analysis could be offered than the Talmud's maxim that when virtuous women marry wicked men, the men become virtuous, but when pious men marry wicked women, the men become wicked (Breishit Rabba 17:7).

A woman's rights—sexual, emotional, and financial—were stipulated in the *ketubah*. Her husband was exhorted "not to drink from his wife's cup" while eyeing a more interesting alternative (Nedarim 20b). (The Talmud in Kidushin 2b acknowledges that the way of a man is to pursue women.) Clearly, women were to be appreciated, cared for, and loved as mothers and helpmates (Isaiah 49:15; 66:13). Men were told that if their wives were short, they should bend down to listen (Baba Metziah 59a). Maimonides declared that "a man should honor his wife more than his own self and should love her as he loves himself. He should constantly seek to benefit her according to his ability, not impose his authority on her, to speak quietly to her, and be of good spirits" (Yad Ishut 15:19–20). Proverbs (18:22) reminds us that those who find a wife find favor, while Yevamot (62b) declares that without a wife, men live without joy, without blessing, without goodness. Eshet Chayil, the famous woman of virtue and valor, is singled out for thrift, wisdom, and kindness: "Her worth is far above rubies…. Grace is deceitful, and beauty is vain: but a woman who honors the Lord will be praised" (Proverbs 31:10–31). Tradition suggests that Abraham dedicated this tribute to Sarah, who devotedly accompanied him to an unknown land. It was through such women that God's blessings were vouchsafed to the family (Genesis 24:67).

Mothers offered elementary religious instruction, protected their daughters' sexual innocence, and taught them dietary laws, how to kindle Sabbath and festival lights, and how to assist with home and farm tasks. Above all, they loved and comforted their children when they were distressed (Isaiah 66:13), but were "shamed" if they were rebellious. The mother's duties were many: "She rises while it is yet night and provides food for her household.… She stretches out her hand to the poor. Her children rise up and call her blessed"

(Proverbs 31:10–31). Not all children. Some were burdened with clinging or overbearing mothers. Sarah insisted that Abraham expel his son Ishmael in order to secure the patrimony for Isaac (Genesis 16:6). Largely because of her, the brothers were never able to bond. A generation later, Rebecca connived at securing Jacob's blessing from Isaac, displacing Esau; her sons lived much of their lives in conflict and friction.

The greatest tragedy that could befall women was an inability to bear the children that represented the future and the continuance of the family name (Genesis 30:23; Samuel 1). Barren wives often endured polygamous husbands. Kings, of course, did as they pleased, although eighteen maidens were considered enough for a modest harem. Excessive wives were discouraged because tensions between the women could be troublesome or because inheritance rights might be compromised. The fourth-century Babylonian scholar Rava pointed out that supporting—or satisfying—more than one wife (and one mother-in-law) could prove difficult if not oppressive (Yavamot 65a; 118a).

So much for parents. What about the children? They are a divine trust (Proverbs 964). If the mother and father were married, the children were legitimate and could inherit. They were taught that their parents stand in God's place (Exodus 20:12; Kiddushin 30b-31a). If they were wise, they would heed the instruction of their fathers and the teaching of their mothers. "Ask your father, and he will show you, your elders, and they will tell you," instructs Deuteronomy (32:7) and Proverbs (13:1). Children were to honor and be responsible for needy parents (Proverbs 1:8). The Talmud teaches that "honoring" includes providing adequate food, drink, clothing, and an occasional outing (Kiddushin 31b). According to some traditions, reciting the *Kaddish* is incumbent on sons for eleven months after a parent dies, as well as every year on the *Yahrzeit*, or anniversary of their death. Rabbi Eleazer of Mainz needed no such reminders to honor his father. "Put me in the ground at the right hand of my father," he stipulated in his will (c.1337). "If the space is a little narrow, I am sure that he loves me enough to make room for me by his side."

God was well aware that children often resent parental lectures and restraints and rebel against authority. (Grandchildren often rebel against the rebels.) When the prophet Malachi closed the last book of the Bible, he predicted that Elijah would eventually "turn the hearts of the children to their parents." Elijah, however, was not scheduled to arrive until "the coming of the great and dreadful day of the Lord." Until that time, the first part of the Fifth Commandment remained a very clear mandate: Was it necessary to *command* filial honor? Yes, it was, since love, or even respect, requires emotional or social conditioning and is not subject to command or duty. Was there a *natural* instinct to honor parents? No, there wasn't. The Torah commands love of neighbor, love of God, and even love of the non-Jew who lives among us, but does not include love of parents. Keeping this in mind, God added the second part of the Commandment: "in order that your days might be lengthened." Although no penalty was exacted, the promise of a long life was a useful bribe if ever there was one.

Although we are told in Kiddushin 71 that "God dwells in a pure and loving heavenly home," men found that dwelling in a pure and loving *earthly* home was never easy, not even the very first home. Since Adam knew nothing of loving parents, what could he know of caring for children? He had been told only enough to sustain life outside of Eden. Neither he nor Eve was given any parental guidelines. They had no conversations with God to help them deal with contentious children, nor did they understand that one of their sons had committed a grave sin. God, therefore, did not hold Adam or Eve responsible for the first murder in history: the first father and mother, having survived troubles enough, were at least absolved of faulty parenthood. If God had offered some Divine advice about law or morality, about family relationships and responsibilities, about guardianship or brotherliness, their children's lives might have been very different.

Although God did not demand sacrifices or offerings from Cain and Abel, they somehow felt the need to propitiate the force that made their lives as farmer and shepherd possible (Genesis 4). Whatever their motives, whatever God's inclination, He only recognized Abel's gift—"from the firstlings of his flock and from the choicest." Cain was understandably upset, but God did not empathize with him. Instead, he was warned to conquer his hostility. The warning did not take. At his first opportunity, Cain rose up against his brother and killed him. "Am I my brother's keeper?" he asked in one of the Bible's best-known—and most arrogant—quotations (Genesis 4:4–9).

The text carries a vital message that family well-being is a family care and duty, that violence and bloodshed are abhorrent, and that the sanctity of human life dominates all. Cain had abrogated ties of personal loyalty. He had sinned, and he knew it. He feared not only the dreadful punishment of everlasting wandering but also that he would be killed by anyone who recognized him. (Who was around at the time to recognize him?) At any rate, Cain repented. God showed mercy and mitigated the curse.

The purpose of the story was not so much to explain the past as to influence the future. And so it was: rivalry, resentment, and competition were introduced to the world. In *Legends of the Jews,* Louis Ginzberg suggests that there was more to the story: Cain was jealously motivated by his love for Abel's beautiful twin sister. When Abel protested that God would know what's going on and would impose appropriate punishment, Cain slew him. It wasn't all his fault: the rabbis tell us that the evil inclination is born with mankind, perhaps

Cain beating and killing his brother Abel with a jawbone. Sacrifices burning on altars appear in the background. Engraving, 1576. By Jan Sadeler.

4. The Family: More Questions Than Answers

at the time of conception. (The good inclination is not manifest until the time of birth or until the age of thirteen.)

Barely ten generations later, mankind sinned again. God regretted His creation and grieved in His heart, threatening to destroy all the families of the world. Which brings us to Noah, the only individual worthy of His concern because "he walked with God."

So, what kind of man was Noah? He was righteous *for his generation*—barely an enthusiastic endorsement. Are we asking too much that he didn't stand up to God and plead for the sinners? He apparently was satisfied that his own family would be saved. Was he concerned that all human and animal life outside the ark would be destroyed? And what kind of father was he to his three sons? What kind of Father was God who destroyed His corrupt children in a flood, keeping only a remnant to repopulate the earth? True, He saved the good and destroyed the evil, but it was He who created evil in the first place (Isaiah 45:7). Once afloat, Noah and his family had ample time to ponder these considerations. When the forty days that they spent in the ark ended, God promised never again to destroy all life—although He recognized that man's heart, with all its flaws and imperfections, would remain tied to the "evils of his youth" (Genesis 8:21). A new code would be based on compliance with God's covenant: the family would be ruled by law and social justice. The family would be fruitful and multiply. It would learn to protect the sanctity of life—or be

Artist's depiction of Noah and his family constructing the impossible Ark. From H. Schedel's *Nuremberg Chronicle* of 1493.

held accountable. And at the end of the rainbow, redemption might give mankind another chance.

But Noah, however anxious he was to connect with God, was not the ideal leader for such a monumental task. Nor was he much of a role model for his children, who were told to replenish the earth, and, presumably, to evolve a better, holier transition from a primitive world to a socially responsible one. Neither Noah nor his sons were ready to address that challenge. Sometime after exiting the ark and making a proper offering, Noah, recalling that, like his ancestors, he must eat and drink by the sweat of his brow, revived the science of agriculture, grew grapes and made wine. All too soon, his son Ham and grandson Canaan found him drunk and naked in his tent. Viewing a debauched father's uncovered genitals was a violation of privacy and respect. The concept of parental honor was not understood by Ham, who gazed at, and perhaps touched, his naked and drunken father (Genesis 9:20–27). He could have—should have—averted his eyes and covered him. He didn't. His brothers Shem and Japheth did. When Noah awoke, he knew that Ham had "done something to him," some sort of sexual activity—castration or sodomy (Sanhedrin 70a). The Biblical text remains silent, perhaps out of modesty or shame. The story of Noah and his family constitutes the earliest (but not the last) example in which fathers and sons contend with each other.

The Bible now moves on to the adventures of the Patriarchs and their families. As noted above, God singled out Abraham and told him to go to an unknown land where great rewards awaited him (Genesis 12). Did God sense that Abraham was seeking something more spiritual than idols in his life? Did Abraham know that the unidentified voice he heard was God's? Did he know God at all? He didn't ask for some show of proof. He heard a command—he trusted, and he obeyed. He was told to leave his people and his father's household, to break with the past and all that was familiar. He was already seventy-five, and his wife, ten years younger. What was he to make of God's offer to give the land of Canaan to his seed, knowing that Sarah was barren? At that point, his only heir was his nephew Lot, who had traveled with them from the prosperous city of Ur to famine-stricken Canaan and finally down to Egypt. As the grazing for their flocks diminished, arguments between their shepherds created conflict. Abraham, wishing to keep peace, offered to part company with Lot. Both agreed to an equal division of their lands, Lot choosing the more desirable Jordan plain near the wicked city of Sodom (Genesis 13:5–11). Separation did not end their quasi-paternal relationship. When war broke out between Sodom and the invading kings of the north, Lot, taken captive by Canaanite tribesmen, was rescued by his uncle, who believed that he was honor-bound to redeem the prisoner (Genesis 14:12–16). That's what families did—or were supposed to do.

But if families were honor-bound to demonstrate allegiance to one another, did Abraham honor or esteem his father? We will never know, because although Terah lived for two hundred five years, after Genesis 11, he is never mentioned in the Bible again. If he had venerated the sacred idols that Abraham destroyed, as the popular story goes, Abraham could no longer respect him. For many years father and son remained estranged. What to do? Legend says that God finally excused Abraham from the Fifth Commandment. (If He hadn't, where would the Jewish people be today?) Terah finally repented—at least the Midrash tells us so—thus establishing the triumph of monotheism over paganism. God rewarded Terah: he and his son currently live amiably together in Paradise (Bereshi Rabba 58:5).

Although Abraham had never wavered in the belief that God would give him children, nevertheless, he began asking disturbing questions: "What will You give me seeing I am childless?" (Genesis 15:2). "Do You still plan to provide me with an heir and make him a founder of a nation as plentiful as the stars?" Yes, He will, in spite of the fact that Sarah is childless and 90 years old. Enter Hagar, the Egyptian maidservant who, at Sarah's urging, became pregnant with Abraham's child. The more Hagar boasted of her good fortune and scorned Sarah, the more odious she became to her jealous mistress, and Sarah treated Hagar so harshly that she had to flee. Abraham shrugged his shoulders and removed himself from a potential hair-pulling match between his two women—with seemingly little or no concern for Hagar or his son. Did he wonder who would care for Hagar and his child? It took the Angel of the Lord to hear her cries and come to their rescue. He promised her a son who would greatly multiply her seed (Genesis 16). Ishmael, it was foretold, would father a great nation although its members would live in great diversity; the land of Canaan, however, would belong to Isaac's descendants. In return for that gift, God commanded that every child born into the covenant was to be circumcised, a divine distinction between His progeny and the rest of mankind (Genesis 17:20). Paternity changed Abraham: he would be responsible for transmitting a unique mission to the future. He would walk in God's ways.

And now, some good news! Sarah, having been told by God's agents to expect a son, within a year bore Abraham's true heir, Isaac. But Ishmael, now thirteen, was still a torment to her. Although it grieved him, Abraham sent Hagar and the boy into the barren land of Beersheba with only a bit of bread and water to sustain them. (He had offered considerably more to the "three men" who visited him when he sat in his tent's door.)

It had come to Abraham's attention that the corruption of Sodom and Gomorrah exceeded all reasonable bounds. He pleaded with God to save the towns if a few righteous men could be found. They could not be found. What followed was an unruly mob of homosexual men who forced their way into Lot's home, demanding that he surrender his male guests. Lot begged them to desist, finally offering to substitute his own two daughters (Genesis 19:5-8). Should Lot have bowed to this abomination? Had he learned anything from Abraham about what families did—or were supposed to do?

God razed Sodom and Gomorrah to the ground, saving only Lot and his daughters, allowing them to settle in the nearby town of Zohar. Desperate for a secure home, they moved into a large cave. As events unfolded, the daughters, under the apprehension that all the males of the destroyed cities—or perhaps the whole world—had been killed, took it upon themselves to perpetuate the human race by getting their father drunk and seducing him. (Were there no viable males in Zohar?) If the daughters believed they were acting nobly, what can be said of their father? Even if he had been too well lubricated the first night to know what was going on, he should not have been unaware of the dishonorable act the next night (Genesis 19:30-38). He considered the consequences of drunkenness as well as of incest, later condemning both in the strongest terms (Proverbs 20:1; Leviticus 18:6). No doubt God was upset, but busy as He was, He still had a lot of other problems with which to contend.

God had not yet finished with Abraham: "Please take your only son, whom you love (first-time mention of *love*), and sacrifice him as a burnt offering." Abraham must reconcile himself to the loss of Isaac. He rose early in the morning and proceeded to do as he was told, although service to the Almighty meant he would be giving up all that he held most dear. Still, Abraham was a father. Why did he neglect to bargain for his son as he had bargained for righteous inhabitants of Sodom and Gomorrah? Can we explore Abraham's emotions—frustration, fear, questions about justice, uncertainty as to how the Covenant

Fleeing from Sodom and Gomorrah. Engraving, 1860. By Julius Schnorr von Carolsfeld.

could be established without Isaac? Abraham did not believe that he was in the middle of a cruel joke. His faith overcame seeming contradictions. He obeyed.

And so, Abraham and Isaac went up the mountain, father and son (Genesis 22:5–6). At first, Isaac hadn't a clue about the meaning of the fire and wood they were carrying. If his father was planning to offer a sacrifice, where was the lamb? If Isaac was suspicious that he was being prepared for a grisly death, he remained passive; his opinions, if he had any, were not consulted. God, now assured that Abraham stood in awe and reverence, hastily dispatched an angel to intercept the deadly blow; a sacrificial ram materialized in the thicket. Isaac was spared (Genesis 22:13).

The test was now concluded. What was it all about? The task had demanded faith and obedience beyond logic, divinity over humanity, trust above fear. Was it a worthy test? Didn't God already know the outcome without putting father and son through a harrowing ordeal? Did God learn something? Yes, He did. He never repeated the experiment. By Deuteronomy 6:5, He asks man to love (not fear) Him. Son and father parted company, never to meet again in life. Isaac had learned acceptance but not forgiveness. Only at their father's death did he and Ishmael come together to bury him beside Sarah in the cave at Machpelah. Isaac mourned his mother but not his father. Having been emotionally scarred by the trauma, he became distant to his own children.

It was now Isaac's turn to be examined. Did it bother him that, unlike Abraham, who argued with God over Sodom and Gomorrah, he had submitted quietly to the *Akeda*—and didn't ask why? Even if he believed he was doing God's will, a less passive man might have demanded some clarification. At age forty, he was still relying on his father to secure him a wife from among his own people. Without having done anything to deserve it, he was the recipient of an everlasting blessing: "I will give to you and your seed all the land which you can see—and your seed will be as numerous as the dust of the earth." All this, not on his own behalf, but on his father's merit. Aware that Abraham had conversed with God, even that gift was denied him, his having experienced only one-sided monologues with the Lord.

However, he was fortunate in the selection of Rebecca as his wife—fortunate in that she was intelligent and crafty enough to bridge the thorny issue of primogeniture—unfortunate in that she not only deceived him but also abetted the sibling rivalry that destroyed the harmony and integrity of his family. His children's successes and failures stemmed from their places in the birth order and from Isaac's negligent role in family affairs. Both children grew up with severe disadvantages—parents who failed their most important obligation, equal love for each child. Rebecca loved Jacob, possibly because he was more like she was. Isaac loved Esau for the game he prepared (Genesis 25:28). Isaac let himself be hoodwinked into giving a blessing to his son Jacob that rightfully belonged to the elder twin Esau. As parents, their inequitable choices led to predictable troubles. They were unsound models for their children, who lived out much of their lives in distrust and antagonism, never able to establish a compatible life together. Nevertheless, Isaac and Rebecca succeeded as patriarch and matriarch, securing a final blessing for Jacob, granting him, through Abraham, inheritance of the Promised Land.

When Isaac—in his old age, blind and infirm—unknowingly bestowed blessings on Jacob, he omitted mention of Abraham and the Covenant. But it was too late to retract or correct the blessing, too late to ease Esau's anger at being swindled out of his birthright, too late to notice Jacob's scheming to secure the benediction that made him Isaac's heir (Genesis 27:1–29). Displaying no anger at his own father, Isaac displayed no anger at his son. In his passive role, he allowed Jacob to keep out of sight and run from confrontation.

Jacob, meanwhile, had fled from his brother's anger to Haran, where he eventually (mostly) overcame his manipulative skills, learning to solve problems through cleverness and self-reliance rather than by guile. He already knew the meaning of familial struggle, both in his parents' home and in Haran, where his devious uncle Laban tricked him by substituting the unloved Leah for his beloved Rachel on his wedding night. They say that there is a substitute for everything except the first love of one's youth (Sanhedrin 22a). Megillah (13b) tells us that in spite of the differences and tensions between the sisters, it was Rachel who ensured the future of Jewish life by graciously accepting the unhappy misalliance.

Eventually, with a large family of his own, Jacob became a man of property, independent of Laban. As he prepared to return to his home in Canaan, he recognized the need to mend the relationship with his brother as he faced—and feared—their inevitable meeting. Might Esau be harboring revenge, waiting to kill him, his wives, and his children? He had not been in the habit of seeking God's help, but now the situation was desperate. Humility having never been his strong point, Jacob admitted his unworthiness and threw himself on God's mercy (Genesis 32:10–12). Not relying altogether on heavenly assistance, he hedged his bets by sending servants ahead with lavish gifts. Would they be accepted? Would they assuage Esau's enmity?

Too tired to wrestle with such questions, Jacob went off quietly by himself to get some needed sleep. Instead, he found himself wrestling with, and prevailing over, an apparition of God (Genesis 32:24). He had entered the dream as a man-child and emerged as a leader blessed with a new name—Israel. Having experienced a personal vision of God, he became worthy of the patriarchy with which he was endowed. Now that God had redeemed him, he must submit to the struggle with his conscience as he was about to confront his brother. Although Esau resisted murderous intentions against him, it must have been difficult to show forgiveness at their reunion, particularly as he had superior forces and livestock. However, magnanimity overcame resentment: "Esau ran to meet him and embraced him and fell on his neck and kissed him, and they both wept." It was a churlish Jacob who refused Esau's invitation to travel together. It was a churlish Jacob who was too suspicious to believe in the sincerity of his brother's gesture (Genesis 33). Did he feel additional guilt knowing that Esau had stayed home caring for their parents while he was unable to fulfill that mitzvah? Some Biblical commentators, finding it necessary to establish Jacob as the righteous agent and progenitor of the Jewish people, did not sufficiently credit Esau with filial duty. Rabbi Shimon ben Gamliel differed: "All my days I attended to my father, but I didn't give one-hundredth of the attention that Esau gave Isaac" (Genesis Rabbah 65:16, 82:14; Devorim Rabbah 1:14,15).

When it became *his* turn, what had Jacob learned about fatherhood? Not much. Knowing how devastating favoritism could be, he did not avoid it in his own family. He gave a beautiful coat to his son Joseph by Rachel, nothing to his sons by Leah. (Tractate Shabbat 10b tells us that it was this lapse of parental sensibility that caused Israel's exile in Egypt.) When Leah's daughter Dinah was abducted and raped by the prince of Shechem, Jacob did not stir or take immediate action. Worried that neighbors would band together and single him out for retribution, he kept silent, waiting until his sons returned from the fields to plan a response. Her brothers, on the other hand, defended her honor, refusing to allow their sister to be treated as a common harlot (Genesis 34). They rejected Shechem's offer to intermarry with their family but accepted his offer to circumcise his subjects. That accomplished, Simeon and Levi took advantage of the Canaanites' weakened condition, ravaged the city, massacred the men, took the women and children captive—and rescued Dinah. Did Jacob regret settling in Shechem, a land of gods unfamiliar with God? Had he done all in his power to instill mercy in his sons or to protect his young daughter from the dangers of "going out" alone in a rough neighborhood?

And yet, it was Jacob more than the other patriarchs who embodied love. He had received unconditional (but uncritical) love from his mother, Rebecca, as well as from his wives Rachel and Leah. He gave unrestrained (but uncritical) love to Rachel's son Joseph. Genesis is sparing with its characters' feelings, particularly with the word *love*. It is associated only once with Abraham (22:2) and twice with Isaac (24:67; 25:28), but seven times with Jacob (29:18, 20, 30, 32; 37:3, 4; 44:20). And yet, he suffered from love because it came with tragic baggage. Frustrated or thwarted, love for Jacob meant dealing with the emotional pain of his less-loved first wife, the loss of his more-loved second wife, and the mystery of what had happened to his beloved child.

As the years passed, neither Jacob nor his children had any idea of what had happened to young Joseph. The last they saw and heard of him, an immature and obnoxious seventeen-year-old tattletale, was as a shepherd of his father's flocks. The beautiful coat of many colors had aroused insane jealousy in his siblings. And they hated him as well for his boastful dreams of dominating them. Jacob, who had "kept the matter of the brothers' envy in mind," didn't calculate the danger of sending Joseph and his beautiful coat into the den of his enemies to bring back word of them and their animals (Genesis 37:14). The brothers saw the "dreamer" coming and callously plotted to throw him into a pit. And they would have done so had not Reuben, the eldest son, prevented them. Instead, they dipped the beautiful coat in animal blood and sold Joseph to some wandering merchants. And the brothers? They sat down to eat, satisfied that they were well rid of an irritant, and prepared to explain to their father that Joseph had been devoured by a vicious beast. If Jacob was suspicious, he said nothing. Silent again when faced with a horrendous deed. Did the brothers feel any guilt? Did they care that Jacob was distraught with grief? Did they believe that sins between men are worse than sins between man and God? No, no, and no.

The merchants bought Joseph for twenty pieces of silver and sold him to Potiphar, an Egyptian government official (Genesis 38:28–36). The Bible speaks of the brothers as righteous men. They represented the tribes of Israel on the breastplate later worn by Aaron. Yet, their "righteousness" was more heinous than the sins of Sodom, for they had contemplated murder. They were inured to the sensitivities of their father and the emotional anguish that he would have to endure. They had yet to learn the principle of mutual responsibility. Although brothers are born for adversity, according to Proverbs 17:17, God did not punish them. Perhaps it was His way of teaching higher values to His yet undiscriminating children. Or, it just might have been a roundabout technique to bring Joseph to where he had to be in time for the Egyptian famine.

Joseph had not died. As the famine spread to their own homes, the brothers set out to buy grain from the storehouses that Joseph had built after being elevated to prime minister, a position acquired by impressing the king with his dream-interpreting skills. They now came before their brother, who, no doubt, was wearing a beautiful coat, looking showy and magnificent. They did not recognize him but bowed exactly as he had dreamed they would. Joseph was ready to toy with them.

Joseph Being Sold by His Brothers into Slavery. **Woodcut, 1852. By Julius Schnorr Von Carolsfeld. Published by George W. Bertron, 1913.**

"Are you spies?"

"No, no, we are brothers here to purchase food. We left our youngest brother back home in Canaan."

"Maybe yes, maybe no. Until you produce your brother you will be accommodated in my jail."

Although Joseph had planned to keep only Benjamin, when Judah volunteered himself as hostage, Joseph finally revealed himself. Until that moment, for all the brothers knew, they had been responsible for Joseph's death. They had made their father's life an aching trial. Now they were caught in Joseph's web, frightened and manipulated, probed, and tested. "I am Joseph, *your brother*" (emphasizing his readiness to revive their relationship). "Is my father still alive? It is I whom you sold into Egypt.... Come close to me" (Genesis 45:1–4). Joseph wasn't faulted for his little ruses—he may have been a Perfect Man, but still he was a man and must have relished the farce now that his brothers were in his power.

Joseph Makes Himself Known to His Brethren. Engraving, 1859. By Gustave Doré. From the Dore Gallery of Bible Illustrations.

Nevertheless, he showed nobility of character: he could have, but didn't, exact retribution (Genesis 45:4–8). Although God had not taken an active role in the charade, Joseph instinctively knew who had planned and executed the drama. He was but the vessel appointed to carry out the mission promised to Abraham.

When Joseph finally reunited with his father, both wept in bittersweet greeting. There are few more poignant words than Jacob's, "Now I am ready to die, seeing your face and knowing that you are alive" (Genesis 46:30). (Ramban elsewhere has perceptively commented: "It is well-known whose tears are more present, the aged parent who finds his long-lost son still alive after having despaired and mourned for him, or those of Joseph, no longer a young son, but married with grown-up children of his own.")

The curtain was now falling. The family, including Jacob and seventy of his descendants, collected their belongings in wagons kindly provided by Pharaoh. "Thus Israel settled in the land of Egypt ... and they were fruitful and multiplied greatly."

One question sticks: How did Joseph deal with his neglect of his father over many long years? Genesis (48:1–10) tells us that when Jacob became ill, Joseph was informed and brought his sons Manasseh and Ephraim to their grandfather for a blessing. Joseph was *informed*? Apparently, he didn't see his father very often. Jacob didn't know his grandchildren. "Who are these?" (In an ironic twist, Jacob might have remembered that his own blind father had failed to recognize him when he impersonated Esau.) Jacob, however, was not so blind that he would not have known the boys if they had been frequent or even occasional visitors; perhaps he had never seen them. He was grateful that God had shown him his grandchildren, pleased that Joseph had brought them to say goodbye.

The scenario wound down. Jacob foretold the separate futures of his sons, assigning specific roles to them in accordance with their characters and bestowing his final blessings and admonitions. As he reviewed the list, each son received more or less welcome news; each was accorded his appropriate status. Did they expect him to overlook their past shortcomings, to forgive their sins? Reuben was charged with incest for "mounting his father's bed," thus forfeiting the leadership due to the first-born. Simeon and Levi were unworthy for their part in the sale of Joseph, as well as for their brutality in Shechem after their sister's rape. Judah was suspected of complicity in Joseph's supposed murder, although he would be connected to the royal destiny of King David and the messianic age. Jacob finally arrived at Joseph, still his favorite (although he had not heard from him for twenty-two years). Joseph received blessings beyond those extended to Abraham and Isaac or his brothers. He was given every possible gift that a father could bestow. And yet, he was excluded from the righteous trinity of Abraham, Isaac, and Jacob: he had married an Egyptian woman, assimilating into an alien culture and hiding his Israelite identity.

How did the brothers relate to each other over time and to Joseph's success in particular? Did their newfound security result in a grudging leadership struggle, or were they satisfied that the mantle fell to the persuasive powers of Judah? Did Joseph vaunt his superiority, or did he assume that God had planned it all and that his brothers had incurred no blame? Was he ever able to fully trust them again, or did he sincerely try to overlook the unhappy past? In its typical cryptic manner, the text gives no clues, but we have already seen how fragile compatibility within families can be. Were they jealous of each other? Or did they make peace as in the words of the Psalmist: "How good it is when brothers dwell together" (133:1). And last—did they finally become their brothers' keepers?

The Founding Parents were subject to unique responsibilities, duties, priorities, and penalties. As founders, they lacked coaches to help them understand God's messages—that family meant social stability and that conflict between its members could result in the collapse of society itself. They labored under awkward tasks, often feeling their way in unknown territory. It was thanks to their collective readiness to weather frustration and accept disappointment that the family, more than the individual, remained central.

What the Founding Parents achieved, above all, was the implicit knowledge that God was with them. They had been chosen to guide the Children of Israel away from primitive idol worship to a profound redefinition of ethical behavior and moral principles. If they had limitations, it was because they had started out as ordinary individuals. Though they didn't always live up to the high standards demanded of them, they knew what God required and that His love, merciful as it was, was contingent on obedience. When they failed, it was because those models were difficult, if not overwhelming. They instinctively understood that every family was a source for reinforcing and intensifying His expectations. They knew what was expected of them.

The Book of Exodus begins with a new Pharaoh who knew not Joseph. The Hebrew population having grown in numbers that constituted a threat to his regime, he decided to destroy them through brutal slavery. When that didn't slow the birth rate, he instituted a system of male infanticide. One mother defied the decree, hiding her infant for three months. Refusing to drown her "goodly child," she placed him in a waterproof basket and floated him down the Nile under the watchful eye of his sister Miriam. Moses' survival—against all odds—was made possible by a royal princess who noticed the little ark, rescued the frightened baby, and raised the Hebrew boy in the palace as a royal prince.

Nevertheless, as an adult, Moses identified with the Hebrews and killed an Egyptian

Moses killing an Egyptian trying to protect a Jewish slave. Because of the killing, he will need to escape from the wrath of Pharaoh. From *The Book of Books in Pictures* **by Julius Schnorr von Carolsfeld. Verlag von Georg Wigand, Liepzig, 1908.**

who was attacking a fellow Hebrew. Fleeing from Pharaoh's wrath, he escaped to Midian, where he married a local woman and fathered two sons, Gershom and Eliezer. For forty years, we are told, he quietly tended his father-in-law's sheep (Exodus 2).

God had not been quietly asleep. He chose the time and place for action, and this was the time and place. He dispatched an angel to appear in the midst of a brightly burning bush that was neither charred nor consumed. As Moses turned to examine this phenomenon, a Voice called out his name: "Moses, Moses." And then God introduced Himself and explained the fearful situation of His people in Egypt. He heard their cry, witnessed their

A 1907 Bible card depicting Israelites dancing and celebrating the casting of the Golden Calf, as in Exodus 32:1–8, 30–35 (Providence Lithograph Company).

oppression, and chose Moses to confront Pharaoh and demand that he set them free. Moses modestly demurred, but God insisted and promised that He would not only stand with him but also would appoint his brother, Aaron, a more fluent and expressive speaker, to be spokesman on his behalf (Exodus 3, 4:14; 7.1). We think we know Moses, teacher and role model, television and movie hero. But who was Aaron?

Aaron was three years older than Moses. When Pharaoh didn't receive the brothers with hoped-for civility, but on the contrary doubled the slaves' work quota, Moses angrily challenged God's commitment to His people. Perhaps his bad manners led God to wonder if He had picked the right prophet. Nevertheless, at God's command, Aaron produced signs and wonders with his magical rod and pronounced ten plagues that would fall upon Egypt unless the Israelites were freed. But in spite of his exemplary performances, he was clearly subordinate to Moses, passive but supportive, receiving God's instructions almost always through his brother. Aaron was not to speak to the king alone. He was not to approach God. Except when he received the laws regarding the functions and duties of the Priests and Levites, he played no part in the escape across the Sea of Reeds. He did not accompany Moses when he ascended Mount Sinai for his forty-day meeting with God, although he was trusted, along with Miriam's son Hur, to handle any problems that might arise in the interim.

And then came the great sin of the Golden Calf, fashioned with Aaron's complicity as a replacement for his brother, on the mistaken belief that Moses was dead. Aaron hadn't tried or wasn't willing to stand up to the rabble who demanded a visible god, attempting instead to placate the people with a riotous celebration. God, however, was angered by Aaron's audacity and the blasphemous goings-on. Aaron acknowledged that he had "exposed them

Moses and Aaron, two of the greatest heroes in Jewish history. Engraving, 1526. By Hans Sebald Beham (1500–1550).

to disgrace." He blamed the people, not himself, and said he feared for his life if he had opposed them. Besides, he could not help it because the sinners were out of control and had been habituated to idolatry—and, besides, the calf had made itself (Exodus 32:24).

Aaron's humiliation is not expressed in the narrative. Surely it would have been too painful to describe, as his sin was the cause of the deaths of three thousand Levites as well as a plague. According to Rashi, Aaron's shame was manifest at the Tent of Meeting when the *Shechinah*, or Divine Presence, refused to appear in the Tabernacle following the inaugural service: "What have you done to me," he cried, "that you let me pronounce the Divine Service and be disgraced!" At which Moses immediately prayed for mercy—and the *Shechinah* returned to Israel.

Aaron was not invited to join his brother at the foot of Sinai to receive the second set of tablets and is absent from the remainder of Exodus except as Moses brings him forward. No mention is made of him in the initial theophany. No mention was made of him until he became Moses' interpreter. He was absent in the construction of the portable sanctuary. Although he supported Moses' hands to ensure victory against the Amalekites at Sinai, he was a minor participant in that drama (Exodus 17:8–13). Aaron was a prophet, yet subordinate to his younger brother. None of which was good for his ego. Was he jealous of Moses, whom he called "my master?" (Numbers 12:11). Probably not. They did not experience the bitter rivalries of Cain and Abel, Jacob and Esau, or Joseph and his siblings. Rather than compete, they supported each other. Or did they? When Aaron's oldest sons died after offering an unauthorized fire to God, Moses might have said some comforting words to his brother. He

An engraving of a Jewish family in the *Illustrated News of the World*, after a photograph, March 31, 1860.

didn't. His response was faith-based: priestly leadership requires a single-minded acceptance of God's judgment. (A little show of affection wouldn't have hurt.)

In spite of the uneven rewards that God had bestowed, the end result was harmony, thanks to the brothers' elevated level of mutual regard and respect. Well, not quite. Was it only to Moses that God spoke face to face? (Numbers 12:2). Aaron joined his sister Miriam in roundly criticizing their brother for avoiding sexual contact with his wife Zipporah because his heightened status presumably demanded ritual purity. God did not sympathize with them. For challenging Moses' leadership and conduct, Miriam was afflicted with a painful skin condition until Aaron interceded on her behalf. But it was Moses who offered the successful plea: "Please, God, heal her!" (Numbers 12:10–13). And He did.

Although Aaron was relegated to second place (or third behind Joshua?), when he died, the entire house of Israel, men and women alike, wept for thirty days (Numbers 20:29). For Moses, only the men mourned (Sifra 45d). Rashi commented that people loved Aaron because Aaron loved peace—especially between husband and wife. Moses was viewed as a stern lawgiver and judge. He apparently ignored his sons Gershom and Eliezer. Was he so preoccupied with his duties that he had no time for fatherhood? Did he complain when God told him to pass the symbols of office to Joshua rather than to his children? His final blessings to the different tribes of Israel omitted mention of his wife or sons—or the faithful brother who had served so many years at his side.

More questions than answers. The Jewish family has survived beyond history. It has been brought forward and brought down. It has survived through remembering to forget, through marriage with another Jew, and through settling down with a warm pastrami on rye with a kosher pickle.

5

The Golden Middle Ages

When Samuel ha-Nagid (993–1056) sang of love, it was to a fascinating young man who came to him at midnight: "*I'd sell my soul for that boy who said, 'Come drink the red wine that flows to you between my lips.'*" The father of secular Hebrew poetry of the Spanish Middle Ages, a versatile scholar of Talmud and Arabic literature, vendor of spices, political and military leader honored as ha-Nagid (Prince in Israel), Samuel is generally credited with the introduction of erotic verses exploiting intense moments of beauty and desire. He was among the leading courtier-rabbis of the Golden Age of lyric poetry in eleventh-century al-Andalus and Sefarad—Muslim and Jewish cultural Spain. "Before Samuel's time, poets had barely begun to chirp, but in Samuel's time their voices were loud and strong." So remembered the philosopher-historian of Spanish Jewry, Abraham ibn Daud (1110–1180), who revered Samuel not only as a poet but also as the champion of Jewish life under Muslim rule.

Under the liberal tenth century-caliph Abd-ar-Rahman III (890–961), Jews had experienced a high level of autonomy: they were exempt from military service, and they enjoyed religious freedom and a prosperous secular existence. But when civil war between the Arabs and the Berbers broke out in 1009, the intellectual environment that had encouraged philosophy, science, and literature failed, and Samuel fled to the safety of Granada. When Samuel's unpopular son, Joseph ibn Naghrela (1035–1066), succeeded him as vizier, massacres of Jews erupted. Joseph was charged with abuse of his office, ostentation, and benefitting his Jewish friends by employing them in government service. Muslim mobs attacked the palace, crucified Joseph, and killed thousands of Jews. Expulsions, plundering, forced conversion, or exile followed. The Golden Age collapsed, presaging the onset of systematized Jewish persecution during Muslim wars of expansion.

Once the riots spent themselves, spiritually evocative, graphically suggestive, or homoerotic literature emerged, establishing a major theme of carnal, as well as idealized, love in poetry. These earthy verses, experienced as stylized clichés rather than as personal emotions, were expressed in traditional fantasies that served as wish fulfillment or in visionary daydreams of sensual pleasure, pain, and unresolved passion.

Religious Hebrew poetry had been sharing its values with secular Hebrew works (often Biblical in style). Both were stimulated by the cosmopolitan character and favorable patronage of wealthy Jewish courtiers and business and professional men at the Spanish courts, as well as in distant countries such as Egypt and Iraq. Sephardic Jews became well established in Iberian lands, a center for spiritual and cultural life in a wider environment. In *History of the Jews* (1853), Heinrich Graetz suggests that, whereas relative isolation and geographical distance from parts of Arab and European civilization brought about the decline of some

Jewries, Hispanic Judaism "rose to the height of universal importance.... When Judaism had come to a standstill in the East, and had grown weak with age, it acquired new vigor in Spain, and extended its fruitful influence over a wide range." Jane Gerber's more recent *Jews of Spain: A History of the Sephardic Experience* (1992) linked Sepharad to new-world vigor: "What they did do, and admirably, is establish pioneering new style settlements in Western societies, successfully sustaining their encounters with dominant non-Jewish cultures, and in effect laying down the guidelines for the modern Jewish experience."

The Spanish Golden Age—or its remnants—continues to flourish through modern evocations of ballads, erotic poems, and wedding and wine songs in Hebrew, Spanish, Arabic, Aramaic, and Ladino—not always recognizable as Jewish, but happily broadening the scope of traditional life. Satiric and humorous lampoons are performed at popular social gatherings where songs are sung, dissipation is encouraged, and physical pleasures, famously indulged.

But, for Solomon ibn Gabirol (1021–c. 1057), it was not erotic love but the mystical contest between human fate and devotion to God that dominated his pessimistic view of life, much of which was spent in loneliness, physical pain, and spiritual doubt. Yet, in his philosophic ode to the kingship of God, *Keter Malkuth* (*Royal Crown*), he employs the power of Divine love to express humility in the face of sickness and alienation from his contemporaries: humbly yearning for God, he manifested his faith: "I will cling to Thy mercy ... until Thou bless lights on me." He wrote personal secular and devotional expressions as well as unconventional love poetry. His sexual images may have been addressed to an imaginary lover, although they remain spiritually linked to God and His beloved congregation of Israel. When God eventually returns to His people, "He will comfort Himself between their breasts.... In the time of love, I will fall upon you like the dew of heaven."

Moses ibn Ezra (1060–1135?) welcomed the great literary activity that now emerged in secular and religious poems "as water first moving slowly and then gushing forth in torrents." However, the controlling power of his family clashed with his erotic and emotional despair. The girl he wanted was his brother's daughter, but her parents decided he wasn't "substantial" enough. He left home and happiness behind before sending her a passionate letter: "Without you the whole world is a prison.... Sweet as honey are your lips but they are not for me.... Though you are false to me, I will be true to you." He learned that before she died in childbirth, she urged him to return home and find peace in sorrow. He remained a bitter wanderer, hoping for forgiveness for his youthful lapses, dwelling on women's breasts, thighs and lips, wine, music, and dance, and showing up drunk at some anonymous girl's door. In another mood, he celebrated homosexuality, recalling the nights and dawns he and his lover caressed each other and drank the fleshly succulence of their mouths. The pious reader need not blush—after all, it was God Himself who provided the desire and the wherewithal to proceed.

Judah Halevi (1075–1141?), a versatile master of devotional and secular expression, as well as Arabic and Jewish theology, moved prose from rational literature to romantic poetry, from sensitive tradition to popular culture, where graceful Arabic lyrics and Biblical Hebrew scripture were expressed in secular and religious stereotypes. His innovative love poems modified or altered the conventional artistic style of the time, wandering from blithe ease to brainy wit. He became a successful physician until his need to communicate ecstatic feelings prompted him to give up economic security—as well as his wife, daughter, and grandson—for the Holy Land and affective poetry. He sighed, "Not for gold, but for the girl's smiling mouth.... She half blinds my sight." By invoking the *Song of Songs*—and

Omar Khayyam's *Rubaiyat*—he dreamed of sensual desire indulged without inhibition or restraint, of being captured by beauteous flesh, the apple-roundness of breasts, the dream of kissed lips. Heinrich Heine called him "the light and star of his generation."

Abraham Ibn Ezra (1089–1164) possessed a sharp intellect, a lively personality, and a roving spirit which kept him poor, luckless, and dependent on wealthy, but weary, benefactors: "If I come for a handout in the morning, the great man has just left; if at night, he is asleep." Again, he describes his wretched state: "If I were to deal in shrouds, no one would ever die. If I sold candles, the sun would never set."

While many of his poems were dedicated to God, he didn't neglect a nod to a beautiful lady with breasts "like clusters of grapevines." "Do not worry," he helpfully advises her. "If you sin, just say you have been enchanted!"

Maimonides encouraged modesty and charity, rejected astrology, warned against false messiahs, and defended the death penalty for witchcraft, heresy, or willful disregard of Sabbath laws. In his *Essay on Intercourse,* he counseled treatment for Saladin's nephew, who sought to achieve an "augmentation of his sexual potency on account of the increasing number of his female slaves." As the rational guide to the perplexities of his time, he denied the authenticity of supernatural intervention, the devil, and Satanic worldviews. His ethics prohibited sacrifice and frowned upon slavery, but he made pragmatic accommodations to the times.

Statue of Yehuda Halevi (1080–1141), an Andalusian Jewish physician, poet and philosopher. Halevi is considered one of the greatest Hebrew poets, celebrated both for his religious and secular poems. A statue in the Ralli museum yard, Caesarea (Wikimedia Commons).

He advised scholars to marry only after they had learned a trade and bought a home. He allotted them four wives each, but restricting cohabitation with each to once a month—and then only when accompanied by pious thoughts. "He should not always be with his wife, like a rooster," he cautioned, "but should reserve Friday nights for his sexual activity." And, he added, the wife should be awake. Although most sages focused on the role of women as worldly sex objects, the more philosophically-grounded Maimonides explored women's status in the Talmudic world: *"It is through the merit of righteous women that our ancestors were redeemed from Egypt"* (Sota 11b). He recognized the snares of assimilation and conversion, as well as the failure of social coherence and the corrosion or disintegration of Jewish life. As a philosopher, he attempted to reconcile the conflict between the rational and reason. His philosophy impacted educated Muslims and Jews, requiring their reexamination of the theological concepts of revelation, the logical difficulties and allegorical interpretations of Biblical material, and the anthropomorphism attributed to God. (The perplexed are still seeking guidance about their emotional lives. With luck, they may succeed.)

In the Golden Age, folktales, myths, fables, mischievous creatures, pithy sayings, and love stories were often set in enchanted Sephardic lands in which every field or forest was occupied by good or evil spirits and every hearth and homestead, by a miracle-working rabbi. *The Flight of the Eagle*, a twelfth-century Spanish fairy tale in Howard Schwartz's 1987 *Jewish Tales of the Supernatural*, recounts the story of a childless rabbi in Guadalajara:

> It happened one night in medieval times when a rabbi had a dream in which he was promised a son who would disappear at age eighteen, not to be seen again for many years. Sure enough, at the appointed time, young Shlomo, who had studied all the sacred texts and was accounted a fine scholar, was whisked off by an enormous eagle and dropped off at the palace of a king who was so charmed by the boy that he offered him kosher food and a comfortable bedchamber. What the king did not offer was the hand of his beautiful daughter, who had promptly fallen in love with the handsome Israelite. They secretly spent every day learning Torah, but when he pointed out that they could not marry because he was Jewish and she was not, the princess converted. Who would perform the ceremony? Well, none other than Gabriel, Michael, and Uriel, who had just arrived from Paradise to prepare a proper wedding contract. But trouble arrived when the eagle showed up on schedule and returned Shlomo to his parents.

It wouldn't be a love story if it ended on a sour note, so we are pleased to report that while the princess almost died of loneliness, a Jewish doctor cured her, and a resourceful rabbi restored her to the beloved husband, who had almost died of the same affliction. Gabriel showed up with the proper *ketubbah*, the Seven Blessings were recited, and they lived happily all the days of their lives.

MORAL: There is no moral. This is a fairy tale.

Let us take a look at another manifestation of love between brothers. Unfortunately, as we have seen, it is not universal. Here is *The Man Who Went to Hell*:

> There was a rich brother and a poor brother. The rich one used to send the poor one a generous gift of Passover matzos until one day he decided he would keep all the unleavened bread for himself. When his brother inquired as to why, he was told to go to Hell. The poor brother, on the way to find that destination, walked and walked until he came to a small house where three maidens sat spinning threads of gold, wool, and silk.
>
> "Alack! Alas! We have been spinning away our lives waiting for three young men to marry, but not one has come."

"Don't worry," he said. "I will try to help you. Remember that God is good and He will look after you."

He kept on walking until he came to a large apple tree. Like many desirable objects, the fruit was beautiful on the outside, but bitter inside. The tree was anxious to know why.

"I will find out if I can," offered the poor man, and kept on walking until he met a ferryman. "For years, I have waited for passengers; nobody has come, and yet I am not allowed to leave," he explained as tears fell from his eyes.

"I will try to find out why you can't leave the ferry."

Because of his efforts to help others, he did discover why the maidens, the tree, and the ferryman were troubled—for which they so lavishly rewarded him that he was able to host a Passover celebration of his own that excelled all known holiday feasts. This did not sit well with the jealous brother.

"Where did you get this wealth?"

"My brother, it was you who sent me to Hell. That's how I got it."

So the rich brother decided to take his own advice. "I'll go there myself." He walked until he came upon the ferryman.

"Perhaps you know where Hell is?"

"Certainly. This ferryboat is Hell."

When the rich brother boarded the boat, the ferryman stranded him in Hell for the rest of his life because he had been concerned only with his own well-being and had ignored the needs of a brother.

MORAL: Reward follows redeeming qualities; punishment follows evil traits, just as the Good Book says.

Some brothers were different.

There was once a large farm where two brothers lived in close proximity and grew their own wheat. One of the brothers supported a growing family, while the other was single. There came a bountiful harvest for which they thanked God and wished to share their good fortune. Recognizing that his married sibling had many mouths to feed, and having more than he wanted, the unmarried brother decided to increase his brother's store by taking some of his own grain and secretly bringing it to his kin's house. At the same time, the married brother was concerned for his single brother, who had no wife or children to look after him, and decided to increase his brother's share. Each secretly carried wheat across their fields to the other's house until they once crossed roads, discovered their mutual devotion, and fell into a loving embrace. The example of their mutual love earned them a great reward. The Holy Temple was built on the very spot where they farmed. God was very pleased, particularly since the first Biblical brothers had caused Him nothing but grief.

As the Psalmist reminds us, "How good and how pleasant it is for brothers to dwell together in harmony" (133:1).

Here is another happily-ever-after story: *A Daughter Who Was Wiser Then Her Father:*

There was once a young king in Grenada who was determined to marry a wise and intelligent woman. As he traveled incognito throughout his country in search of such an uncommon jewel, he fell in with an old man, and they decided to walk on together. The king asked if he should carry the old man or if he, the king, should be carried. The old man didn't reply but thought it was a foolish question. When they came to a field of barley, the king asked if the barley had been eaten or not. Again, the old man thought it was a foolish question. Finally, they came upon a funeral procession, and the king inquired whether or not the man in the coffin was dead or alive.

The old man, now disgusted with his companion, returned home where his daughter explained the mysterious questions: "The way seems shorter if one tells another a story—as if the teller were carrying the listener. As for the barley, if it hasn't been sold, it hasn't yet been eaten. Regarding the corpse, if there were surviving children, the man could not be considered dead."

The father was impressed, found the king, and invited him to a delicious chicken dinner. As the king began to carve the bird, he gave the legs to the old man's wife, the wings to the daughter, the head to the old man, and the rest to himself. Again, the daughter explained: "The chicken's head went to the old man since he was the head of the family, the legs to his wife because she was on her feet all day, the wings to the daughter who would soon be flying off with a husband, and the rest to the stranger because there was no one else with whom to share it."

The King found his true mate in the lovely daughter. May they live happily.

Jewish moral and ethical customs and practices steadily moved across Christian and Muslim Europe, relayed by preachers who spun legends and homilies drawn from the non-legalistic parts of the Torah and *Midrashic* parables. They told of Jews who were isolated from mainstream life by religious prejudice, sumptuary laws, lack of security, and an inability to acquire freehold property. They learned that Papal policy was not consistent and that some popes loosened the restrictions. They experienced the laws of the Third Lateran Council of 1179, which called for toleration (but not equality) of the Jews "on the grounds of humanity alone." They welcomed the ruling of Duke Frederick of Austria, who, in 1244, granted them privileges were soon extended to Jews in Poland, Bohemia, and Hungary.

While Jews valued the ties of civilization to the past, they stressed the lessons and profits offered by the contemporary world. At its best, this world regarded reason and faith as the ideals for raising man to his highest potential of toleration, peace, and ecumenical love, a philosophy expressed by the thirteenth-century German lyric poet Walther von der Vogelweide in *My Brother Man*: Christians, Jews, and heathens serve the same God Who cares for all of creation. "Many call Thee Father who will not own me as brother.... We are alike both within and without."

Such homilies were popular wherever Jews lived, especially in small isolated communities such as Kurdistan in southwest Asia. *The Folk Literature of the Kurdistani Jew* by Yona Sabar (1982) and Ken Blady's *Jewish Communities in Exotic Places* (2000) explore the history and literature of ancient Jewish communities dating from the eighth century BCE, when Jews had been exiled from Israel by Assyrian conquerors. These Jews claim lineage from the Ten Tribes of Israel and take pride in living in the land where Noah's Ark came to rest and Ezra the Scribe is buried. According to their tradition, King Solomon, who ruled over the nether world, ordered a tribe of genies to fly north and round up a bevy of enchanting maidens for his enjoyment. Unfortunately, he died before he could enjoy their attractions. The genies then inherited the lovely ladies, remembered as the mothers of the Kurdish people.

By the latter half of the twelfth century, such fairy tales had been largely displaced by more truthful reports. We learn of two Sephardi travelers, Benjamin of Tudela and Petachia of Ratisbon, who penetrated the flourishing communities of Amadiya and Arbel, which boasted large wealthy Jewish populations and many synagogues. Their descriptions of major towns such as Mosul and Zakho suggested that Jews had brief periods of self-rule and well-run civil services. However, when one of the last great Golden Age Spanish poets, Judah al-Harizi (1165–1225), visited Kurdistan, he reported that, regrettably, the synagogues were filled with people largely ignorant of Jewish law, prayers, and ceremonies. Because of high rates of illiteracy, legends, songs, and sayings were transmitted orally in Kurdish, Neo-Aramaic, Arabic, Turkish, and Persian dialects (and later recorded by twentieth-century redactors). Synagogue services were often memorized; perhaps few understood their meanings. Nevertheless, their recorded literature is imbued with deep spirituality, as was their love of Sabbath and holiday ceremonies. Because much of this folk literature was derived from non–Jewish sources, the preponderance of the material was secular, with busybody kings and animals available to cheer or frighten the locals. Please meet The Happy Carpenter:

> A king and his counselor were passing through a market town one day when they noticed a carpenter simultaneously working at his job and shaving his head with a sharp ax without hurting himself. The counselor, having explained to the king that the fellow remained unhurt because he was satisfied with his lot and that he and his wife loved each other, decided to test this unusual state of well-being. He hired an old woman to inform the carpenter's wife that his source of pleasure was actually the attentions he was receiving at a house of ill fame. Loud screams, bitter tears, self-imposed exit from his once happy home. Nevertheless, he continued to connect the axe to his head. The good king was appalled at his counselor's devious test and immediately ordered the old woman to restore the loving relationship of the husband and wife. After which the carpenter, cheerful again, was able to shave his head in peace and tranquility.

Does the story have a point? Certainly. Marital happiness is secured when the wife is satisfied.

Kurdish townsfolk were apparently obsessed with axes and head injuries. Here is a tale about a lion that suffered from a woodcutter's sharp blade as well as a wife's sharp tongue:

> A formerly loving couple were having a difficult time because the woodcutter husband barely earned a decent living. Loud screams, bitter tears, self-imposed exit from his once happy home. This time there was no good king to come to the rescue, only the king of the beasts, a friendly lion. "O lion, I am filled with despair," cried the woodcutter. "No food, no clothes for my children, only a wife who quarrels and curses. Please kill me and get it over!" Now, this lion was a kind beast and provided the poor man with a gold coin. The wife was now so pleased that she urged her husband to invite their new friend to dinner. The lion accepted, enjoyed a hearty welcome, thanked his hosts and prepared to leave. The wife, who understood neither loving relationships nor the finer points of etiquette, whispered to her husband that the lion suffered from bad breath. Unfortunately, the lion overheard her unfeeling words with suffering and distress. He insisted that the woodcutter take his axe and strike his head until it was split in two. The injury to the lion's head healed in a few weeks, but the injury from her hurtful words did not.

MORAL: Love and concern for others' feelings is highly valued. Ingratitude is hurtful. Be careful.

And a few more Kurdish folk tales—these about love and romance:

> A young fellow has fallen so deeply in love that he would not exchange the girl for the entire world, although she has caused him much torment before bringing him happiness. When he asked for a kiss, her father came by unannounced. End of story. We will never know what happened, but we can guess that if her father made a habit of prowling around young lovers, sadly, there would be a dearth of kisses.

Oral stories were often more direct and clearer than those written down. Socrates had judged that "writing gives us not truth, but only the semblance of truth … written language has its limitations because it seriously erodes the intellect and psyche, creating forgetfulness because listeners will no longer use their memories." However, these tales, whether written or oral, were not only intended to instruct or indoctrinate, but also to communicate in imaginative terms aesthetic or personally valid experiences. Such simple folk material was not to be despised, for as the Dubner Maggid Rabbi Jacob Kranz (1741–1804) pointed out, "with a penny candle one may find a gold coin."

Although most of these tales are not inherently Jewish, many were recited and collected in Jewish communities for generations. Stressing dependence on God and His role in the struggle between good and evil, they are cast with Biblical figures—kings, princes, princesses, rabbis, and scholars—who operated in a variety of cultures. Dozens of these sacred and secular mystical parables and fables found their way into popular culture. Some were love stories:

> In a palace on the shores of the Aegean Sea, there once lived a king with his second wife—the first having died after giving birth to a lovely princess. While the king was away on a hunting trip, the queen, who hated her stepdaughter, kept the girl secluded for fear that she might marry and have a son who would supplant her. However, she was unable to keep a handsome young Jewish cantor from gazing at the princess, who was on the balcony of the palace tower. He immediately fell in love with her. Although he was aware that he stood little chance of succeeding, he hoped he might win her with his heartfelt voice. Night after night, he serenaded her with songs sweeter than those of a nightingale. Carried away by their beauty, she tossed him a ring that sealed their love. But they remained far apart, she on the balcony, he on the beach. He could sing; she could sigh.
>
> The wicked queen, too, heard the heavenly melodies that he had learned in the synagogue, but, as they were unfamiliar to her, she believed the voice was that of a mermaid. When she discovered that he was not only poor but also Jewish, she ordered her servants to do away with him and the grieving princess as well. The lovers decided to run off, but the evil queen had them caught and put to death. But wait—the princess was turned into a dove, and the would-be groom, into a nightingale, and they flew away to a tree where they sang together in perfect harmony. But when the lovebirds were caught, the stepmother ordered their throats slits under her very eyes.
>
> *(Don't stop reading. There is a relatively happy ending.)*
>
> The souls of the birds entered two fish—a perch and a flounder—and they swam away, but the wicked queen's vengeance knew no end. She ordered the fish killed and prepared for her lunch. Fortunately, she choked on one of the fish bones and was no more. When the king returned from his hunting trip and discovered what happened, he had the fish buried together in a grave where a carnation and a rose miraculously grew entwined in love, never to be separated. As for the evil queen, her body exuded an offensive smoke for many years.

MORAL: Sometimes love wins; sometimes evil is punished.

Medieval Jewish life in the Iberian Peninsula had been see-sawing between Muslim and Christian rulers for centuries—occasionally tolerant, but mostly not good for the Jews. When fanaticism, religious conformity, and forced conversions led to mass expulsions, the Sephardim developed new commercial and cultural centers, finding a niche as indispensable "capitalists" financing much of Europe as it proceeded from a barter to a money economy. Persistent Catholic resistance to "usury" had made an opening for Ashkenazim from France and Germany until the establishment of free loans dispensed by the Catholic Church put a crimp on Jewish lending. Jews were reduced to petty dealings, and their usefulness was eroded.

But they still read. Translated secular works titillated them with doomed and bawdy lovers. They were less attuned to classical Arabic or Hebrew forms, more drawn to the courtly literature coming out of Italy: Dante (1265–1321), Boccaccio (1313–1375), and Petrarch (1304–1374) set the latest standards of style and design. The poems contributed to the development of stories in which infatuation was seen as an ideal of a worthy life, in which generosity between lovers was valued over wanton sex, and in which intellect was occasionally valued over appetite. The parables enriched the imaginative cross-cultural literature as it moved from medieval Jewish spiritualism to the lyricism of the early Italian Renaissance. These themes were also found in the witty, lascivious poems of Immanuel of Rome (Imanoello Giudeo) (1261–1328), a Jewish contemporary and friend of Dante's who introduced the sonnet form in Hebrew. As a lively, satirical commentator on loose living, he wrote Biblical commentaries and dabbled in humorous riddles and questionable wedding songs. But as his heresies moved him away from Synagogue (and Church) towards the incoming spirit of Humanism, his fortunes dwindled, and he took to the road, impoverished and bitter. His sonnets, which may have shocked the local provincials, were collected in *Machberoth*, twenty-eight chapters of verse and rhymed prose offering snippets of contemporary Jewish life in its scholarship, strengths, weaknesses, and extravagant talk of fair ladies. Hell was his preferred destiny, he judged, for that is where beautiful women and passionate girls dwelt, while heaven, he was convinced, was full of withered crones. His erotica was criticized or praised by later rabbis, who accused or commended him for his story of a virgin who laments that being poor and alone, her ripe breasts and pubic hair remain undiscovered and unexplored by approaching suitors.

It is no surprise that Joseph Caro (1488–1575), in his 1565 abridged compendium of Talmudic laws and practices, *Shulchan Aruch* (*Prepared Table*), forbade the reading of the *Machberoth*. What would Caro have said to Immanuel's report that "although he has a penis, for fear of wearing it out when he has sex, he uses somebody else's"?

As the Jewish diaspora moved to distant areas, its literary excellence embraced many other exotic cultures. In their *Folklore Literature of the Sephardic Jews* (1986), Samuel Armistead and Joseph H. Silverman organize five centuries of such ballads and related melodies, exploring their origins and comparing them with later texts from Portugal, North Africa, Israel, and Hispanic America. One version, printed in Zaragoza in 1550, but probably following an older Judeo-Spanish tradition, was recorded in Tetuan, Morocco, in 1962.

Here is King Fernando's Invasion of France and the Saga of Sancho and Urraca:

> Following his conquest of France and his usurpation of unlimited power, King Fernando Sancho unfairly imprisons his brother Alonzo in an illegal seizure of sovereignty. We are not told of the charges against him, nor why any of his defenders were subject to severe punishment. Although the king believes that he answers to no one, he is challenged by his sister Urraca, who demands Alonzo's release. She reminds Sancho that, after he slapped her when she was a child, he offered her a gift if she would not cry. She did not. Now she shows up in fine royal garments to claim her due. Although she is a princess, she risks her rank and status as she begs him to carry out his promise and free the captive. Sancho equivocates, offering her money and a choice of his cities, both of which she proudly refuses. What she wants is their brother's immediate freedom. What she got was a hollow assurance of his liberty and a curse against insistent women. The king will not be defied.

In one version of the story, Alonzo is murdered. In another, he lives, as Urreca's determination overcomes Sancho's authority.

MORAL: Sibling relationships remain courageous and loving.

The Hispanic-Jewish author Vidal Benveniste (c. 1380–c. 1439) was among a small group of fifteenth-century poets whose work marked the climax of major Hebrew poetry from medieval Spain. Anti-Jewish activity was blamed, but acculturation and conversion on the part of sophisticated Renaissance Humanist Jews was more likely. Benveniste's drama *Efer ve-Dinah* tells of an ill-suited couple and a greedy father who symbolically represent the deterioration of conventional moral and religious standards during the fourteenth and fifteenth centuries. The tale, proudly written in the Hebrew Holy Tongue, deliberately avoided "barbarous" vernacular as a literary device. The text is intended as a parody of the marriage *ketubbah*. As a source of fun, the allegory has its place, Benveniste explains, but its lesson was serious—sexual gratification is not the goal of life, and the "vanities of sin" must make way for more temperate values.

Here is *Efer ve-Dinah*:

> A money and status-hungry father, his beautiful young daughter, Dinah, and Efer, a rich elderly widower, participate in a humorous (or horrendous) game of deceit and immorality. Efer promises abundant wealth to her greedy father in return for Dinah. The ill-fated wedding vows concluded, the bride expects sexual gratification from her husband as he attempts to perform his conjugal duties. Alas, he not only deals in pleasure for a price but is impotent as well. In desperation, he resorts to a strong aphrodisiac. When it fails to arouse his manpower, he recklessly increases the dose. Soon he is gone.

MORAL: The need for supercharged benefits destroys those who make a mockery of love. Good riddance.

The Golden Age of Hebrew poetry that flourished in the lifetimes of these philosophers and writers was brought to an end by massacres, persecutions, and the inroads of assimilation that turned their thoughts from love to the need to survive. The Sephardic heydays of the tenth and eleventh centuries collapsed, but it was not the end of the rabbinic, mystical prose or great secular literature that has outlived time. Medieval Jews are acknowledged for their achievements, prospering through cross-disciplinary scholarship, kinship relationships, trading skills, deft craftsmanship, legendary romances, beautifully printed books—and soaring lovesick lyrics.

During their brief halcyon days of peace and prosperity, they flashed a brilliant incandescence on the mind and heart of the Golden Middle Ages.

6

Midrash and Magic

It was once believed that spirits had free will and were able to manipulate humans as they chose. As legends of angels, demons, ghosts, Messiah, Satan, and other paranormal phenomena were described in Jewish folklore, reality and fantasy morphed from make-believe into sorcery, superstition, magical charms, riddles and the hidden texts of allegory. Miraculous stories lent a sense of wonder to powers that defied known physical laws, powers that were not seen, understood, or explained, powers with no apparent existence outside the imagination.

It all began when Judaism evolved from a prophetic religion to a post-Biblical society following the destruction of the Second Temple in 70 CE. Fearful that the Oral Torah would be lost or forgotten in the scattered communities of the diaspora, or subsumed in Hellenistic rationalism, rabbis under the guidance of Yehudah ha-Nasi (1735–213) redacted existing debates and commentaries, editing and canonizing them as the Mishnah—Torah by word of mouth. Interpretations, digressions, and arguments regarding written and oral law (Torah and Mishnah) were collected as Midrash. Often predating the Mishnah, they were anthologized and compiled in the post-Temple period, originating as rabbinic exegeses or clarifications that commented on, rationalized, and analyzed the Bible and Talmud, often achieving the status of divine revelation. By attaching themselves to the communal memory, their creative and often fantastic explanations drew the texts close to contemporary life, accepting the ephemeral over the mundane. Focusing on original constructions to carry theological and social records of Judaism across neighboring or diverse communities, Midrashim looked beyond stereotypes, investing the Bible with deepening pertinence and comprehensibility. Although many of its narratives were derived from the intercultural, non-Jewish, or classical literature of Babylonia, Rome, and Persia, by the twelfth century, they became fixed religious or moral accretions to Jewish life and character. Their familiar stories tied the twilight world to the material world, extracting ambiguous, hidden, or multiple meanings from terse, compressed, or reworked Bible stories; because the scriptural words in themselves were often unfamiliar, editors judiciously balanced knowable facts with eccentric fiction. It was largely by reformulating and universalizing these imaginative dreams into fictional entertainment that the Torah, with its beliefs in a single God and a universal morality, became accessible to the wider Jewish populations.

Midrash exists in two forms of rabbinic literature. It includes *Halachah*'s binding rules of everyday behavior and rituals, as well as the ancient *Aggadot* or written homilies that equated magic with idolatry. They suggested that humans fall into disorder and confusion through the potency of occult manifestations (Sanhedrin 7:7), as well as through reliance on devils, witches and soothsayers. While all of this was forbidden as anathema to God

Saul and the Witch of Endor. Engraving, 1820. By Washington Allston (1779–1843).

(Deuteronomy 18:9–14, 32:17 and Leviticus 19:26 and 20:6), nevertheless, tractate *Berakhot* offers instructions on how to catch sight of supernatural beings and demons whose idolatrous abominations have no real existence. But just in case they do, human agents were directed to catch them or drive them off by loud noises, circumcision knives, and by affixing a *mezuzah* to the doorpost. Rashi, the eleventh-century French scholar of the Bible and Talmud, gave credence to the malevolent demon Lilith, who seized newborn babies and killed them or their mothers—unless childbed charms or amulets undid her control. *Caution*: Don't mess with demons. And then there was 1 Samuel in

A fanciful woodcut of Rashi, an 11th century French scholar, 1539. By William of Paris. Appeared in a printing of *Postillae maiores totius anni cum glossis & quaestionibus.*

the Bible, which tells of King Saul who, having disobeyed God, turned to the Witch of Endor to summon the prophet Samuel from the dead to advise on combating the Philistine army. It didn't work. Saul and his three sons perished the next day; worse, Israel was lost to the enemy (1Samuel 28:6–19). *Caution:* Obey God. Pay attention to Ecclesiastes 9:5,10—"the dead know nothing ... there is no knowledge or wisdom in the grave."

Such superstitious beliefs were prevalent among the Jews in the Mizrachi (Eastern non-Sephardic) world. Prophylactic measures were taken to be on guard against witches, ogres, ghosts and goblins among the Jews in the Caucasus. Obsession with the Evil Eye among the Jews of Kurdistan required facial and body tattoos and bracelets made from wolves' teeth to ward off its pernicious effects.

On the other hand, the twelfth-century Rabbi Moses ben Maimon (Rambam to the Jews, Maimonides to the Christian world) denied their efficacy, believing they are lies and falsehoods accepted by gullible fools, uneducated women, and children (Avodat Kokhavim 11:16). While rabbis optimistically tried to distance fearful Jews from such deviant practices, reliance on the power of darkness remained alive and well.

Demonology surfaced in the mystical side of the Torah developed in the Kabbalah, the cosmology of the Torah, the essence of God's communication with the world that effectively turned traditional texts into allegory. It became pronounced in the twelfth and thirteenth centuries in Spain and Southern France, taking form in the *Sefer ha-Zohar (Book of Splendor)*. Although many authorities disapproved of this folk religion, they were not able to restrict its influence or sense of community. Through its interpretations and revelations,

The study in the alleged synagogue in Worms where Rashi did his work, completed in 1034, Hintere Judengasse 6, Worms, Germany (Ilsemarie, Wikimedia Commons).

Kabbalah sought unity with God in the ten Divine manifestations or *sefirot*. By reconciling relationships between the eternal and the finite worlds, messianic dreamers attracted scores of followers as they transcended the ordinary. Revered as wonder-workers seeking reality within or outside the limits of God, they promoted piety and righteousness over strict observance, believing that salvation was attainable by observing certain ethical and intense spiritual principles. Fables and parables of God's immanence, often extending into magical practices, were passed down through generations, keeping alive messianic hopes for an approved and improved world. Kabbalah warned persons who died without repenting serious sins that they would suffer eternal torture, or that *dybbuks* or wandering souls might enter young women's vaginas and control their sexual behavior until a Kabbalah-trained rabbi exorcised the intruder.

Although men were possessed less often, they were able to arouse love in a chosen prospect by adopting the magical practices outlined in the apocryphal thirteenth- or fourteenth-century manuscript, *The Wisdom of the Chaldeans,* from *The Sword of Moses*:

> Take a tablet of fine silver and draw on it a picture of the woman you desire. Write the names of those who also love her on her shoulder. This will gain you her strong and unbreakable passion. Follow this up with conjurations to a variety of angels to inflame her with your love and cause her destiny to be united with yours as Adam was united with Eve. She must not eat, drink, sleep, stand or sit until she is in love with you … and fulfills all your wishes and desires. Then heat the tablet and you will see marvelous things.

While similar narratives are found in many other collections, Jewish literature recognized few cultural or geographic boundaries; it floated along wherever Ashkenazi, Sephardi, or Mizrachi listeners gathered to enjoy recycled tales in their own mother tongue. What mattered was not whether anyone believed that these incidents really happened, or whether the Messiah was actually on his way, or whether miraculous happy endings were ever realized. What was more important were the messages and values they reclaimed and communicated. They lasted because they were told with fervor and the presumption of truth based on improbable reasoning.

With time, writers backed away from traditional *Midrashic* stories, Talmudic literature, or the Biblical canon, and moved on to popular tales distributed in widespread communities. Jacob Pollak's 1602 *Ma'aseh Buch* (*Book of Stories*) included humorous Yiddish legends or parables that were the delight of Jewish audiences as well as sources of consciously derived moral or useful lessons, mystical inspiration, or fantastic and supernatural wonders. Fictional histories and romantic fables of the lives of Biblical heroes, however, were styled independent of didactic ideology, ethical works, or legalese Midrash.

With respectful deference to the originals, we begin with the Genesis tales that ushered daylight into the powers of magic:

> One day, as God was regarding the empty spaces of an uncompleted heaven and a vacant cosmos, He decided to flesh out His imagination with a universe of plants, animal life, and human tenants. Capping six days of unsparing work, He fashioned male and female beings equipped with emotions, basic intelligence, and the ability to communicate, reserving for Himself the attributes of divine love and justice. While He was shaping them into His own likeness, He consulted the Angels to get their opinions of His great adventure. The Angels of Love and Justice were in favor because they believed that man would be caring and just; the Angels of Truth and Peace disagreed because they believed that man's lies and disobedience would always triumph over virtue. None could understand why God would even consider mankind at all: "What is man, that Thou art mindful of him?" they asked.
>
> Answered God: "What is the use of all the appetizing dainties I prepare, if no one is there to enjoy them?"

Unfortunately, He soon became aware that, dainties or not, His first venture in humankind was incomplete. Adam lacked a companion to cure his loneliness and enlarge his world; all the animals that had come to him to be named had come in pairs. Behold, here comes Lilith, his very own partner! But when her demands for equality and rights were unceremoniously rejected, the first registered feminist flew away in a pique. That made room for his second wife, Eve, who was beautiful and compliant, causing his heart to tremble and throb. God planned a magnificent wedding for the couple. But when Satan/Snake learned he was excluded from the festivities, he used his malicious tools—disguise and duplicity—to arouse sexual desire in Eve, planning to direct her lust to him as soon as he could get rid of Adam. Misled about the consequences of eating from the Tree of the Knowledge of Good and Evil, Eve cajoled Adam by flattery and caresses to taste the forbidden fruit. The snake's strategy backfired: his unbridled libido brought about mankind's first sin as everyone knows and regrets. Confronted by a punishing God, he not only lost the power of speech, as well as his hands and feet, but also received eternal curses, including perpetual enmity between himself and woman.

Moral 1: Don't try to override God; it won't work.

Moral 2: Unbridled libido is destructive.

Because of their sin, Adam and Eve were forced to live in great distress outside of Paradise. He worked the unyielding land; she suffered painful childbirth. So far, nothing had been said about love. But they did learn to care. When Eve saw that Adam failed to produce enough food, she blamed herself, offering to die if God would return them to the Garden. Finally embarked on a rigid penance, Adam, noticing that Eve was not as strong as he was, took on most of the hard labor. When he was about to die, Eve wept and begged him to give her half his pain and anguish. "Lord of all powers," she prayed, "do not separate us now."

That was love as unifier.

But they weren't able to pass it on. Eve gave birth to Cain, the child of Satan (who finally had his way with her). Adam adopted Cain, after which he and Eve begat Abel. Fratricide was inevitable. It turned out that Cain desired his brother's beautiful twin sister, of whom we have thus far been ignorant. Deprived of her, and embittered because God preferred Abel's offering, Cain was primed for blood. When he picked a fight over some sheep, the situation became ripe for mayhem. Brotherly enmity had come into the world.

That was love as divider.

Other than siblings, there were uplifting biographies of heroes, heroines, and even anti-heroes on whom we may pass judgment. Some probably amused God.

Although Abraham and Sarah had been married for some time, Abraham, chaste as he was, had never looked at her. How she responded to this type of affection we do not know. Perhaps it should not concern us. At any rate, when he saw her reflection in the water as they waded through a stream, he finally noticed that she was very lovely. Since he was afraid that the Egyptians, who were known to be very sensual, might covet her, he bravely decided to hide her in a casket so that no harm might befall him.

"Does the casket contain wheat, pepper, gold, or precious stones?" inquired the officials.

"Yes," Abraham answered. He was prepared to pay the required taxes. Not being fools, they demanded he open the casket. Suddenly, all of Egypt shone with Sarah's beauty. Every other beauty was like an ape! Eve herself was outdone! Pharaoh approached her, intending no good. But wait. An angel appeared, gave the king several smart blows, turned his palace leprous, and thwarted all carnal desire.

The story does have a happy ending. Sarah remained pure and untouched, and Abraham received apologies and lavish presents from the king. And that was not all. He taught the Egyptians astronomy and astrology, unverified before his time.

Moral: Beauty demands its due, but virtue carries the day.

Surely you know what happened to Jacob when he traveled to Haran in search of a wife. As soon as he arrived, he noticed his cousin Rachel coming to water her father's flock. He instantly fell in love, impressing her with a dazzling display of superhuman power—love gave him the strength to roll away a heavy stone covering the well. He kissed her and wept with joy.

Why did Jacob weep? Genesis Rabbah, which expounds the book's chapters and verses item by item, suggests that Jacob had recently been robbed and was unable to offer her proper gifts. Or maybe he was saddened because he knew that they would not be buried together. Or was it because he had forgotten proper behavior and reproached himself for succumbing impetuously to love's call?

In the end, it all worked out. Following fourteen years of hard labor exacted by his uncle Laban for the beautiful Rachel, whom he wanted—and for weak-eyed Leah, whom he did not, but whom Dad sneaked into his marriage bed—Jacob eventually overcame deceit, coped with double wives, patched up the quarrel with his brother, Esau, and fathered the twelve tribes of Israel.

Love, or what passed for love, had conquered all.

> Moving on from Biblical sources, we meet three sons of a pious and very rich man who bequeathed to them a locked chest containing great wealth, stipulating that they not open it except in extreme need. The wicked youngest son counterfeited the key, removed all the money, and filled the box with stones. When the chest was eventually unsealed, the rascal claimed that his brothers had secretly pillaged its assets. The honest brothers instantly became suspicious of each other. A rabbi, called to judge between the once-amicable men, identified the guilty son who was tortured and soon confessed. Disobeying his father brought adversity to the wicked son who muddies the possibility of a happy ending for this ill-starred family.

MORAL: We learn that families that live together don't necessarily love together.

Some of these tales revolved around the ins and outs and ups and downs of folks in the snares of romantic love. Because the Midrash tells us in Genesis Rabbah (68:3–4) that God superintends the union of boys and girls even before they are born, love stories found a place in Pollak's *Ma'aseh* anthology:

> One day, as a fine young man was on his way to invite his family and friends to his wedding, he met the Prophet Elijah, who said, "Do you not know that you are about to die and that the Lord wishes to take your soul? At the wedding feast, a bareheaded man in tattered garments will approach you. It is the Angel of Death." The frightened bridegroom said he would willingly die if that is the will of God, but begged leave to bid farewell to his dear parents and loving bride.
>
> The father prayed.
>
> The mother wept.
>
> The bride spoke up: "The Angel of Death, you say! Stay right here. I will speak to him myself." And this is what she said: "Please remind God that Deuteronomy 24:5 stipulates that a man who takes a wife shall be free for a whole year to rejoice with her. Would the Lord, blessed be He, violate His own law?" Of course, the Lord would do no such thing. He prolonged the bridegroom's life for seven years, corresponding to the seven days of the wedding festivities.

When a loving woman calls on the Lord with her whole heart, He will hear her prayer and fulfill her desire (Psalm 145:19).

Some stories involved rabbis who decided that, although papa ruled, strict paternal discipline should give way to gentler notions, hide-bound tradition should be displaced, and family structure, loosened. The following tale acknowledged that such newfangled wrinkles were possible only if dogmatic or obstinate fathers would not interfere with progress. Although many folktales have universal origins, this one is definitely Jewish:

> Once there was a simple man, unlearned in the Torah, who was determined that his slow-witted son should master holy works. Despite his best efforts, the boy found it difficult to cope with the texts.

The father's solution was to lock up the child without food or drink for three days: God would make the child literate or leave him to die in his solitary room. The mother quietly decided to overrule her husband's behavior. Because she loved her son, intellectually gifted or not, she invoked the heavenly gates to admit her tears—which they did. A heavenly spirit immediately taught the boy all of the Torah and permitted him to sing its laws with a beautiful voice. The father then kissed and hugged his son, whom he accepted as a great scholar—but not as a mediocre student.

MORAL: Motherly love superseded fatherly rigidity long before the dawn of modern psychology.

The first systematic collector of Jewish folklore, Mischa Yosef Bin Gorian (1865–1921), reclaimed a trove of *Talmudic* and *Midrashic* homilies, animal stories, old wives' tales, songs, and riddles that had long been overlooked or forgotten. His editions were collated and edited by his son after his death and published in 1965 in *Mimekor Yisroel*. They evoke Jewish life about ordinary Jews, heroes and sinners, witches, demons, and evil spirits, as well as lovers, families, and troublemakers in all their amusing, harmonious, and incompatible affairs:

There was once a wealthy Jew (wealthy Jews were apparently plentiful) who loved the beautiful wife of a poor man (beauty and poverty were amenable as well). The husband, troubled by his empty purse, urged her to sell herself to a pious, wealthy Jew for enough money to bail him out of debtor's prison. She appealed to the rich Jew who agreed to provide the funds in exchange for her favors to "make him whole again." But when she explained that he would thus lose his reward in The World to Come, he subdued his lust and sent her home in peace and prosperity. The foolish husband, believing her guilty, became wildly jealous and belligerent. Fortunately, because Rabbi Akiba noticed that the pious would-be transgressor sported a mystical brightness and restraint, he assured him a place in the heavenly world. The foolish husband took note, apologized to his wife, studied Torah, and was granted many blessings.

MORAL: Illicit love in the world above could result in hellfire in the world below without the saving grace of Rabbi Akiba.

Other than wealthy Jews, many were pious. Many were wealthy and pious:

There was a wealthy man who nevertheless had no pleasure in life because, at age seventy, he had no children. After a time, God in His mercy gave him a handsome son. Happily, the old father set about teaching the boy the Book of Genesis, which was fortunate because the lad was able to heal a sick king by reciting its first chapter from memory. God's wisdom and love, evident from His creation of the beautiful world, brought solace and good health to the king, who rewarded the boy with many favors and sent him home with many gifts to his parents. The sages then declared that while God had already given the boy many blessings, even more would follow as he studied Torah and Mishneh with his father.

MORAL: Rewards are especially great to those who study diligently and observe the Commandment to honor parents.

Bin Gorian found ample resources in the Commandments for simple, but telling, parables of God's love and concern for His often-recalcitrant children:

A rich man who had been very generous to his son was sadly denied a comfortable life in his old age. One very cold day, he begged his son to supply him with a warm coat. Finally, after repeatedly ignoring his father's request, a grandson was sent to fetch a worn old garment, which he then cut in two. One half, he said, was intended for his shivering grandfather; the rest he would save for his own father's later years. The negligent son, fortunately recognizing that he had shamed his father, took the elderly man into his home, treated him with Fifth-Commandment reverence, and lived on for many years.

MORAL: Treat the old folks well and be assured of a long life.

Read on:

Two sisters were identical in looks. When one of them was suspected of adultery, her husband decided to test her by giving her bitter waters, which only the pure could drink without peril (Numbers 5:17–31). Knowing that because of her sin she couldn't pass the crucial trial, she begged her innocent and unpolluted sister to drink the deadly brew—which she did. The guilty sister, believing that she could secretly entertain her lover without her husband detecting the truth, kissed her pure sister in gratitude. But when the smell of bitter waters on the lips of the innocent girl drifted past the wicked sister's mouth, the depraved girl turned green, her belly swelled, and she died.

MORAL: Adultery leads to bad things, as what is performed in secret is known to God.

Sefer Ha'Aggadah (Book of Legends) (1908–11), edited by Hayim Nahman Bialik (1873–1934) and Yehoshua Ravnitsky (1859–1944), likewise recorded many popular stories from the Talmud and Midrash, one of which reminds us that the Eighth Commandment makes stealing counterproductive. However, we are assured that if stealing leads to love, we can overlook the sin:

A couple married for ten years without having a child applied to Rabbi Shimon ben Yohai for a divorce. "As you were paired over food and drink in your marriage feast," he told them, "so you must now be parted over food and drink."

The wife threw a gala party, giving her husband one too many cocktails. "My dear," he said to her in great good humor, "pick any desirable article you want from my home; you may take it with you to your father's house."

As soon as he fell into a drunken sleep, she had her servants carry him to her father's house. When he sobered up, he wondered what he was doing there. "My dear," she answered, "I stole you. Did you not say that I might pick any desirable article and take it with me? There is no desirable article that I care for more than you."

MORAL: When a couple gives a proper party as ordered by Rabbi Shimon, they will be remembered by God who will grant them love, and before long, a beautiful child (Pesikta de Rab Kahana 22:2).

Another story about family love:

It was a Friday afternoon. Rabbi Joshua ben Levi normally spent time listening to his grandson reading from the Bible. Once, however, as he was relaxing in the baths of Tiberius, he forgot the appointment with his grandson. He immediately turned to leave when Rabbi Hiyya bar Abba reminded him that if one has begun his bath, he may not interrupt it even for prayer. "On the contrary," Rabbi Joshua replied, "Listening to my grandson reading from the Scriptures is as though I were hearing it at Mount Sinai."

No moral necessary.

Then there is another story which Rabbi Shimon ben Yohai used to tell about an old profligate who complained that he couldn't find a satisfying wife: "You ill-fated wretch!" he was admonished. "With your dripping nose, your deaf ears, and your dim eyes, what woman would be willing to have you?"

MORAL: Man that is born of woman is full of troubles (Job 14:1).

Here is a vignette about Rabban Gamaliel: When he bathed on the first night after his wife died, his disciples reminded him that a mourner is forbidden to bathe. "I, being very delicate," he replied, "am not like other people."

Humility is irksome, *mikvah* notwithstanding.

And a touching love story:

A king ordered an officer to guard the dead body of a knight hung on a tree for disobedience and rebellion. Came midnight, and the officer was startled to hear the sound of a woman's loud and bitter wailing.

"What troubles you to be weeping and complaining so?"

"My soul is bitter because my beloved husband was taken from me," sobbed the grieving widow, "I shall wail and sorrow until I too shall return to dust!"

The officer kindly conducted her home where, he told her, she could better mourn her husband in peace and quiet. The moaning and groaning were repeated the next night, with the officer consoling her with sweet and gentle words. At which, the widow forgot about her husband, declared love for the friendly officer, and followed him to where the knight had been dangling. However, while they had been gone, the dishonored knight's body was stolen by a kinsman who wanted to give it a proper burial. "Never mind," said the heartbroken widow. "I will dig up someone else's remains and hang them on the tree. No one will know the difference, and because I love you, we can marry without sin."

At which she quoted Rabbi Joseph Caro's *Shulchan Arukh* that the dead may be removed from the grave if it is unprotected from robbers. He said nothing about moving bodies to please the living.

Such interpretations required a high level of invention and a determined woman. Here is "The Finger," a story about a famous rabbi and a determined demon:

A young man out for stroll came upon a most unusual sight—a finger waving at him. In a playful mood, he slipped his ring over the mysterious digit. Sometime later, when he was about to get married, a strange woman interrupted the ceremony shouting that he was already married to her finger and that she would kill him and the bride unless a divorce were arranged according to the Torah. Rabbi Isaac Luria ascertained that the woman was a she-devil who normally kept herself hidden out of fear of God. Ordering her to marry a demon of her own kind, the rabbi nevertheless required the groom to give her a proper divorce, even though the Law was not applicable to demons. Satisfied, she departed, and the rabbi was able to perform the rites according to the laws of Moses and Israel.

MORAL: Fun and games have no place in marital affairs.

In Hyman Goldin's 1946 book *The Magic Ring*, we again meet a golden circlet:

Amol iz geven (once upon a time) the good and learned Rabbi Eliezar took a group of his students to a forest to hide from the wicked king of Uz, who had decreed that any Jew found studying holy works would be killed. Having left his home and belongings to his loving wife, Abigail, he spent months of suffering in the hinterlands from lack of food and water, finally calling upon the Lord: "How can we study Your law without sustenance?"

Suddenly, a small weasel with a ring in its snout appeared and dropped the ring in front of the amazed rabbi. And he certainly should have been amazed, not only because he suddenly felt cool and refreshed, but also because of the ring's engraved inscription: "Beware of those who wish for things, lest they wish for evil things." Nevertheless, the rabbi wished for the bad king to be replaced by good Prince Joseph, who would supply money and a bag of gold for his students. Wishes answered.

Back at home, his wife plagued the rabbi until he revealed the secret of the magical ring, which she then pocketed. She amassed great wealth for herself and transformed her husband into a werewolf. Alas, she was not as loving as he thought.

One day, as Prince Joseph was riding in the forest, he became puzzled by strange markings in the snow. Fortunately, a learned Jew wandered by and recognized them as Hebrew characters that revealed the wife's evil behavior. The prince immediately saw to it that the wonderful ring was retrieved, that the werewolf was transformed into his human form, and the cruel wife into a donkey. Rabbi Eliezar and his students then studied Torah for the rest of their lives. As for the ring? The weasel snatched it and vanished forever.

Does this frightening story have a moral? Indeed, it does: Whoever forfeits love by destroying a good and learned scholar will be destroyed herself.

Extravagant tales compiled from centuries of Jewish life in many parts of the world were among the works collected by Louis Ginzberg in his monumental *Legends of the Jews* (1909–1939). Its huge cast of characters and singular episodes are unparalleled in Jewish literature, the "spontaneous creations of the people by the people." Although many of the

Midrashim are narrowly didactic, they represent the deep cultural and emotional needs of a population with limited resources for entertainment or information—and sometimes finding it. The story is told of the second-century Rabbi Meir, who remained steadfast despite suffering the loss of his beloved children:

> When Rabbi Meir returned home from a short absence, his troubled wife told him that two exceedingly valuable jewels, which had been entrusted to her while he was gone, had been recalled that day by their rightful owner. The rabbi acknowledged that she had done well in returning what they could not keep. She took him into the bedroom, where their sons lay dead. "God gave us two sons," she told him. "Today He has recalled them. We rejoiced while He granted us these precious jewels, and now we must willingly surrender what we only temporarily possessed. The Owner has a right to reclaim His property." And Rabbi Meir blessed God: The Lord gave, and the Lord has taken away. Blessed be the name of the Lord (Job 1:21).

Can't think of an appropriate moral, can you?

> There was a poor man who spent all his time in the House of Study. After being harangued by his starving family, he took up his staff and went on his way to unknown lands. He was not unknown, however, to a very black and ugly man—a demon!—who took him to a synagogue where the cantor recited the verse in Psalms 90:17: "Let the favor of the Lord be with us and credit the work of our hands." Suddenly everyone vanished. The poor fellow understood that he was among evil beings that would keep him from his beloved family and force him to marry a demon-wife and raise children with her.
>
> After a while, he begged her permission to return home, which she allowed providing that he would remain for only one night. Otherwise, he would lose his soul. When he explained the situation to his human wife, she urged him to go to the House of Study and pray—which he did. The demon then agreed to depart if he would kiss her goodbye, saying, "If you do, I will never bother you again."
>
> She was as true as her word for a demon, for with his kiss she drew out his soul and vanished forever.

MORAL: Never kiss a demon.

One more:

> The son of a certain scholar died, causing the father bitter tears. "Joseph, Joseph," he called, "come and study, come and eat." But Joseph did not come. A demon, however, overheard the sorrowing parent and maliciously appeared in the likeness of Joseph. Fortunately, the father did not mistake the apparition for that of the child he loved so well. "Depart, depart, you tainted polluter," cried the father, at which the demon flew away.

From which we learn that a father's love beats evil spirits.

Moses Gaster (1856–1939), a prolific Rumanian scholar translated a number of such stories in his 1934 *Ma'Aseh Book,* a compendium of humorous, entertaining, and disturbing Yiddish folktales, typically centered around Biblical characters, rich merchants, treacherous men, virtuous women, wicked kings, and wise rabbis. Here is one about a yeshiva student who needed to acquire more learning before he could marry the daughter of Rabbi Judah. Unlike most folk tales, no moral is implied or suggested, no social anthropology is injected to hinder the reader—just a bit of fun.

S'iz an emese myseh (This is a true story):

> Rabbi Judah the Pious was anxious to marry his daughter to a learned man, for, as she told him, "Marriage to an ignorant man is like being tied to a lion." The girl settled on Rabbi Hanina, a young fellow of great merit. The problem was that he was in no hurry to tie the knot, stipulating that he must first complete his studies with the esteemed rabbi of Regensburg, a hundred miles from home. A fixed time for the wedding was set, but an unfortunate dream informed the family that Hanina would be late for the ceremony. In fact, ten years late. But, once equipped with the necessary learning,

he remembered that the following Sunday was set for his wedding. A trip of a hundred miles could not be made without recourse to witchcraft. And so, Hanina found himself on a Sabbath afternoon in a beautiful house filled with incredible objects of silk and silver, as well as an incredible old Jew who was so pious that his beard nearly touched the ground. Prayers were led by Moshe Rabbeinu, the Patriarchs, and the prophets Elijah and Jeremiah, after which Hanina was sent on a magical cloud that bore him, first to a privy where he could relieve himself, and finally to an on-time performance of the marriage ceremony.

In what other body of folklores is a bathroom stop consistent with the need to show up on time for a wedding?

Another one:

This happened in the time of King Solomon. The daughter of a rich man fell in love and asked her father for the young man as a husband. To which the father agreed. Soon the happy couple started off on their honeymoon, but they were waylaid by some robbers, who tied the groom to a tree, forcing him to watch his wife cheerfully disporting herself with the most handsome of the lot! After drinking a lot of wine, the bad fellows were soon sound asleep. At that point, a snake came by and poisoned them, and they all died. The wife untied her husband after he promised not to kill her, but when he told his father-in-law how she had behaved freely with the robber, the father killed her.

And then there is a happier love story about the adventures of a lucky woman whose fortune changed when a beggar showed up at her door:

She was rich; he was thirsty. She invited him to her room, offered him a glass of wine, and softly crooned, "You are mine, and I am thine." The song revived memories of their past affair, for in the morning when the children awoke, she told them to say hello to their papa.

Luck and love together. It can hardly get better.

Rabbi Yohanan related the story about the ties that bind parents to their offspring:

Once there was a man who planted a carob tree. A rabbi asked him how long it would take for the tree to bear fruit. When the man answered that it would take seventy years, the rabbi reminded him that he would no longer be around to enjoy its growth. The man replied that as his father provided for him, he would provide for his children and his children's children.

Love lasts.

Then there is the story of the pious father who refused to allow his son to read for the congregation on Rosh Hashanah and Yom Kippur:

Apparently, the young man was not deemed sufficiently worthy of the honor. The old father believed it was his duty to punish his son, as Eli, the priest, had been punished because his sons were corrupt and did not know the Lord (1 Samuel 2:12). Eli had failed to rebuke them, aware that his sons were not sufficiently worthy. The sons died, after which Eli fell down and broke his neck (1 Samuel 4:18). But, by rebuking his own son, the pious father believed he saved himself and his sons from similar fates.

MORAL: Punishments between parent and child may seem harsh but are sometimes necessary.

The American humorist Nathan Ausubel (1898–1986) edited the *Treasury of Jewish Folklore* in 1948, gathering stories of wonder-workers, droll characters, rogues, demons, and matchmakers. Many of his animal fables, in which non-humans assume human virtues, vices, and absurdities, stem from ancient Hebrew, Greek, and Indian tales. Not all affirm the Jewish experience or were sparing of Jewish sensibilities; they gave power to moral lessons but pointed as well to ineffective Jews regularly outwitted by the shrewd, cunning, or devious strategies of their foxy non-Jewish neighbors:

Natural enemies, a fox and a leopard sparred in uneven campaigns. The credulous leopard depended on his sharp-witted wife to protect him from the crafty fox. Although the leopard dearly loved his wife, he was easily beguiled by the fox, which advised him not to trust her but to ask her advice and then do the opposite.

"My dear, do not heed the fox, for I am afraid of his wiles," the leopard's wife warned. Did the leopard heed her warning? He did not, which got him into much trouble.

"Woe is me," he sighed, "that I did not listen to my wife!" And he died before his time.

MORAL: Do not consult women on important affairs.

Many elements of Jewish folklore, in their cultural, religious, and soulful elements, are present in these evergreen stories: wish-fulfillment in the face of actuality and insecurity, reliance on spiritual faith, and confidence in the sacred ancestors and heroes on whom they rest their hopes and dreams. Jewish folklore may be different from other types of orally transmitted stories or literary forms in that the study of Scripture requires unusual unvarnished mind-sharpening activity. The application of knowledge, thought, and reason, though subject to casuistry, often produces brilliant insights not always vouchsafed to others. What shines through this material are the life-affirming, humanizing, and revealing tales of natural phenomena, brought down from the ivory towers of the Bible, Talmud, and Midrash, where magic and make-believe, philosophy and admonitions are made explicit and instructive to generations of believing Jews.

The naïveté of these myths often belies the heritage of Jewish rationality and pragmatism. They explain interpretations of subconscious fears, supernatural phenomena, hostile forces, or forgotten customs that perpetuate or make sense of lost traditions. Nevertheless, as the twenty-first-century rabbi Jay LeVine says, "When things aren't going great, great stories help." They met the needs of powerless Jews who could only daydream about worthy heroes, pious rabbis, rich men, and beautiful daughters. Angels, fools, and fantasies filled their imagination when there was not enough food to fill their stomachs.

7

The Many Languages of Love

If a God-given language was spoken in Eden, it must have been one of love. Surely, Adam and Eve had voiced the need to support each other against imagined terrors, whispered about ways to continue the species, spoken of their vulnerabilities and dependencies, and confessed to temptation and frustration.

Genesis (11:1–9) tells us that the world was once of one language. Some ancient interpreters believed it was Hebrew, the language spoken by God in the Bible: "Let there be light, let us make men." Following the Great Flood, the arrogant descendants of Noah, not knowing that the unity they enjoyed was only an unsteady moment before the arrival of confusion and disorder (i.e., Babel), attempted to investigate the situation by building a tower high enough to probe the heavens, mighty enough for self-rule, compelling enough to examine God's intentions for mankind. God, however, was in no mood to have His omnipotence challenged. Realizing that men might soon have the power to check or oppose Him, He destroyed the skyscraper, scattering the people of Babel into communities with unknown languages so that they no longer had a single voice in which to demand answers. If God ever imagined that He had designed a compatible humanity that was willing to live within prescribed limits, He now understood that what He had wrought was a work in progress.

If the Babel languages were God's gift from which all subsequent languages flowed, not all of the local vernaculars were mutually understandable, although some were connected to Aramaic and Hebrew. The lingua franca of Abraham and his family when they lived in Canaan was probably proto-Aramaic.

Life for the native populations was influenced not only by the many diverse cultures that they had encountered in the years of Israelite exile but also by the exotic fables and myths they had absorbed in their travels and incorporated into their own traditions; their stories transcended ethnic boundaries. When Ezra the Scribe returned to Jerusalem from the Babylonian Captivity in 538 BCE, he introduced the new Assyrian script in which the Hebrew Bible was redacted or revised into its present form.

During the following centuries, Jews picked up new speech patterns as they settled in Spain, Holland, Turkey, North Africa, and Italy with their treasured Torahs to await the Messiah and return to Zion. While they were waiting, new and diverse vernaculars evolved that combined the Hebrew language with indigenous tongues: Judeo-Berber (Tashilhit) in the mountainous regions of Morocco; Judeo-Arabic in the Southern Arabian Peninsula; Jibali among the small communities in Kurdistan; Judi in Iran; Judeo-Spanish (Ladino) in the Iberian Peninsula and Turkey; and Judeo-German (Yiddish) in Central and Western Europe. It was these Jewish dialects that preserved

Tower of Babel. Etching, 1728. By Anton Joseph von Prenner. Metropolitan Museum of Art.

outmoded words and expressions as well as enriching and energizing the languages of the countries in which they now lived.

Perhaps during no other period were Jews more actively engaged in everyday life than in Sephardic Spain where expressive language skills prompted cross-disciplinary interaction with their Christian and Muslim neighbors. During the fourteenth and fifteenth centuries, Sephardic poets emulated or recreated models from the Moorish Golden Age. Some, like Don Vidal Benveniste, chose Hebrew over the Spanish vernacular because he was concerned that lapsed Jews were deserting Jewish traditions. He hoped that young people would relate to his use of irony in his language to criticize foolish conceits, while at the same time imbibing the lesson of avarice and love gone astray. He mourned the painful period when *conversos* forfeited Judaism for personal safety and social position in the secular Spanish environment, ultimately bowing to assimilation, acculturation, and materialism.

Wherever Jews lived, they remained mobile. Although in exile, they were determined to carry on communal life, preserve their poetry and folklore, and maintain, as best they could, their language and religious identity. The achievement of these aspirations was made possible by the fifteenth-century invention of printing, which turned handwritten and oral material into printed books. Ancient Jewish stories of Biblical prophets and sages, as well as of ghosts and the Evil One, were now available in published form. Pious rabbis believed that printing was a divine craft and that books would be among the greatest wonders of the heavenly world. But even in this world, the enormous value of the printing press was clear. More and more people availed themselves of the parables, allegories, and folktales that were collected for those hours when the eye and mind sought entertainment or spiritual guidance.

Among Jewish playwrights who took advantage of the divine craft was the Spanish author and dramatist Fernando de Rojas (c. 1465–1541), charged by the Inquisition for secret Jewish practices and skirting conventional morality. Having written and labored under the insecurity of *converso* life, he was cut off from one language but never fully part of another. He was plagued by doubt or disbelief in the precepts of love, while at the same time questioning the systems of parental authority and arranged marriages. His only known work, *Tragicomedia de Calisto y Melibea*, published in Spanish in 1499, marked the close of the Middle Ages and the birth of the Spanish Renaissance in its depiction of characters as authentic, non-stereotypical personalities. The psychodrama, popularly known as *Celestina*, reflected the abandonment of Jewish ideals and beliefs by Jews who had succumbed to apathy or disinterest.

As tragedy or comedy, *Celestina* became a paradigm of Spanish Renaissance literature—emotionally distant from its medieval predecessors. The bachelor Calisto, who exemplified the amorality and cynicism of intemperate love, is consumed with hunger for Melibea, the object of sexual appetite, but not of marital bliss:

Calisto, master of wicked intrigues, pays Celestina, a former prostitute, to arrange a secret rendezvous with the lovely Melibea, who, having been warned by her parents, has rejected his romantic overtures. Celestina's commanding presence and magical powers, however, soon overcome her qualms. Calisto is eager; she is willing. He is concerned with gratifying his lust; she views moral standards as hypocritical. Together they seek a life of freedom and sensuality over conventional behavior, of passionate love over spiritual love and honor. In the end, the real world prevails: notions of autonomy and license turn out to be illusions when Calisto's servants murder Celestina for refusing to share her ill-gotten wages. Calisto, in turn, is killed while keeping a forbidden tryst with Melibea. After confessing her guilt to her father, she throws herself to the ground and dies. Shattered by the turn of events, Dad ruminates on bitter fate in a world devoid of love.

Fernando de Rojas was a Spanish author and dramatist, known for his only surviving work, *La Celestina*, 1499. It is variously considered "the last work of the Spanish Middle Ages or the first work of the Spanish Renaissance." Unknown contemporary artist.

The sexually explicit story was considered lewd by Abraham Farissol (c. 1451–c. 1525), a prominent fifteenth-century Italian rabbi who urged his students to turn to higher-minded matters. Because it was widely published in Latin, French, English, German, and Flemish versions, however, European as well as Jewish-language writers quickly adopted similar themes. They were also probably acquainted with the sad history of Judah Abravanel (1465–1523). When Portugal briefly accepted Jews fleeing Spanish tyranny in 1492, Abravanel smuggled his one-year-old son Isaac there to escape conversion. When, in 1497, the baby was baptized, his father suffered the rest of his life for having abandoned him. In his poignant 1503 ode, *Tlunot al Ha-Zman (Laments Against Time)*, he expressed his longing to see his "treasured heir to wisdom." Loneliness deprived him of sleep: "I cannot tell day from night." He implored his son to study the Sacred Tongue and remember the language of Holy Works. They never met again.

Abravanel's *Dialoghi di Amore (Conversations of Love)*, published in Italian in 1465 but based on Greek legends (and possibly also originally composed in Ladino, unusual for its time), appeared in Italian, Hebrew, French, Spanish, and Latin editions. Widely acclaimed for its lively language and its discussion of love as a universal rule or truth, it polarized two idealized "beings": Philo, representing sensual desire, and Sophia, representing intellectual love. Together as *Philosophy*, they evoke the strain between faith and experience as well as the tension between sensuality and spirituality. They agree that love of the ultimate good—which is love of God—is the prime focus of all reality. That controversial principle, which had appealed to pagan Greek humanists, eventually found its way to the Judaism of the early Renaissance period.

Collections of medieval Hispano-Semitic songs, poetry, proverbs, and folk stories continued to yield accounts of love-sick lovers, indifferent husbands and neglected wives, as well as faithful partners and supernatural prophets. Both secular and religious storytellers remade these tales in numerous languages, lending color and variety to traditional folklore and Biblical *Midrashim*.

Dan Ben-Amos, in his edited collection *Folktales of the Jews from the Sephardic Dispersion* (recorded in 2006), adapted ancient stories of God's love for man and man's love for God. We learn how the magical properties of the Prophet Elijah's cave proved that trust:

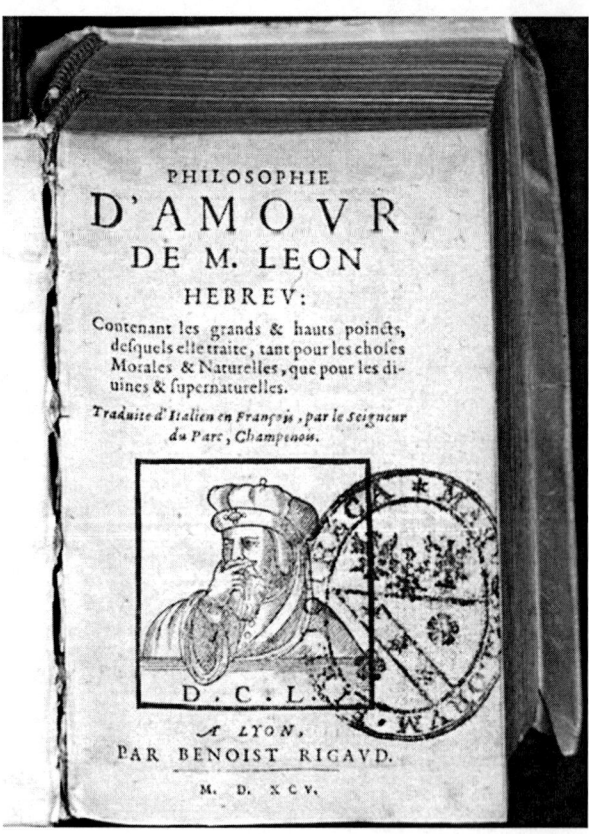

Front page of *Dialoghi d'Amore* (1595) by Judah Abravanel (also known as Leone Ebreo)(1465–c. 1523), poet and physician whose Dialogs of Love were one of the most important philosophical productions of the 16th century.

> There once lived a virtuous woman known for her advice to the Sephardi community. One day an unhappy neighbor came to her home tearfully explaining that because each of her pregnancies ended in miscarriages, her husband had vowed to divorce her. Like Sarah and Rachel and the holy mothers in the Bible, she was aware that his love for her was contingent on her fertility.

"First go to the mikveh and then hurry to the cave of the saintly prophet Elijah where you must spend three nights," said the virtuous woman, "God will help you." And, of course, He did, sending her three separate dreams of a baby waiting to be fondled and nursed. And, of course, He sent three similar dreams to her husband, who promised to love her tenderly in the future. And indeed, she gave birth to a healthy and wise son who performed many good deeds. She named him Elijah in honor of the prophet whose cave remains to this day a refuge for troubled souls seeking love and progeny.

MORAL: Dreams of love and babies come true with the help of God.

Then there is the story of Noah, a pious man who has three sons but only one daughter. She is so perfect in beauty, wisdom, and goodness that suitors come from around the world to claim her for their bride. Noah checks them out:

Number one comes riding on a white horse.
"Have you planted a vineyard?"
"Not yet."
Number two shows up on a black horse.
"Yes, the vineyard is planted."
"Have you built yourself a house?"
"Not yet."
Number three has a brown horse.
"Yes, the vineyard is planted, the house is built."
The wedding takes place.
Hold on.
Number one returns, having built the vineyard and house. Sorry, but the beautiful girl has been taken. Not to worry. Noah has a fine donkey, which has just been turned into a lovely girl, a miracle from God who doesn't want the righteous to suffer. Off they go on his white horse. Unfortunately, she turns out to be, like the ass, lazy and stubborn.
Number two arrives, having fulfilled the demands. Can God repeat His wondrous feat? Yes, He can, with the help of a dog who is transformed into a beautiful girl. Too bad, for she is like a dog, angry and loud.
Number three is intelligent, quiet, and industrious, a true and appropriate mate. Ring the bells.

Has anyone consulted the girls? Doesn't God believe in women's lib?

Here is another one from the Ben Amos collection—about a bear, a poor musician, and an offensive wife:

Every day poor Avram prayed to God to help his family. His wife thought that if he got up, went out, and found work, it would be more helpful. After many years, during which God appeared busy elsewhere, his wife finally convinced Avram it would be useful to get a drum, beat it in the graveyard, and sing all day long—which the poor fellow did until one evening he spotted a bear dancing to his beat. Song over, the bear deposited a large number of silver coins for the musician. The largess was repeated until poor Avram became rich Avram. His wife prepared a fine meal for the guest who had made their fortune, but she was alarmed when he showed up on her doorstep. Loud shrieks!
"Filthy bear!"
The bear, too humiliated to eat, hung his head in shame. "Cut my hand," he said. Avram was reluctant, but the bear insisted. "My wound will heal, but your wife's words cannot restore me to spiritual wholeness. Leave your cruel family and go to the Land of Israel, where God will comfort and sustain you with love of the Holy Books." So Avram went to learn Torah in the holy city of Jerusalem.

MORAL: Words can hurt. Be careful how you use them.

Love of Torah helps.

Many of these tales came to light after the creation of the State of Israel. Most of the communities from which they emanated had largely disappeared following forced migrations, shifting cultures, and Holocaust atrocities. Fortunately, Italo Calvino collected and edited many such exotic stories and published them in *Italian Folktales* (1956). One of these tales reminds us of what happened in Tuscany:

> An Italian Jewish nobleman, having lost his beloved wife in childbirth and unwilling to cope with the care and responsibilities of their infant daughter, Olivia, places her with a poor-but-kind Christian family. The understanding is that if he does not reclaim her in ten years, the family will keep her as their own. When the allotted time comes and goes without his reappearance, the child is baptized. Nevertheless, the father eventually shows up and secures the release of Olivia: he needs her as a heavy-duty homemaker, not as a loving and devoted daughter. Alas, he is a hard and unbending master, not a loving and devoted parent. She flees their home, is captured, and is punished by having both hands amputated. But in spite of her handicap, a rich young Christian king falls in love with her and marries her. While this troubling story should have ended happily here, Italian folktales are often endless. Her wicked mother-in-law throws Olivia out of the palace and convinces the king that, unbeknownst to him, she and their two babies have died. The king finally discovers the truth, she and the children are safely returned, and her hands are wondrously reattached. The foster parents are generously compensated for the years they sheltered her.

(Unauthorized *Midrash* by the auhor—with apologies to Signor Calvino: Jewish Olivia undergoes baptism in Spain, suffers under hard and unbending Inquisitorial masters, is expelled by a wicked queen [who but Isabella?], flees to Italy where she adapts to a new language, and rewards the country for its kind tolerance. Her children and her children's children safely return to their original faith to construct a new and vibrant Judaism in the Diaspora.)

The invention of printing spurred an upsurge in reading in the many languages of Jewish literature, which depicted actual events or was adapted from fictional sources. Before long, Jewish publishing houses were established in Amsterdam, Bologna, Brescia, Venice, Naples, and other Italian cities, and issued a mix of religious, mystical, messianic, and romantic anthologies. Communities with blended identities and languages were thus enabled to tighten bonds across geographic borders, opening a variety of hybrid Jewish languages and dialects to the literate world, making it possible to preserve earlier oral stories.

So, from where did Yiddish come? It showed up in the late Middle Ages in Poland and Ukraine, where it incorporated Polish and other Slavic words into the Judeo-German vernacular. Yiddish, 10–15 percent Hebrew and Aramaic, with infusions of Latin and Greek, developed out of a world of native folktales, mythologies, and traditions. It relied heavily on banter, accents, inflections, figures of speech, puns, and just plain gift of gab. Much of its vocabulary (at least 60 percent) is of Germanic origin, although in its written form, it uses the Hebrew alphabet. Possessing their own Yiddish language gave Jews a number of advantages over their non-Jewish neighbors: they could trade more readily across international borders, share religious practices, and find marriage partners with familiar backgrounds. Wherever Ashkenazi Jews were oppressed, at home or on the road, they could feel secure and take pride in their own national literature, which was shared by all ranks, scholars and butchers, artists and salesmen—all the Chosen People.

On the other hand (and there is always the other hand), Yiddish is a type of nihilism with a grievance against the outside world—and for your deadliest enemy. Yiddish curses are universally acknowledged as the ultimate vehicle for character assassination, somehow unique to the Jewry of Eastern European origin. Here is a dreaded sample—*mea culpa* if I tread on your sensibilities:

Shtik drek. *Piece of excrement; contemptible individual.*
Di zolst lign in drerd; a meeseh meshineh zul dikh trefn. *May you lie six feet under eternally and in Hell; may a horrible death be your fate.*
Ale tseyn zoln bay im aroysfaln, nor eyner zol im blaybn oyf tsonveytoog. *May all his teeth fall out except one for a toothache.*
Az es iz dir bashert tzu dertrinken veren, vest di dertrinken veren in ah lefel vasser. *If it's fated for you to drown, you will drown in a teaspoon of water.*
Feh! *Enough already!*

Beginning in the sixteenth century, Jewish publishers in the Italian, Dutch, Germanic, Polish, and Balkan areas commissioned collections of romantic Yiddish anthologies. The best known among these imaginative gatherings, *Bovo-Bukh*, (1541), was compiled by Elia Levita (1469–1549). It is the first secular book known to be printed in Yiddish. Its sentimental themes were planned to counteract Christian values and romanticized Gentile heroes in popular literature by substituting Jewish equivalents. (The title was later misconstrued as *bubbe meise*, "old wives' tale."). Here is one of these stories:

Prince Bovo's mother arranges the murder of her old husband, the king, in order to marry his assassin. Because Bovo gets wind of her plot, son or not, he, too, must be eliminated. He escapes to Flanders, where he becomes a stable boy to the local ruler, who, of course, has a beautiful daughter, Druzane. Naturally, they fall in love, not aware that she is destined for Lucifer, the ugly son of the sultan of neighboring Babylonia, who kidnaps Druzane's father. Comes Bovo on his magic horse. He kills Lucifer and rescues the king, who promises a grateful Bovo the hand of the princess. But before that happy day can take place, Bovo is lured to Babylonia and tossed into jail where he languishes for a year before escaping. In the meantime, Druzane, imagining that her gallant lover is dead, agrees to marry the knight Macabron. Are you still with me? Comes Bovo disguised as a beggar. He rescues Druzane and dashes off to a forest with her—where, in the fullness of time, she gives birth to twins who are duly circumcised. Hunted down for making off with Druzane, Bovo attempts to find safety in Flanders with his intended father-in-law. Druzane, believing him dead, follows with the twins. Bovo, returning to the forest in hopes of finding them, believes them dead, enlists in the army, kills his stepfather, packs his mother off to a convent, becomes king in his own right, and finds his children and his queen, the lovely Druzane.

Nothing, no matter how bizarre, seemed to diminish the supply of Yiddish tales, legends, and love stories. Here is another one:

Amol iz geven—*Once upon a time:*
A beautiful Jewish girl from Danzig sets out to find her missing husband but must travel as a man in order to avoid unseemly behavior. However, she is spotted by the local princess, who falls in love with her. A serious problem. They are unable to communicate because the Jewish girl speaks Yiddish, and the princess does not.
Nevertheless, talk or no talk, the princess wants her as a husband. The king obliges his daughter and immediately arranges a proper wedding with the local rabbi. (A rabbi?) What to do? The missing husband, fortunately found, sizes up the situation, slips into the marriage bed, and without saying a word, performs a groom's duty. By the time the unfortunate princess discovers what happened, the Jewish girl and her young husband are gone—jabbering in Yiddish all the way home.

MORAL: Be careful to fall in love with someone who can chitchat in Yiddish.

S'iz an emese mayse—*This is a true story:*
A tailor and his wife had enjoyed a loving relationship until she passed away, leaving the widower sad and lonely but determined to test marriage once again. A voice exhorts him to choose a beggar woman who had been the recipient of his late wife's charity. "Marry her or die." Although neither alternative appeals to him, he chooses life, as the Good Book advises, and marries her. The poor lady can hardly believe her good fortune but insists that for one year he join her in her begging profession around and about Yiddish-speaking shtetls. All apparently goes well. So well that when she

agrees to settle down with him and create a loving home in time for the coming High Holy Days, he hesitates.

"What's the hurry?" he asks her. "People are so free with holiday gifts that we will do better to keep on traveling."

MORAL: We learn in every known cynical language that greed outweighs the attractions of a loving home. Another:

There were two close friends, neither of whom had children, who pledged that if one ever had a son and the other a daughter, they would make a match. Both went to the rebbe in hopes that the holy man would intervene with God and bless them accordingly. God chose to bless one with riches and a son who was sent to a yeshiva to study; the other, with poverty and a daughter who sold bagels from a basket.

Unbeknownst to their parents, the youngsters meet and fall in love when the yeshiva student buys one of her bagels. They are kept apart because the rich family insists on a rich daughter-in-law. The poor family knows that, given their unfortunate finances, the best husband she could expect would be an old man.

Ever alert and resourceful, the yeshiva student borrows some money from his father and hurries to the unfortunate wedding where he pushes aside the elderly groom, wedges himself next to the bride, and marries her. After the ceremony, one of the guests discovers a box of money and a letter in Yiddish explaining that a rich man had once asked the bride's father to hide some money for him until he returned. He didn't return. The money is delivered to the young couple by none other than Elijah the Prophet.

MORAL: True love wins out, especially if you can read Yiddish and know a prophet.

Did you know that flowers play a symbolic role in Jewish life? White is for friendship, red for true love. This is what happened to a fellow who should have known the difference:

A yeshiva student had become friendly with two lovely girls after he returned home from a study session with his rebbe. One of the girls fell in love with him but said nothing although he presented her with a bouquet of white flowers—while her friend received one of red, the color of passion. Not a good omen in the color-coded language of flowers. The white-flower girl suffered in the belief that she lost out to hot-tempered sex. Her parents sent her to America to help her forget. When that didn't help, she moved to the Holy Land and opened her own flower shop to keep the memory of her lost love alive.

One fine day a customer came in. "What color flowers do you want?" she asked him, trembling from head to toe. "I'll take white, though I'm not sure it matters."

Oh, yes, it does.

Can you guess? It was the young man she secretly loved. And she sold him a beautiful bunch of red roses.

And then there are busybody storytellers who intrude on the love lives of their characters. I'll tell you what happened when a meddling author intercepted a pair of candidates on their way to Heaven:

It was late Erev Shabbos when a righteous man arrived in the next world expecting to sail right through the Pearly Gates. But what's this? A fly challenging the character of a God-fearing rabbi? "Yes, one day I landed on his forehead, and, contrary to the Commandment, he killed me." Since a beit-din doesn't meet on Shabbos, the court had to wait until Sunday to judge the merits of the case, while the Yiddish-speaking rabbi and the Christian fly were confined together in a room, unable to communicate because of the language problem.

On another Erev Shabbos, a skeptic arrived at the place of happiness, likewise seeking entry. Should such a freethinker be invited in or automatically be sent to Hell? Had he ever done a good deed?

"Indeed, he did," said a lovely Gentile girl who was listening behind the Gate. "He secretly ogled me as I bathed naked in the river, but when I began to drown, out of love, he jumped in and saved me."

Because the decision could not be rendered until the beit-din met on Sunday, the agnostic and the lovely Gentile girl were confined together in a room, where there was no language problem at all.

I ask you: Who had it better, the God-fearing rabbi or the skeptic?

The Talmud says that a single kind act of compassion may save even an impious person from Hell (Shabbat 32a).

Who would argue with the Talmud?

∾ ∾ ∾

Jews found comfort and strength in their own native tongues and literatures whenever or wherever persecution and banishment became intolerable. Until the 1394 expulsion of its Jews, Jewish Frenchmen spoke Judeo-French, a dialect written in Hebrew characters. None of that had any resonance for Abbe Henri Gregoire (1750–1831), who frowned upon vernaculars, Yiddish, in particular. The erudite bishop and revolutionary leader proposed that Jews be incorporated into the national culture and that government considerations should be conducted in the language of the country in which they lived. For him, that included eliminating Yiddish, the *"German-Jewish-Rabbinical jargon, which the Jews employ and which only they understand, the main aim of which is to increase their ignorance or camouflage their lust."* He believed that without Yiddish, their customs and language would soon be discarded. Although the French Jews assimilated quickly, many declined to "improve" themselves as a prerequisite to entering mainstream life and went right on speaking and writing as they chose—until they assimilated.

When Russia swallowed up chunks of what had formerly been the Polish-Lithuanian Commonwealth into the Pale of Settlement, despite great adversity, "Russian" Jewry gathered strength and came alive as a people with a renaissance of Yiddish language and a vast literature. Jewish folk culture, wedded to the Jewish language and religion, developed a sense of intense commitment to the metaphysical world. But with the rise of the nineteenth-century Jewish Enlightenment in Western and Eastern Europe, the revival of Yiddish "jargon" was denigrated.

To overcome the projected loss, as well as to preserve the ethnological and linguistic documentation of the Jews in the Russian Empire, Shloyme Zanvi Rappaport, better known as S. Anski (1863–1920), roamed the countryside collecting thousands of Yiddish tales that were later published in 1924 in Vilna by the Institute for Jewish Research (YIVO). Following World War II, this material, containing many stories, poems,

Catholic Abbe Henri Gregoire (1750–1831) proposed that Jews should be recognized, made useful and incorporated into the nation's culture (The New York Public Library's Digital Library, digital ID 1244276).

and other matter drawn from Eastern European communities, was rescued and is currently preserved in YIVO archives in New York City.

One such story is about an earthly match scheduled in heaven:

> A poor unmarried Hasid appeals to his rebbe for help in making him the happiest of men. Advised to accept the first marriage proposal that comes his way, he sets off to the village inn to fortify himself for this critical undertaking. There he encounters a group of pranksters who suggest that he meet one of their "sisters." Their idea of a good joke is to introduce him to the daughter of the rich innkeeper. The young heiress, amused by its possibilities, finds herself duly married with a proper ketubbah under a hastily patched-up chuppah. Lots of fun until the innkeeper shows up, not amused at all. Offered a hundred rubles to agree to a divorce, the young husband refuses. Naturally, they appeal to the rebbe for his counsel. He ups the bribe to one thousand rubles, which the father of the bride ruefully accepts. The poor Hasid is now a wealthy Hasid.

Mazel Tov!

Another ... Once there was an unwelcome guest:

> A poor man finds himself host to a stranger whose only belongings are some ragged garments.
> "Who are you, and what are you doing in my house?" inquires the poor man.
> "Ich heis Nakitkayt und Ich bin du tzu bleibn." *(My name is Nakedness, and I am here to stay.)*
> The poor man feels obligated to supply him with some decent clothes because he learned from Leviticus 19:18 that he must love his neighbor as himself. Accordingly, he orders a tailor to make a suit to the pauper's measurements. Unfortunately, it doesn't fit.
> "S'iz nisht der shuld fun dem schneider," said Nakedness. *(It's not the tailor's fault.)* "Ich bin gevaksn greser." *(I grew larger.)*

Because Leviticus mandates love, the poor man orders another suit.

Early twentieth-century Persian Jews spoke in Judi, a Judeo-Persian dialect, although its letters were scripted in Hebrew. Stigmatized as *dhimmis* (in Arabic) or Subject Peoples of the Scriptures, they lived as second-class citizens in Sunni Muslim lands, and as third-class citizens under the more repressive Shiite Muslim lands, such as Persia and Yemen. *Shariyah* laws granted certain rights, including freedom of religion, but consigned them to unpleasant or offensive jobs, in some places forcing them to serve as executioners, those hauling off animal carcasses from the streets, or those cleaning public latrines. Their tales of fear and humiliation were kept alive in their oral and written narratives, among which is Farideh Goldin's haunting *Wedding*

S. Ansky (1864–1920), author of *The Dybbik*, who led the first Jewish ethnographic expedition in 1912 to the Pale of Settlement. From the Jewish Ethnographic Museum, St. Petersberg, 1916–1917.

Song (1953), a memoir of her battle to overcome religious and authoritarian discipline and to unlearn her native language. This is Goldin's abbreviated and edited story:

> I was born to an intimidated mother and a domineering father. I tried to write the harrowing tales of my extended Jewish family in Judi, but my father burned my carefully hidden books when I was fifteen. My mother taught that our language pollutes the air. They believed my writings were destroying my chance for marriage—cooking and cleaning were to be my lot. I rebelled against their destructive, superstitious beliefs, using stories as testimonials to our history, surviving by distancing myself from relationships, rejecting family tradition, and fleeing to America. Although I eventually pursued graduate studies in the United States and married well, I no longer retained the Judi dialect that had grounded my youthful identity. My demons have since died, and the past has faded, my life ultimately renewed through relearning the Judi language of forgiveness and love.

Inshallah. If God is willing, love will make amends for suffering.

Although Jews were often forced to adapt to divergent authorities and languages, Midrash tells us that by the end of time, all people will speak in a purified form of Hebrew. But this much we know in the present time: wherever Arabic, Hebrew, Ladino, Italian, Russian, Yiddish, Near Eastern, or Persian folktales flourish, they all share the many languages of love.

8

Age of Reason—
Challenge of Tradition

A wide range of traumas afflicted large sectors of the Jewish cultures as well as the entire European community: the devastating Black Plague, instability and weakness in the ruling classes, and military conflicts in France and England all pointed to the transformation of the medieval world into the early modern period. The Sephardic culture was dissipated. Jewish poets no longer sang of love and lust. Christendom was rid of the Jewish spirit (or so it thought), but it had not disappeared. What the Church now learned was that it could no longer control or wipe out information inconsistent with its theology. Ideas and ideals persisted, although the technique of breaking people's principles by the destruction of their literature was nothing new. More than a thousand years earlier, the pagan emperor Diocletian (244–311) attempted to eradicate Christianity by purging its "abominable scriptures." Shakespeare (1564–1616), too, was aware that a civilization could be wiped out through the loss of its written history:

> …thou mayest brain him,
> Having first seized his books, or with a log
> Batter his skull, or stab him with a stake
> Or cut his throat with thy knife. Remember
> First to possess his books, for without them
> He's but a sot…. Burn but his books.
>
> [The Tempest (Act III, Scene 2)]

Jewish literature likewise was under constant attack. When charges were made that Hebrew texts maligned Christian faith, huge bonfires of "blasphemous" holy books lit up the streets of Renaissance Europe. The widespread success of the printing press assured much of Europe that readership could not be controlled, that the written word could no longer be kept out of sight. The printing press changed civilization in the arts, sciences, and philosophy. For the Jewish world, it reached a vast population unfamiliar with current secular social, political and cultural complexities.

The Jewish Renaissance was manifest in the works of the statesman, poet, and physician Judah Abravanel (Leone Ebreo, 1460–c. 1523), who emigrated in 1497 from Portugal to Italy where he wrote moral and religious tracts on perfection and harmony through love. In his *Dialoghi d'amore* (*Dialogues of Love*) (1535), dialectical reason confronts mysticism, challenging faith and contemplative life, examines love as opposed to desire, and poses divine love of God against human love of friends. He brought Renaissance idealism to Spain, comparing intellect and reason to soul as they broke out of old molds of pedantic scholasticism.

Early wooden printing press, depicted in 1568. By Jost Amman.

Love, Abravanel cautions, is not equated with pleasure-bent possession, but with the pleasure of the beautiful and the good to be as it exists in the sublime intellect and goodness of God. But God is not the sole source of love. Abravanel introduces dialogues, or invented conversations of differing philosophical ideas, between Philo, lover and teacher, and Sophia, beloved pupil (i.e., Philo+sophy):

> Philo is more concerned with the desire for sexual union, the object of which is pleasure, the physical manifestation of human love that is the dominant principle of life. Sophia claims that love and desire are mutually exclusive, opting for the spiritual or ideal love that meets, beyond physical delight in mind and soul. Love's highest level, she informs him, is the triple marriage of body, intellect, and soul, the origin of happiness. Not necessarily so, he argues. Love and desire are a mix, a pleasure to be enjoyed, not rejected.

Things are at an impasse because she can only be satisfied with an intellectual life, doesn't return his version of love, and leaves him in torment and grief. And so they part, promising to meet and argue again.

Will they? Abravanel doesn't tell.

Abravanel apparently influenced Miguel de Cervantes (1547–1616), the acclaimed author of *Don Quixote* (1605), when he references Hebrew as a better and older language than Arabic (Part I, Chapter 9). History is silent about his Jewish or New Christian origins or sympathies. Still, as his ancestors were barber-surgeons and in the clothing business, both Jewish trades, he could have been of *converso* origin. Dominique Aubier, a Catholic convert to Judaism, hints in *Don Quixote, Prophet of Israel?* (1966), that, as the hero of free expression, Cervantes is the standard-bearer of Jewish resistance to the Inquisition.

While Jews loved books and philosophy, they also admired figurative art, which had apparently been outlawed by the Second Commandment (Exodus 20:4,5). Fear of paganism, as expressed in idol worship, was the likely motive, given that nude statues of the Jewish hero David, carved by Donatello (1386–1466) and Michelangelo (1475–1564), were highly regarded and regularly visited by wide-eyed Jews who stopped by to watch the artists at work. Not to be outdone, Jews occasionally undressed their own notables in the interests of humanism or voyeurism. A 1526 Prague Haggadah, illustrated by Hayyim Shahor (d. 1547), featured a skimpily clad woman: "…thou camest to excellent beauty; thy breasts were fashioned, and thy [pubic] hair was grown; thou was naked and bare" (Ezekiel 16:7). A Mishneh Torah printed in Venice in 1574 by Meir Parenzo included the love goddess, Venus, standing on a seven-headed Hydra wearing nothing but a smile and a crown, declaring that "…the king desires thy beauty" (Psalm 45:11). The racy illustrations are rarely found in complete copies of the books since many of the original owners removed them—for what purpose, they didn't say.

Women were notable for their brains and reason as well as for their bodies (they say). One of the brainiest and most magnanimous was Beatrice de Luna (1510–1569), born into a wealthy Portuguese family of forcibly converted Jews. At eighteen, she married Francisco Mendes, who, with his brother Diogo, established thriving banking and commercial interests. Eight years later, under inquisitorial threats, she fled Portugal for Antwerp with her daughter Reyna and nephew Joseph. By then a rich widow, she reunited with her younger sister and brother-in-law. She was thirty-two when Diogo died, leaving her the

Printer's Trademark: Venus, 1574–1575. By Meir Perenzo. From Mishneh Torah.

sole administrator of his vast estate. It fostered bitter feelings between the sisters that never abated.

Antwerp was an up-and-coming city, known for its diamond cutting, wool, cloth, and spices. Emperor Charles V (1500–1558) looked with covetous eyes at the Mendes fortune—which he attempted to confiscate. When that didn't work out, he offered—for a very large fee—to arrange a marriage between young Reyna and an elderly nobleman who was a friend of his sister, Mary, Regent of Hungary (1505–1558). When the Mendes clan refused the offer, Mary threatened to expose them as Judaizers. Now known by her Jewish name, Dona Gracia Nasi, Beatrice and her family took the precaution of escaping to Italy, where her sister concocted a delayed revenge by outing her as a Jew. (Sibling relationships had not improved since the time of Cain and Abel.) She moved to Istanbul, where she spent her remaining years helping fugitive Jews and supporting synagogues, scholars, and religious academies. The Sultan of Turkey, honoring her economic and social contributions to his country, granted her concessions in his Palestinian territory of Tiberias, where she endowed a yeshiva.

And, oh yes, her nephew Joseph Nasi married his cousin Reyna. How better to wind up the family fortunes than with a love story!

While Judaism had historically emphasized physical love as consistent with spirituality, there is no sign of physical or spiritual love in Shakespeare's principal rival, Christopher Marlowe (1564–1593), whose *The Jew of Malta* (1590?) never knew if he was slave or master of his wealth. The play's Prologue introduces the "tragedy of a Jew" in a world steeped in racial, religious, and political hostility. Barabas, a ruthless villain and murderous psychopath, has become inhuman in a world that he believes made him inhuman—an outsider, rejected by a Christian society as duplicitous as he. When he refuses to surrender half his wealth to the government, his home is seized and turned into a convent. His daughter Abigail, the only loyal and loving character in the play, helps him retrieve the gold and jewelry he has secreted there by pretending to become a Christian. If he has a redeeming quality, it is his love for Abigail, although she absconds with his fortune. He equates her with money and is willing to sell her to either of a pair of knaves. Foiled, he goes on a killing spree. Abigail, embittered by guile and treachery—*"I perceive there is no love on earth"*—repudiates her Jewish heritage as the *"folly of the world."* She becomes a nun. It is more than her father can bear. Her conversion leaves him without love, without an anchor to sanity. With a homicidal curse, he disinherits her, plots her murder and the murders of friends, enemies, and the convent nuns. Without her (and his gold), he no longer knows who he is. With love gone awry, he meets death in his own trap, caught in the grotesque hypocrisy of the Machiavellian society in which the end always justifies the means.

Love and deceit, unchanging and eternal, are revisited in Shakespeare's *The Merchant of Venice* (1600), set in sixteenth-century Venice and its ghetto, home of the hated usurer Shylock. Although Jews were rejected, they could not be disregarded. In the absence of a credible banking system, they were useful as middlemen, consumers, taxpayers, and moneylenders. The authorities protected them because canon law forbade Christians (but not vulnerable Jews) to take interest: *"For the commodity (privilege) that strangers have with us in Venice, if it be denied, will much impeach the justice of this state, since the trade and profit of this city consisteth of all nations."*

Despite trade and profit, however, a compulsory separation for Jews was imposed by Pope Paul IV in the papal bull *Cum Nimis Absurdum*, published in 1555: "It is highly absurd and improper that the Jews, condemned by God to eternal slavery because of their guilt, *should, on the pretext to dwell in our midst, show such ingratitude to Christians as to insult them for their mercy, and presume to mastery instead of the subjugation that beseems them...."*

It was the presumption that Jews deserved their lot that may have prompted Shakespeare to dredge up old folktales that simmered with anti-Jewish prejudice, although he had probably never encountered a Jew: no practicing Jews had lived in his England since 1290 when King Edward I banished them from his lands. Shakespeare could neglect the invisible Jews who were perceived as responsible for the death of the Christian savior. Nevertheless, without "the People of the Book" there could be no Redeemer. So the Jews were needed. They were needed as foils for the devastating plagues, for rumored poisoned wells, for economic setbacks, for mankind's original and eternal sin, for Jewish smells and Jewish vulgarity, and for murdered children's blood.

But they were conditionally allowed to love. Like Barabas, Shylock loved his daughter—and his gold. But, unlike Barabas, Shylock was no monster. True, he had demanded a pound of flesh from Antonio in place of a defaulted loan, but only because the merchant had vilified and spat on him as a Jew: *"The villainy you teach me I will execute ... but I will better the instruction."*

Shylock is cast as a merciless Jewish creditor, an artful (or sympathetic) victim who is urged to show mercy but who contends that mercy must be earned, not dropped as gentle rain from heaven. Charged with lacking Christian grace, he questions Christian love. While the court acknowledged his legal right to remove flesh, it did not extend reason to shedding blood; one drop forfeits his lands and goods and effects the reversion of his estate to his daughter Jessica and her Christian husband, Lorenzo.

While his losses were already great—*"My daughter! O, my ducats!"*—they were not as great as the misery of Jessica, who already suspects that her lover is up to no good: *"In such a night did young Lorenzo swear he lov'd her well, stealing her soul with many vows of faith, and ne'er a true one."* It is when Shylock learns that Jessica traded the turquoise betrothal ring, given him by his late wife, for a monkey, that Shylock is hurt worst: *"I had it of Leah when I was a bachelor. I would not have given it for a wilderness of monkeys."*

Forced to accept Christianity, denied life in the ghetto home he knew, denied revenge, and bereft of half his wealth as well as of love, at the end Shylock submits to conversion to save his life. The conversion is a sham. Although humbled, his sense of self is intact. He charges the Christian world with hypocrisy, the immorality they believe they have inflicted on him. Was he villain or victim?

> I am a Jew. Hath a Jew no eyes? Hath not a Jew hands, organs, dimensions, senses, affections, passions, fed with the same food, hurt with the same diseases, healed by the same means, warmed and cooled by the same summer and winter as a Christian is? If you prick us do we not bleed? If you tickle us do we not laugh? If you poison us do we not die? And if you wrong us shall we not revenge?
>
> [The Merchant of Venice (Act III, Scene 2)]

The traditional Jew survives, has always survived—with love, or without.

∽ ∽ ∽

While the Church was coping with Jewish moneylenders, Jews were dealing with the offbeat Leone da Modena (1571–1648), an acclaimed Italian rabbi whose sermons charmed Jewish and Gentile audiences, but whose compulsive gambling almost led to his ousting from the Jewish community. Yet his sins were fewer than his misfortunes. His love for a widowed daughter, care for an insane wife, and grief for the deaths of four children—one of whom was a teenager hanged for teasing Christians—was chronicled in his

1648 autobiography, *Hayye Yehuda (Life of Judah)*, the story of Jewish life in the waning years of the Renaissance. He tells that because one of his books, *Historia de'riti hebraici* (*History of Jewish Rites*, 1637), had contained "a few things which I was afraid might not find favor with Christians ... I cried aloud in terror." Three years earlier, his beloved grandson and some friends had been "thrown into a dark dungeon and the house was sealed up" for an indiscretion reported to officers of the Inquisition. After fifteen days, the boys were allowed daylight but were kept in prison for another two months. "I came daily in great distress and at great expense. Finally, by God's mercy, they were acquitted."

Love came hard in those days.

Societal differences in Holland produced a very different kind of rabbi than Leone da Modena. Manasseh ben Israel (1604–1657), born into a Portuguese "New Christian" family, grew up in Amsterdam's liberal atmosphere. At age eighteen, he could deliver lectures in several languages, including one in English composed in honor of Queen Henrietta Maria, who visited his synagogue in 1642 and allowed that she was charmed by his sermon. He established the first Hebrew printing press in Holland operated by a Jew, publishing over seventy works in five languages. In 1651, the Calvinist church council prohibited him from issuing books in his native Dutch to avoid offending local Christians. Manasseh was outraged as a rational Jew—and a messianic Jew at that—whose love of Israel overcame his fear of the Church. He began a campaign to resettle Jews in England, from where Edward I had exiled them in 1290.

Hearing that a crypto-Jewish adventurer had encountered Native Americans in Colombia, South America, Manasseh became convinced that the Indians were one of the legendary Ten Lost Tribes of Israel. He dispatched a letter to England's Lord Protector, Oliver Cromwell (1599–1658), a missive in which he shrewdly pointed out that the prophecies in Deuteronomy 28:64 and Isaiah 11:12 precluded the return of the Messiah until the dispersion of the Jews had reached from "one corner of the earth to the other." As England was homonymous with "corner of the world" (*Angle Terre*), he suggested that the Second Coming awaited only the admission of the Jews. Having composed and translated his *Hope of Israel*, he dedicated it to Parliament, reminded its members that God and the world were watching, and, at Cromwell's invitation, betook himself to London in 1655. The religious potential of the rabbi's arguments should have been irresistible to Parliament.

Rabbi Menasseh ben Israel (1604–1657) was the founder of the first Hebrew press by a Jew, in Amsterdam. Etching, 1636. By Rembrandt van Rijn.

It was not. The response was to rehash Christ-killing, to dredge up tales of Jewish lust, and to renew charges that Jews would circumcise Christian males and convert them to Judaism, encroach on England's commerce, and buy up St. Paul's Cathedral for use as a synagogue. (Jews may have admired its architecture but could hardly have afforded to buy it had it been for sale, which it was not.) Cromwell bypassed public opinion—and permitted crypto-Jews to quietly, but unofficially, return. A Sephardi congregation was established in 1657, followed by an Ashkenazi synagogue in 1690. Manasseh didn't live to see the fruition of his dream, but his love for his co-religionists and his efforts to secure them a safe harbor have earned him an honored corner in their history.

Manasseh's role in Amsterdam's Jewish community likely extended to serving as a teacher of Baruch Spinoza (1632–1677). As a young man raised in an influential Sephardic family, Spinoza had duly studied the basic texts—Bible, Talmud, and Kabbalah—but soon left tradition for the blandishments of the emerging rationalist spirit. Secularism based on reason could not be tolerated if Jewish life, as it was traditionally practiced, was to survive. Spinoza championed a "natural" religion that emphasized intellectual precision over spiritual fulfillment, one that stressed moral values as opposed to a "revealed" Judaism. His antagonism toward religious authority upended theories of a logical basis for a divine Judaism. His reading of the Bible as parable or myth, suitable only for the ignorant or naïve, offended traditionalists. The corroding impact of Renaissance "paganism" was not a healthy transition in a community that feared that worldliness would lead to godlessness.

Dutch liberalism might be real, but it was conditional. Spinoza's philosophy undermined the traditional foundations of Christianity and Judaism: Did God exist? And if so, was He all-powerful? Did he care about the troubles of his chosen people, the Jews? And, for what were they chosen? Certainly, they were on the receiving end of unimaginable suffering. Was a communal code still viable to the majority of modern Jews who questioned its rituals and laws in the reality of prejudice and hostility? Spinoza rejected the doctrine of chosenness, the divinity of the Bible, rabbinical authority, and the immaterial nature

Old St Paul's as imagined before the fire of 1561 in which the spire was destroyed. Engraving, 1875. From *Early Christian Architecture* **by Francis Bond (1913).**

of God's body. He spoke of separation of church and state, intuitive philosophic systems, and a universal god that reveals itself through nature alone—clearly heretical concepts in a three-millennium-old Judeo-Christian creed. In 1656, from the synagogue pulpit, the rabbinate ordered him barred from every Jewish contact. He was twenty-four years old. He never converted, but remained an alienated Jew, neither close to his own religion nor officially part of any other. He had lost his faith but believed he had found reason—and hoped he would find love.

Spinoza was a disciple of the Dutch scholar Francis van den Enden, whose daughter Clara Maria offered to coach Spinoza in his Latin studies. While she was teaching him conjugations, so the story goes, he was proposing conjugal love, but his curly hair, full brows, and soulful eyes did not stir her. The shy suitor spoke of "rational piety" and the "science of faith" rather than of her endearing charms. She married a man more adept in the ways of romance. Lost to love, Spinoza retired to a single life, grinding lenses for a living and writing the books that established him as the precursor of modern rationalism and the eighteenth-century Enlightenment.

Although love may have eluded Spinoza, it manifested itself in the surreal drama of a beautiful six-year-old Jewish girl who was orphaned during the catastrophic 1648 Chmielnicki massacres. Sarah was placed in a convent where she was converted to Christianity. At sixteen, she managed to escape and make her way to Italy, where she developed a reputation in magical arts, love potions, and prostitution. But her dream was to be the bride of the Jewish Messiah. She couldn't know that far away in the Turkish port city of Smyrna, Shabbtai Zvi (1626–1676), a gifted but psychologically unstable thirty-nine-year-old Sephardic rabbi, also had a dream. He would marry a profligate woman, as did Hosea, who took a "wife of whoredom" (Hosea 1:2). If that was good enough for a prophet, it was good enough for him. In 1665, steeped in the Renaissance cult of transcendent individualism and rationalism, Shabbtai declared himself the incarnation of the Redeemer worthy of sharing the stage with the Heavenly Host.

In their on-and-off-again relationship, during which both were sexually promiscuous, Sarah's allure and eccentricity lent excitement to Shabbtai's reign as "King of the Jews." With all the panoply accorded to divinity, they mobilized thousands of impassioned followers in Europe, Africa, and Asia who believed in his mission to release divine sparks and heal the world. He apparently never doubted that the Ottoman Sultan (and ruler of Palestine) would abdicate in his favor, after which he and Sarah would conduct all of Israel to Jerusalem where the Messiah was scheduled to make his first appearance. Instead, their popularity so alarmed the authorities that they were settled in prison to contemplate their indiscretions. Offered the choice of death or conversion to Islam, they considered the alternatives and chose the latter. Although he was later graced with additional wives, it is thought that Sarah devotedly remained with him in separate quarters until her death in 1674. He died two years later, having been reviled by many for his cowardly act of converting to Islam but revered by others as a martyr who alone understood Heaven's mysteries. Perhaps God alone understood the complexity of their on-and-off-again love story.

They say that love is the art of perseverance. True enough in the case of Moses Mendelssohn (1729–1786), the philosopher and religious scholar who followed Spinoza in pioneering the enlightened ideas of Haskalah, which introduced secular European literature to Jewish circles through the use of the Hebrew language. By preparing Jews for life outside the ghetto, he intended that his translation of the Pentateuch into German (written in Hebrew letters) would provide a better understanding of Jewish principles and would pave the way for German citizenship. By insisting that knowledge of the German language and literature was essential to adapting rational "universal" truths as embodied in the Torah, he determined to reinforce the spirit of Judaism while keeping Jews within the Jewish fold.

Mendelssohn was a great scholar and linguist. He had many intellectual attributes, but his physical appearance was not that for which a much younger woman might hope. His body was crooked; his features, ugly. Nevertheless, his talent for perseverance paid off in his courtship of Fromet Guggenheim, whom he had tutored at her father's suggestion.

Much of what is recorded about their love story appeared in a February 5, 1904, edition of the Australian newspaper, *The Traralgon Record*:

> How Moses Mendelssohn Won His Wife:
> The reporter related that Moses once met a merchant who revered and admired him. As did the merchant's daughter. Under the circumstances, papa allowed that he would be honored to have the young man as his son-in-law, although he noted that Moses was "very retiring and shy for he was sadly hunchbacked." The merchant told him that, when he had first met Fromet, she was "very shocked over his frightful deformity."
> I thought so," replied Moses, "but still, I will call and take leave of her." He seated himself by her as she was sitting near a window with a piece of needlework in her hand.

The news item continues:

> They talked together pleasantly and intimately, but the maiden did not look up. And Moses did not look at her. At length, the maiden put the question: "Do you really believe that matches are decided in heaven?"
> "Certainly," he replied. "And something very unusual has happened in my case. You know that, according to a Talmudic saying, the birth of a child is announced in heaven. When I was born, my (intended) wife called out to me that she would have a fearful hunchback!
> "'Dear God,' I said, 'a maiden who is deformed will likely be bitter and harsh. Dear God, give me the deformity and let the maiden be beautiful and comely.'"
> Scarcely had he said this when she fell upon his neck. She became his wife in 1762, and they were happy together.

Another story has it that in order to get around the twenty-year discrepancy in age, he suggested that every time she looked at him, she would age by ten years. Every time he looked at her, he would grow younger by ten years.

Moses and Fromet Mendelssohn had ten children, six of whom survived, only two of whom resisted conversion. Mendelssohn died in 1786, never knowing that his future family, including the composer Felix Mendelssohn (1809–1847) and the painter Philip Veit (1793–1877), would choose to live as practicing Christians.

Mendelssohn's mission ultimately failed: most of his family found the drama and soul-stirring qualities of the Church more compelling than the cultural assimilation he advocated. By attempting to find rational proofs of God's existence and the immortality of the soul, Mendelssohn sought to reconcile rabbinic authority with Renaissance ideals of intellectual freedom to help Jews participate in the outside world. It was a slow, uphill struggle considering that, while he believed the Talmud was divinely revealed, he thought certain of its ceremonies were not.

Jewish continuity struggled as rabbinic authority weakened in some areas, separating traditional Halachis, who punctiliously followed prescribed laws, from those among the secular Maskilim who promoted Jewish integration into European society. Rabbis from both camps complained of Jewish eagerness to acquire Gentile manners and behavior, making it increasingly difficult for religious practices to compete with the glamour of romantic adventurism. Nevertheless, ritual celebrations of love and marriage were still widely observed, but sexual relations between Jews and Gentiles were often cynically winked at or conducted behind drawn curtains.

Satire and cynicism targeted the social environment as Enlightenment rhetoric penetrated Europe's Jewish culture. In 1731, William Hogarth (1697–1764), England's first great native-born artist, engraved six theatrical episodes of *A Harlot's Progress*, featuring Moll Hackabout, an artless young girl just off the farm. She soon falls into the hands of a disreputable procuress and an unattractive Jew who ogles her suggestively from a doorway. In the next scene, *The Quarrel with Her Jew Lover*, she kicks over a table to distract him from the stealthy exit of her Christian sweetheart. Hogarth underscored the folly and unsavory relationships based solely on sexual desire by linking a monkey's features and turn of the head to that of the Jew.

Jewish manners—or lack of them—were also easy butts for the wicked etching needle of the English satirist, Thomas Rowlandson (1756–1827), who found his subject matter wherever amusing, provocative, or pornographic treatment of Christian maidens suggested itself. *The Jew Rabbi Turn'd to a Christian* (1772) illustrates what happens when a lascivious

The Quarrel with Her Jew Protector. Engraving, 1732. From *A Harlot's Progress*, by William Hogarth.

Ladies Trading on Their Own Bottom. Etching, 1799. Presumably by Thomas Rowlandson.

Jew, who was expected to know better, tempts a naïve lass to trade her virtue for a bag of gold. A quarter of a century later, Rowlandson was still at it, depicting *Ladies Trading on Their Own Bottom* (1799), an etching with an indelicate title that perceives Jewish mating as a loveless procedure transacted by wicked ladies of the evening.

A very different kind of love sustained Glueckel of Hameln (1646–1724) during a long widowhood nurturing a dozen children. She left behind a memoir of the lives and times of central Europe's Jewish merchants and financiers as they struggled through the Chmielnicki atrocities and the religious and political fallout in the wake of the Shabbtai Zvi disaster. She was one of many competent entrepreneurs who were increasingly useful in developing and expanding Europe's industrial and commercial markets.

Her diary, begun in 1690 following the death of her beloved husband, was recorded "in the hope of distracting my soul from its grief." For thirty happy years, she wrote, they had shared a successful business partnership; now she tells how she managed to live through the many lonely nights, "springing from her bed to shorten the sleepless hours." When the family business foundered, she reluctantly remarried—"the great mistake of my life." Yet she experienced a measure of fulfillment and tranquility through reciting the Yiddish prayers for women and through telling her children stories of love, responsibility, and the stern realities of parenthood:

> There was once a great bird that decided to carry his three young chicks across a restless and stormy sea in order to deliver them to a safe haven. Fierce winds required that he carry them one at a time.

"Will you risk your life for me when I am old as I do now for you?" he asked the first two. Unfortunately, they prevaricated, whereupon he dropped them into the raging waters. Baby three responded that while he would do his best, he could make no definite commitment. However, he promised to do as much for his own children as his father had done for him. With honesty and truth established, the chick was safely carried ashore.

Glueckel's greatest satisfaction, she wrote, was in arranging the marriages and fortunes of her enormous progeny during her remaining twenty-two years. And in a storybook ending, happiness and love finally reached her in the home of a daughter and son-in-law from whom she gratefully received the devotion of the third little bird and "all the honors of the world."

Progressive rulers in Europe were often seeking talented Jewish bankers and physicians and useful Court Jews. If rich, these assimilated paragons attended Gentile schools, shaved their beards, sported wigs, dressed in the height of fashion, served as military contractors, participated in trade and finance, enjoyed political indulgence, and danced in the salons of high society. Living a dual existence as privileged outsiders, they remained subject to many restrictions but also functioned as advocates to the great mass of "useless" Jews, enabling many to remain in the fold during the difficult journey from exclusion to civil equity. One of these "honored" Jews was Jud Suss—Joseph Oppenheimer (1698–1738)—dapper lady's man and financier to Duke Karl of Wurttemberg. His patron's sudden death and the jealousy of rivals sent him to the gallows on alleged charges of embezzlement and making love to Christian women. In 1738 he was offered his life on condition of baptism but opted for strict religious observance. His public hanging over the main street in Stuttgart was attended by a bevy of his forlorn mistresses.

Acculturated Jews, such as Jud Suss, sought social inclusion, educational opportunities, citizenship, and equal economic rights for the first time in modern history. While most remained bound to their spiritual heritage and faith, others hoped to rid themselves of schismatic rabbis, religious fragmentation, dubious cults, stringent laws, and rusty conventions. While these Enlightenment modernists opted for a rationalist man-science relationship, many Eastern European Jews kept their own agenda—they knew their conventions were eternally

Gluckel, a businesswoman and mother of a dozen children, described the lives and times of Central Europe's influential Jewish merchants and privileged financial agents (frontispiece from the 1719 memoir *The Life of Glückel of Hameln, Written by Herself* [1646–1724], translated and edited by Beth-Zion Abrahams).

relevant; critical examinations of their religious principles were rejected. They sought a renewed man-God relationship, a revival of the beliefs that had never quite lost their grip. They longed for a guide who could bring God back to the orthodoxy they had not forgotten.

Behold Israel ben Eliezer (c. 1698–1760), the Baal Shem Tov (Master of the Good Name). Known by his acronym BeShT, he founded the Hasidic movement to explore man's kinship to God, not through asceticism or mechanical liturgy, but through charity, humility, spiritual revelation and fervent prayer. Disciples spread his homilies and messianic teachings, as well as his doctrine of love of God through feasting, ecstasy, dancing, and joyous song. A collection of his legends, *In Praise of the Bal Shem Tov*, was published in 1814, fifty-four years after his death. The tales, which had been derived from earlier narratives, offered glimpses into his life: marriage at the age of fifteen, lime digging, mystical introspection, hidden sainthood, healing powers, and inspiring leadership. Whether the allegories and parables were set in familiar villages or in the World-to-Come, his followers were convinced that his attention to prayer, control of supernatural powers, and communion with God would assure him a special niche within the heavenly gates.

Here is a story as told by one of his followers:

Mocking portrait of Joseph Suss Oppenheimer with the iron gallows as an emblem. Inscription: "He who misappropriates the great favor of the Lord with wicked advice. How this insolent Jew Suss Oppenheimer did that. Like Haman, he came to gallows at last." Engraving, 1738. Anonymous (Württembergische Landesbibliothek Stuttgart, graphic collections/Wikimedia Commons).

A man who had always been favored by the BeShT was very depressed when the great rabbi turned away his face. "I cannot bear this much longer," the man cried with a bitter and broken heart. When the BeShT explained that he recognized the sin of adultery on the man's forehead, the poor fellow vigorously denied the charge, arguing that he had been a faithful husband for, lo, these sixteen years. Nevertheless, he had recently avoided sexual relations with his wife after taking and pawning her jewelry. Since it is forbidden to touch jewelry when taking the vow of abstinence, the Rambam (Maimonides) had ruled that when a man avoids his wife, it is as though he considers her as a mother figure. He had, therefore, avoided sexual relations with her because it could be construed as incest or adultery with a married woman. Eager to be sympathetic and merciful, the BeShT ascended to the Rambam's palace where he successfully challenged that logic. Having opened a new channel of understanding, he succeeded in having the sin erased.

Because the Rambam's decisions in the upper world were compassionately interpreted by the BeShT in this world, we presume that sexual relations between the man and his wife were happily renewed.

The Baal Shem Tov would not

have been dissuaded by those who claimed that miracles and visions were deliberate falsehoods and deceptions or by those who promoted logic or rational scientific principles as the roads to truth and knowledge. He believed that God had infused him with miraculous insights, that they were not susceptible to modification, and that love and compassion were manifest in the oneness between the Creator and human beings.

When his friend Rabbi Abraham offered him his daughter Chana in marriage, her wealthy brother was alarmed at the prospect of an ignorant, penniless family member. Nevertheless, he gifted the couple with a horse, their sole asset. The young pair withdrew into the Carpathian Mountains, where they lived among the Ukrainian peasantry. Through her weekly deliveries of the clay and lime that he dug out of an intractable soil, they were able to scratch out a living. Being married to a non-materialistic man was probably not easy for a girl used to security and affluence. But if he was remarkable, she was a comfort.

The story is told that the BeShT had to die to achieve the human perfection of love:

"My beloved," he pleaded, "let me go."
"Let me die with you," she entreated. "Let me be reborn when you are."

Some Jews were rugged individualists; some were eccentric. No news there, but perhaps few other communities ever produced someone like Lord George Gordon (1751–1793), a scion of the Scottish aristocracy, member of Parliament, and scourge of the Catholics. After consultation with a rabbi, he converted to strict Orthodoxy and became concerned about the proper length of a Jewish beard; indeed, his own extended to his waist. Among his other activities, he libeled Marie Antoinette with indifference to hungry French peasants. (She never said, "Let them eat cake!") Landing in a commodious London jail for fulminating against the queen, he held regular services with a *minyan* of ten Jews and gave formal dinner dances attended by a number of royal princes. When a friend offered to visit him, he declared that only Jews with suitable beards would be admitted. The poor fellow was advised to "tarry until thine is grown."

Then there was Solomon ben Joshua Maimon (1754–1800), a Lithuanian Talmudic scholar who called the holy book a tedious debate without end or purpose. At one point, he considered converting to Christianity but refrained because he didn't believe in that religion, either. If his attitude—but not his erudition—was somewhat awry, it might be attributed to an early childhood in which his father married him off at age eleven in return for a dowry; at fourteen, he was a father himself, with a predilection for drink. Hoping to escape from an unhappy life with a carping wife and meddlesome mother-in-law, he took off to Breslau, where he worked as a tutor with a sideline in medicine. His wife soon tracked him down, offering the choice of a divorce or returning home. He chose the latter.

In his *Autobiography (Lebengeschichte)* (1792–1793), Maimon describes a loveless marriage as well as friction with his mother-in-law. If, as the Talmudic passage in Shabbat (152a) tells us, woman is the joy of the heart, Maimon begged to differ. Sadly, he was unable to cope with a life without love. Alcoholism took its final toll when he was just forty-six:

> I was under the foot of my wife—but what was very much worse—under the tongue of my mother-in-law. Nothing at all that she had promised was forthcoming. Of the six years' board I scarcely enjoyed six months. Now and then she laid hands on me, which I repaid with interest. Hardly a meal passed before we flung plates, bowls, and spoons at each other.... Tired of ceaseless warfare, I hid under her bed and took a large pot into which I spoke loudly to disguise my voice: "Why do you treat your son-in-law so badly? If you do not mend your ways, you will be damned forever." Then I

pinched her cruelly and went back to bed. The next morning she told my wife her "dream," threw herself on my mother's grave, begged forgiveness, and, as was the custom, ordered a large wax candle for the synagogue. She fasted the whole day, after which love returned—for awhile.

We are glad to learn that love and improvement are possible, if only for a while.

So here we have collected a sample of the way Jews loved (or didn't), summed up through intellectual activity, storytelling, poetry, and lively imagination. Lovers still hewed to prescribed manners and traditions—mostly. Religionists still believed that everything is continually ordered from above as needed. King Solomon had unequivocally declared in Ecclesiastes (1:9) that there is nothing new under the sun. Nevertheless, there were credible arguments that suggested otherwise. Emerging from the shadow of the Middle Ages, an Early Modern or Renaissance age was revealed in the new inventions and systematic scientific study of the natural world. Unknown oceans and continents were giving up their mysteries, telescopes were revealing the secrets of the heavens, and guns were laying waste to great swaths of land and its people.

Had rationalism superseded humanist values, concluding that the story of creation, if it ever existed as defined in the Bible, had long since been discredited? Was the Jewish Renaissance correct in arguing that the times indeed were changing, that modern insights had expanded the meaning of love from what was too often a cycle of designated sentiments and assigned behavior to one of greater personal intimacy and steadfast ties of commitment?

Yes, if the meaning of love rests in the authority of the Age of Reason, which believed that a primitive god does not, or cannot, control the world of emotion. But no, if King Solomon was correct in declaring that there is nothing new under the sun, that love is continuously renewed and reaffirmed through an omnipotent God who controls the world of emotion, including everything and everyone under the sun.

9

Chasing Modernity

Troubles were everywhere, but nowhere in such disarray as in France. Political, social, and religious diversity flowed into the vacuum of the Revolution's aftermath: monarchy versus republicanism, aristocracy versus the common man, inequality versus equity before the law, and a propertied bourgeoisie versus the property-less proletariat. With Napoleon's obsessive wars ending in humiliating defeat, the fallout demoralized the nation and undermined the democratic reforms that were the legacies of the Revolution. In an effort to promote a peaceful balance of powers and a regulated system of law and order, representatives of European nations met at the Congress of Vienna in 1815, professing to "depart from evil, to do good, to seek peace and pursue it" as Psalm 34:14 urged. Although some restrictions against Jews had been lifted, and some resolutions favoring Jewish emancipation were offered, entitlement to citizenship with full rights and privileges did not result in the hoped-for improvement. Nevertheless, ghetto walls had come down in Europe's cities: some civil rights and vocational options were granted. Expulsions, resurrected ghettos, and humiliating legislation soon resurfaced.

The road had not been easy for emancipated Juifs, now known as Israelites. Threats of violence plagued Yiddish-speaking Jews. However, despite charges of lax patriotism, usury, and existence as a "nation within a nation," religious courts agreed to trade the concept of peoplehood and communal self-government for secular state supervision. Although complete assimilation was resisted, acculturation resulted in the acceptance of many French manners and practices. Still, most Jews never disengaged from the Jewish community, nor did they leave Judaism in waves of conversion because ameliorating economic and educational circumstances made prejudice less threatening or less likely.

Some loving couples never gave up on marriage and divorce. In 1890, Alphonse Levy (1835–1919) evoked rural customs and humble ceremonies in his gently eccentric, scornful, or unabashed love songs to the traditional *shtetl* Jews of his beloved home in Alsace-Lorraine:

Putting government, economics, and traditional morality aside, much of the effort of nineteenth-century Jewish intellectuals in Central and Eastern Europe was devoted to works in Hebrew and Yiddish. They continued to write their stories, flaunt their sensibilities, and explore behaviors of which parents disapproved. They trusted that the gallant lovers and demure heroines in their shocking novels would leaf through illustrated books now that the relaxed censorship laws of 1881 allowed previously doubtful material to flood the market. Newly obtainable works, clandestinely peeking into modernity, were now *de rigueur*.

Hozen (Bridegroom). **Etching, c. 1890. By Alphonse Levy.**

Through French, German, and English popular translations, nineteenth-century literature was hurried into everyday life.

As novels about people, like or unlike themselves, gained readers, Jews found their growing visibility reflected in characters produced by some of the finest Jewishly intolerant storytellers of the day. George Sand's modern-dress Shylock in *Chateau des Desertes* (1851), the deceptive bankers and art enthusiasts in Honore de Balzac's seventeen-volume *Comedie Humaine* (1799–1850), the Goncourt brothers' *Manette Salomon* (1867), Alphonse Daudet's *Les Rois en Exil* (1879), Guy de Maupassant's *Mont Oriol* (1887), and George du Maurier's *Trilby* (1894) featured Nietzschean stereotypes of greedy capitalists and other disagreeable Jewish types such as Svengali, who corrupts the innocent Trilby. Jewish writers, as well, searched for—and found—provocative and unpalatable material in their own side streets and back alleys. Frequently assigning negative qualities to their cast of Jewish characters, they leaned heavily on distinctive or unpleasant characterizations in works by non-Jews.

The first popular French novel by a Jew, *Rachel, ou L' heritage* (*Rachel, or the Inheritance*, 1833), is an autobiographical memoir by Eugenie Foa (1796–1853), who was born into a wealthy Sephardic banking family but later adopted Catholicism. As the first serious writer of a minority group presenting themselves as Jews, her feminist interest was fashionable at a time: half of the professional storytellers in France were women who portrayed their female characters as emotionally fragile women of cloying moral excellence who were

Rozwód przed Rabinatem.
„Get" Ehescheidungsprozeß vor dem Rabbinate.

The Rabbi Presides Over a Divorce. Engraving, 1850. Anonymous.

saddled with unfulfilled desires. Although she looked fearlessly into the lives of "ordinary" individuals, Foa was criticized for suggesting that maintaining a Jewish identity in an alien society was not a sufficiently viable goal to justify its place in the modern world. Like her namesake, Rachel, Foa had obediently, but unwisely, married young. After abandoning her husband, and because divorce was illegal at the time, she turned to writing to support herself and her children— sublimating any thoughts of the love and happiness she rejected—as the mistress of a Gentile nobleman.

As a woman with a broken marriage and a broken heart, Rachel is on her own, living quietly and apart. Having been brought up in post-revolutionary France, her civil rights were not challenged, and conversion held no social or professional advantage. But life in a Christian environment required remaking herself in an economy and social setting for which she was ill-prepared. With few possibilities for a vocation or even an adequate livelihood, she attempted to earn her keep in a literary career. Disparaged as a female author, nursing thoughts of an impossible love affair, she fed on her body until it could no longer sustain her. Premature death offered the only "respite for her suffering soul," her own unfinished life.

The self-styled prophet of despair, Alexandre Weill (1811–1899), predicted that anti-Semitism would gain momentum even though many French Jews declared themselves opposed to the concept of Jewish nationhood expressed in the incipient Zionist movement. At first responding positively to the Judaism of faith over ritual, which he had imbibed as a young rabbinic student, Weill later rejected the "yoke of the Talmud." Nevertheless, troubled by the impact of modernity and materialism, he decried "profane" or secular life in the small Alsatian village where Jewish tradition was recognized as the best defense against assimilation. His novel, *Braendel* (1860), explores contemporary life where revelation over reason defined the norm. Arguing against rational law, Weill placed his doomed young lovers, one visionary, one freethinking, in a town much like the one in which he was born:

> Braendel is a pious fifteen-year-old girl who is bound to the heroic tales of Biblical prophetesses with whom she identifies; she dedicates her life to the belief that God cares about the covenant between Himself and Israel. Barely earning enough collecting forest wood to support herself and her grandmother, Braendel rejects her passionate love for Joel, a seventeen-year-old Hebrew scholar. She and Joel had once experienced the heights and depths of spiritual love but ended up as disillusioned utopian prophets. The intellectual traditions they once embraced were destroyed by a fledgling modernity and the lure of progressive liberalism.
>
> She fears that Joe's father will force him to marry a rich girl, take on the family business, and leave the synagogue behind. When Joel finds the company of local Catholic boys more compelling than hers, Braendel battles for his soul against the chance that he will abandon his studies. Alas, Joel is tempted by Christianity. She suspects that she is sacrificing herself without hope of success, challenging personal freedom and religious indifference. When Joel injures his foot and collapses into a ditch, Braendel sets off against all odds to find him. Find him she does but at the cost of her life. As the image of Braendel remains "between his heart and his head," Joel, tempted by conversion, rejects heresy in her memory. In accordance with Jewish custom, he places a small stone on her tomb but acknowledges the inevitability of diverging paths.

The sole Jewish officer on the French General Staff, Alfred Dreyfus, was convicted of treason in 1894 for allegedly turning over confidential military documents to the hated Germans. He endured life on Devil's Island for five years, fighting off a breakdown and thoughts of suicide. During his years of incarceration, he was sustained by the censored and delayed letters that he and his wife Lucie were allowed to exchange. His diary, begun in 1894 and concluded in 1899, was first published in 1901 as *Cinq Ans de ma Vie (Five Years of My Life)*. It was filled with a mutual love neither of them believed would ever be realized in freedom:

> My dear Lucie, in the end truth must prevail.... I embrace you a thousand times. As I love you, as I adore you, my darling Lucie. A thousand kisses to the children. I dare not say more about them to you; the tears come into my eyes...
>
> Dear Alfred, Someday justice will be done, and we shall again be happy together, and our children will love you the more.... Wherever you go, wherever they send you, I will follow; together we shall bear more easily our exile. We shall live for each other.

The Dreyfus trial, the signature political and social event in France in the closing years of the century, resulted, among other achievements, in the separation of church and state and the passing of control of the army and navy from a small clique of reactionary officers to more competent hands.

The Dreyfus Affair had a profound influence on Theodor Herzl, an Austrian journalist assigned to cover the explosive trial. Herzl was shocked by charges that Jews lacked loyalty to France, as well as by a rise in anti-Semitism and racist theories that had been declared dead or dying after the tolerant American and French Revolutions. Herzl's nationalist ideology culminated in 1896 in the Zionist movement for the return and reestablishment of the Jewish people to their rightful home as a modern nation. In his book, *Der Judenstaat*, he laid the groundwork for an independent Jewish State in Palestine as a safe refuge for every displaced or dishonored Jew.

∽ ∽ ∽

Early nineteenth-century England was sharply divided by extremes of wealth and want. Rich landowners, poor farmers, and a struggling working class shared a country that supported a growing bourgeois population. Although new pecking orders were imposed, the aristocracy clashed with aggressive parvenus in an effort to keep its fixed divisions intact and its charmed circle closed to Catholics, Jews, dissenters, and paupers. Disease, polluted factories, unholy working hours, and class enmity infiltrated London's East End, where large numbers of Jews met with hostility from the English working classes. When Charles Dickens (1812–1870), in his first full-length novel, *Oliver Twist* (1837), introduced the Jewish villain Fagin, he was cast as a corrupter of boys and receiver of stolen merchandise. Fortunately, young Oliver was rescued from evil just in time. While Dickens claimed, "that class of criminal almost invariably was a Jew," he didn't endow Fagin with stereotypical Jewish features. He attempted an apology for his perceived anti-Semitism in his last complete novel, *Our Mutual Friend* (1864), in which the "gentle Jew," Mr. Riah, is cast as impossibly good.

Sir Walter Scott (1771–1832) famously depicted medieval England in *Ivanhoe* (1820), drawing links between prejudice and frustrated love. Written a dozen years before the emancipation of Jews in England, it reflects the fixed biases of his own century as well as those of the twelfth. Isaac of York is described as a "mean and unamiable" usurer, although he improves with the turning of the pages; no longer the stereotypical Jewish villain, he becomes an advocate of peace and love as befits the father of the saintly Rebecca. The book struggles with the possibility of a union between a Christian knight and a beautiful Jewess, which is, of course, impossible. Ivanhoe marries the colorless Rowena—to the dismay of many readers who were rooting for Rebecca, a modern woman with womanly instincts and desires, the "bride of Song of Songs." The novel marked a profound and welcome change in anti-Semitic Western culture.

Scott also traces the difficulties of blending hostile Normans and Anglo-Saxons who, in spite of mutual interests, fail to live as friends, let alone as brothers:

> Nor is brotherly love available to Isaac of York, a courageous, dignified, and devoted father to Rebecca, who is a thousand times dearer to him than his own life. Her lovely features and high moral qualities, her pride and humility establish her as an ideal woman and a model Jewess. When the brave Crusader knight, Ivanhoe, is gravely wounded during a tournament, Rebecca, known as a skilled healer, undertakes to treat him. She is, however, accused of sorcery and in danger of her life until Ivanhoe secures her innocence. Could it be love that prompts him—injured as he was—to ride his horse to exhaustion in order to save her? Certainly, he was attracted to her and may even have spun fantasies of their life together—until he discovers that she is Jewish. As a good Christian, he has no choice. Love between Rebecca and Ivanhoe is out of the question because she is Jewish, and he loves elsewhere. He must sacrifice love to religion, hoping to find his ultimate reward in heaven—or in Rowena, whom he marries. Rebecca, alas, is in love with her noble champion. Is it a crime to look upon Ivanhoe with longing? Not a crime, perhaps, unless she converts. Which she won't. Or unless he does. Which he won't.

Case over? Not quite. Scott tells us that the memory of Rebecca's beauty and humility filtered into Ivanhoe's mind more frequently than his wife would have approved.

Like most Jewish writers in nineteenth-century England, Grace Aguilar (1816–1847) favored dual attitudes towards Jews, approval and aversion, as they threaded their way across Biblical subjects and social and historical themes. She related her fiction to *Ivanhoe*, but whereas Scott's Jews abandoned England, Aguilar's Victorian Jews were ready to play leading roles in service to their country. Descended from Portuguese Jews herself, Aguilar adapted the Sephardic past to Jewish life in the present.

The Escape: A Tale of 1755, written in 1844, is based on the mid-eighteenth-century earthquake, fire, and thunderous tidal wave that devastated Lisbon and surrounding areas. The novel channeled the memory of the disaster into a poignant story of the Inquisition and

Iberian crypto-Jews, replete with the mayhem that erupted on the morning of November 1, All Saints Day. Aguilar approached the true narrative in Biblical terms as evidence of God's punishment of Portugal for its Jewish persecutions. Evangelical Christians interpreted the earthquake as the divine judgment of a wrathful God who was preparing humanity for the End of Days. Enlightenment philosophers explored its impact and consequences less by theodicy, more by naturalism. If the power of the Church was so strong, they concluded, why were God's temples destroyed while the city's brothels survived?

The story pointed to a better life in tolerant England, where financial and commercial opportunities were opening up, where some fortunate Jews might move from the unwholesome East End to more salubrious neighborhoods with the possibility of non-traditional marriages. But above all, *The Escape* is the romantic tale of Alvar Rodriguez and Almah Diaz, a story in which mutual passion and dependence on God's mercy are miraculously rewarded by heavenly love:

> The wedding of Alvar Rodriguez and Almah Diaz was celebrated with extraordinary excitement in the town of Montes, some fifty miles from Lisbon. The church was decorated with all possible finery, its Catholic altar covered in gold and jewels reflecting the beauty of the bride and the elegance of the groom. True, they were unnaturally calm, but surely that was natural in an affair of solemnity and grace. Why then does Almah shrink and tremble? Is it because she is aware that, in a small room next door, a second betrothal and benediction would take place under a Jewish canopy in the sight of the God of the Exile—may His infinite mercy hide the secret of their faith? For this was the time that Jews concealed their mysterious rites in the midst of inquisitional intolerance, despair, and fear of the flame.
>
> Alvar, betrayed on a business trip to Lisbon, is convicted and tortured as a Jew, but never submits to conversion. Fortunately, a mysterious young Moor produces a file and a rope ladder for him to escape from prison. Who can it be but the heavily disguised Almah, who apparently has come too late to save them! Alas, death by burning awaits the loving pair, but as Almah says, "Love is mightier than death; there is only love in heaven."
>
> Suddenly, under a clear and cloudless sky, with the victims already bound to stakes, a violent upheaval shakes the ground leaving behind mass destruction. Freed from their ropes, Alvar staggers through the ruins with Almah tightly clutched in his arms as a convulsive sea rushes in to carry off what remained of the once-glorious city. Their love is preserved by God in his infinite mercy. Luckily, He also preserves their child and the bulk of Alvar's property, which had been previously secured in humane and liberal England. With the veil of secrecy removed, love and faith are possible in England, the other Eden.

The Lisbon earthquake and tsunami of 1755, which killed about 50,000 people and destroyed some 12,000 homes in Portugal and Spain, was felt all over Europe, as well as in North Africa and parts of South America. The repercussions were particularly tragic in devout Catholic countries that believed that the world was governed by a benevolent deity. If divine judgment was not questioned by true believers, it was cynically questioned by rationalists such as Voltaire (1694–1778)—*"Are you sure the power which could create the universe and fix the laws of fate, could not have found for man a proper place, but earthquakes must destroy the human race?"*

Benjamin Disraeli (1804–1881) was twelve years old in England, a year shy of his Bar Mitzvah, when his father, Isaac, a member of the Bevis Marks Synagogue, declined the honor of his election as a warden on the grounds that he wasn't consulted and that Judaism held little meaning for him. Because he believed that his son, as a Jew, had few or no opportunities for advancement, he had him baptized, thus making him eligible for the high offices of Prime Minister and member of the House of Commons in the British government. Although Benjamin was a bona fide Christian, he was regularly referred to as "The Jew," and he always acknowledged his heritage with pride. It is said that when he was taunted by the Irish leader Daniel O'Connell in 1835 as a descendant of "miscreant" Jews, he replied: "Yes, I am a Jew, and when your ancestors were brutal savages in an unknown land, mine were priests in the temple of Solomon." (A similar statement has been attributed to Judah P. Benjamin, the Confederate Secretary of State.)

Whether those were Disraeli's actual words, they were characteristic of his philosophy. He had campaigned for Jewish national independence, had supported the return of the Jews to the "land of their fathers," had written a semi-historical novel about the twelfth-century messianic pretender David Alroy, and had challenged the Christian Church to acknowledge Jews as the "aristocrats of mankind." His early travels to Palestine inspired a number of historical works involving the struggles toward national unity through the reconciliation of ethnic and religious identities. Disraeli's novel *Tancred; Or, The New Crusade* (1847) was named for the Italo-Norman leader of the First Crusade, which lasted from 1096 to 1099. Disraeli appropriated the story as a highly satiric critique of Victorian political and social conventions.

> The young idealist Tancred, Lord Montacute, a radical aristocrat seeking "higher values," has turned his back on his devoted parents and the frivolous and shallow materialist London society. Instead, he enlists in a pious crusade of his namesake to seek the Jewish roots of Christianity in the Holy Land and to restore to Christianity its moral and religious force. He soon realizes that reaching Jerusalem was not his burning issue—the difficulty was what to do after arriving there. He meets and falls in love with Eva, the beautiful daughter of a Jewish merchant, envisioning her as an angel who advocates the doctrine of equality between Christianity, Judaism, and Islam. He gets caught in political machinations, is kidnapped, is wounded, and is mercifully restored to health by his beloved Eva, who explains that Christianity derives from and is indebted to Judaism. It is their hope that the two nations might be reconciled through the intermediary of interreligious love. But a fateful blow falls on the young couple when Tancred's parents show up in time to rescue him from an unsuitable marriage and to return him safely to England, from whence Britain rules the world.

Tancred was more than a Victorian-era racial or religious analysis of Christian and Jewish origins. It was presumably the author's vision of marital happiness. His marriage to Mary Anne Lewis, an eccentric widow twelve years his senior, was admittedly for financial convenience. Nevertheless, for thirty-three years, they were genuinely devoted to each other. "Love me, love my Mary Anne," he demanded. "Dizzy married me for money," she acknowledged, "but if he had to do it over again, he would marry me for love."

George Eliot (Mary Ann Evans, 1819–1880), published *Daniel Deronda* (1876), in which Jews are described as worthy and ideal members of the human race in pursuit of religious freedom and identity in England. It followed upon the trail of French Revolutionary liberalism and Emancipation when, in 1858, Jews were relieved of oath-taking according to Christian principles and finally permitted to affirm loyalty to France according to Jewish requirements.

The proto-Zionist novel matches Daniel's urge to discover his Jewish origins and the interwoven plot of religious restraints in contemporary racial and nationalistic Victorian society. By contrasting the possibility of a happy marriage for emancipated women with the probability that the nuptial bond is a hostile trap, Eliot expanded (and expanded and expanded) the boundary between the mid-century morality, spirituality, and materialism of Mirah Cohen, a poor Jewish girl, and Gwendolen Harleth, who marries for money and regrets it:

> Gwendolen Harleth is a beautiful girl of great charm who chose economic security when she couldn't have love with a mysterious young man that she met at a roulette table. Because Daniel Deronda did not return her interest, she recklessly gambled, lost her inheritance, and was reduced to genteel

poverty. Marriage to the cruel-but-wealthy Henleigh Grandcourt was the only way for her to acquire financial independence, but she is repelled when she learns of his mistress and their four children. Necessity overruling judgment, she accepts the union out of desperation, although she is in love with Deronda. Nothing will come of that because we learn (after several hundred pages) that he loves someone else. Her pain, however, was not for naught, because, having known him, she vows to help others and become, herself, a better person.

Daniel, too, had been searching for a meaningful life. For him, it was personal identity, since he suspected that he might be the illegitimate son of Sir Hugo Mallinger, in whose home he was raised. After rescuing young Mirah Cohen from drowning, he takes her to the home of his friends. There she allows that she is Jewish and that she is alone in the world, having failed to find her mother and brother. Through Daniel's efforts to help her, he becomes acquainted with Mordecai, a Jewish idealist who hopes to enlist him in a project to secure a Jewish national homeland in Palestine. Daniel discovers that his mother had renounced her Judaism in rebellion against its strict lifestyle and had turned him over to her former lover, Sir Mallinger, to be raised as a Christian. That wasn't his only discovery. Mordecai and Mirah are brother and sister! Daniel and Mirah marry and will leave England, study the tenets of Judaism, and settle lovingly in God's Holy Land. Mordecai's vision is redeemed, and he dies of consumption gratefully in their arms.

Jews who lived in Germanic lands had different concerns: German-Christian nationalist theories partnered with traditional anti-Jewish attitudes. Jews were charged with lack of patriotism, overbearing social habits, fiscal intrigues, and aggressive political and economic activity. Violence swept through towns and cities in 1819 (the infamous Hep! Hep! riots), taking lives and vandalizing property. What generations of German brutality had not accomplished, apostasy, assimilation, and intermarriage might. The challenge was met through the German-Jewish intellectual movement *Wissenschafft des Judentums,* the science or scholarship of Jewish history and culture. Organized in 1819 by the eminent historian of Jewish medieval and modern literature Leopold Zunz (1794–1856), it promoted objective, historical programs to match the level of modern European academic scholarship. His treatise, *Zur Geschichte und Literatur* (*On History and Literature*), published in 1845, showed an impressive knowledge of Jewish folklore and homilies that appealed to middle- and upper-class Jews who discovered that they might acquire the "fine art of living" through the appreciation of popular literature.

Germany's greatest lyric poet, Heinrich Heine (1797–1856), was among those dismayed and disillusioned by the breakdown of liberalism. Cynically and out of sheer expediency, he converted to Lutheranism at age twenty-seven. Later claiming it was only an "admission ticket into European culture," he became bitterly aware that neither the ticket nor the apostate's "crawling to the cross" would ever be honored. Sex seemed a possible alternative. He promptly fell in love with his cousin Molly, he was broken-hearted when her father thwarted the romance, but overcame his sorrow by transferring his longing to her sister, Therese—with similar results. His poems were dazzling overtures to love, naively gained and cynically lost:

> I love this white and slender body, these limbs that answer love's caresses,
> Passionate eyes, and forehead covered with heavy waves of thick black tresses.
> You are the one I've searched for in many lands
> You are my sort, you understand me;
> As equals we can talk together,
> In me you've found the man you cared for,
> And, for a while, you'll richly pay me with kindness, kisses, and endearments—
> And then, as usual, you'll betray me.

9. Chasing Modernity 127

Passion burned too fast. For the last eight years of his life, poor and deathly sick, he was confined to a "mattress grave." He was buried neither as a Jew nor as a Christian.

Corresponding to the interest in the Jewish past, and aligning it with the present, artists portrayed upper-class Jews as they stepped into a cosmopolitan foreign world of exotic Jewish society. Among those prints, *La Noce Juive au Maroc (The Jewish Wedding in Morocco)* (c. 1839), by Eugene Delacroix (1798–1863), introduces newlyweds entering a courtyard to enjoy the performance of a sultry dancer. A wood engraving by Haenen, *Marriage Israelite* (Jewish Wedding) (1886), features a happy bride, a vision in her dressmaker's finest effort, alongside her groom elegantly decked out in *tallit* and tails.

Moritz Daniel Oppenheim (1800–1882), the first professing Jewish artist whose intimate evocations of Frankfort's well-to-do Jews were widely acclaimed, was the first to portray Jews as members of a dignified enlightened tradition "worthy" of emancipation. His mezzotint portrait of *Fanny von Arnstein* (1804) was a daring challenge to the proprieties: neither sermons nor raised eyebrows deterred this woman of the world from displaying her curls or flaunting her bare arms to attract the gentlemen who bought the print either to hang in their clubs or to hide in their closets.

Through an interest in literature and the arts, Jews were no longer automatically relegated to outsider status but could identify as members of ordinary families, (often) divisive, (occasionally) supportive, and (sometimes) endearing. With more and more communities dealing with intergenerational conflict, intermarriage, and apostasy, their popular romances and evocative pictures helped Jews to come to grips with an unlamented past and to project a happier future.

Many stories by and about Jews, set in small ghetto communities averse to social advancement or individual needs, nevertheless were instrumental in defending and preserving literary traditions. The novel by Austrian Leopold Kompert (1822–1886), *Der Dorfgeher (The Village Peddler)* (1849), explored the emotional baggage of family conflict between generations as it collided with the progressive Jewish Enlightenment:

> Emanuel, dressed as an itinerant beggar, arrives unannounced in search of the peddler, Reb Schimme Prager. He asks Benjamin, a young Talmudic student, to lead him to the home he once fled, where, now incognito, he takes a place at his father's Sabbath table. Benjamin attempts to keep traditional Judaism inviolate at the time when religious reforms are subverting cherished conventions and rituals. With the approach of the Sabbath, Benjamin asks Emanuel to attend the synagogue service. At first, Emanuel is repelled by Jewish prayer. He determines to leave the ghetto to renew his love for non-Jewish Clara but immediately returns when memories of the sweetness of the Sabbath become overwhelming. Confused by his painful struggle, he writes to Clara of his difficulties even as he remains with the family. By rejecting the rationalism and glitter of assimilation, as well as the arms of Clara, he slowly redeems the legacy of Jewish self-worth and self-respect and accepts the positive values of religious ritual from which he believed he had escaped.

Neither Christianity nor modernity holds an answer for Emanuel. Rather, it is the pull to national identity, the acknowledgment that the past is crucial to the present, that brings him back to his roots. However, he believes that for Benjamin, a youthful incarnation of himself, "Years will come and go and this iron fortress of faith will be reduced to a heap of rubble." In the meantime, the repentant and reluctant son remains torn: "I shall smile, I shall be happy—but can I ever forget Clara?"

Yes, he probably can, but ambivalence will be a life-long spouse.

Subjects of conversion or assimilation allowed readers to express their opinions or vent emotions through a variety of sentimental narratives. The novel *Aurelie Werner* (1863–1864), by Sara Hirsch Guggenheim (1834–1909), relates the trauma of a beautiful Orthodox heroine, who, constrained from marrying the man she loves because he isn't Jewish, determines to "live in happiness … with love as her religion." Encouraged by her mother, who has overcome her aversion to Jewish "superstition," she is whisked off to baptism in which, she believes, faith, not practice, constitutes the basis for morality. While not explicitly sexual, the novel's suggestive matter was sufficiently melodramatic to ensure its popularity. With such potboilers shaping modern attitudes, permissive notions could be widely disseminated—and they were:

> Mrs. Werner is blinded by the advantages to her family of connecting with a wealthy Gentile son-in-law. Forbidden by her husband to promote the courtship of Count H___ and her daughter, Aurelie, she nevertheless takes every opportunity to bring them together. Mr. Werner explodes upon hearing rumors that the count has asked for her hand in honorable marriage—that is, as soon as she becomes a Christian and is lawfully able to defy her father. After all, he informs her, Jewish and Christian prayers have a lot in common, in doctrines of humanity and morality, as well as in superstitions. Though Aurelie believes that she may be compromising the salvation of her soul, she is egged on by her mother's ambition. Five years pass, and all her father's unhappy predictions have come true. The count has tired of her, is an indifferent parent to their son, has taken mistresses, reminds himself that it was folly to give up the social attractions that would have accrued with a more suitable wife, as well as the pleasures of a bachelor-style life. The Werners learn that, despite perceived religious reforms, social and material acceptance never materialize in the real world; the negative consequences of intermarriage do. In her misery, Aurelie returns to God and her father's home; properly repentant, she is forgiven. The grandchild will be circumcised according to Jewish law.

Nothing can make a Jewish woman the happy wife of a Christian man.

The search for love was forever new and occasionally felicitous, even in fractious Russia. Samuel Gordon (1871–1927) examines love's highs and lows in his novel, *Daughters of Shem: A Study of Sisters* (1898). (According to the Bible, Shem, the son of Noah, fathered the Semitic peoples.) Through the story of the sisters Zillah and Salka, somewhere in the Eastern land of the displaced Jews, Gordon offered the appeal of contemporary Russian life as well as the threat to traditional Judaism. He did not neglect modern arguments in favor of love and intermarriage, but neither did he shrink from the possibilities of religious disintegration:

> It was only a dreary small shop along the Russian frontier that dispensed odds and ends for the use of local officers. It was mindlessly attended by Zillah, a beautiful girl who spends the long hours behind the counter reading secular German novels to distance herself from the mind-numbing home she inhabits with her sickly mother, her businessman father, and her younger sister, Salka. The imaginary world of her books has sustained her during dreams of escape from marriage to an unknown rabbinic scholar, Enoch, when all she asked was to be left to herself, not to a man "into whose face I have never looked, whose voice I have never heard, to be his inalienably, while I am gasping for liberty." Nevertheless, obedience, not rebellion, drudgery, not diversion, and dedication to barbarous folkways were to be her fate, as, indeed, they were the fate of all the women she knew.
> Zillah is tempted in the form of a handsome young Russian Police Commissioner. He falls in love with her. After a soul-distracting struggle, she returns his love and agrees to run off with him. Yet she could not afford to ignore the future, which she knows would be bought dearly. Salka urges her to taste love and life to the full and to teach the world tolerance and respect; that would permit atonement for the grief inflicted on their parents. Her options, Zillah explains to Salka, were preserving

their Jewish heritage or running to a Christian world of which she could never be a part. What Zillah doesn't know is that Salka is in love with Enoch, who, discouraged by Zillah's indifference, decides to leave. In the end, Zillah wordlessly begs Salka to save her from herself. Salka informs the Commissioner that her sister will not come; sadly, he goes off. Zillah gives her hand to Enoch: she will be a true daughter of Shem, ensuring the future of the Jewish people. It was the work of her good angel—her sister, who sacrificed her own dream of a possible union with Enoch.

Shalom Aleichem (Solomon Naumovich Rabinovich) (1859–1916), the beloved Russian-born author of *Tevye, the Dairyman* (1894), promoted Yiddish as the Jewish national language in his comic/poignant story depicting the resilient Russian Jews as they leave the *shtetl* and emerge into the mainstream of European and American life. The book reached millions of devoted fans in dozens of languages, thanks to the 1971 movie *Fiddler on the Roof*.

> Tevye makes the acquaintance of the fictional Shalom Aleichem and talks his ear off in an endless monologue about his trials as a poor dairyman with a nagging wife, Golda, and five headstrong daughters, three of whom dream of marrying for love despite the fact that their choices distance them from Jewish beliefs. Matching his tribulations against those of the Biblical Job, he trades homilies with his captive, but patient, audience:
> Praise the Lord Whose deeds are most just but Who has burdened Tevye with troublesome children, though he mustn't complain. His eldest daughter, Tzaitel, rejected the wealthy butcher for the uneducated tailor, Mottil Komzoil, who can barely read his prayers—which would be fine ... except for the slight inconvenience of his brood having very little to eat. Next is Hodel, who can write and read Yiddish and Russian but lives in exile with her revolutionary husband imprisoned in Siberia. Will he ever see her again in this world? A merciful God will help him to forget those troubles by inflicting an even deeper pain. It is the village priest—may his hateful name perish—who taunts him with arguments about God, libels the Talmud, and laughs while he encourages Tevye's young daughter, Chana, to convert and marry her Gentile lover, Hvedka the Scribe.
> "Don't forget," Tevya cautions her, "who you are and who he is." To which she argues that "God created all men equal," that He favors social progress and individual choice.
> "How have I sinned?" Tevya asks God, "What am I that You keep me constantly in mind and unfailingly bless me with new troubles and calamities?" He and Golda sit Shiva, the prayer for the dead, take up their work, never mentioning Chana's name. He calls on the Lord for comfort and release. The louder he prays, the louder he hears her parting voice.

No one will ever hear Tevya complain—Tevya isn't that kind of man.

What Tevya is, is the kind of man who knows that he should not see guilt in one whom he loves, nor merit in one whom he hates (Ketubot 105b). And yet, how can a poor dairyman blame his precious child or acknowledge virtue in one who has played the devil with his life? But God is good. He and Golda discover that after twenty-five years, they still have something in common, called love.

So why, Tevya might have asked, had a good God permitted Charles Darwin (1809–1882) to turn Biblical accounts of human origins inside out, which led to the concept of favored races? In his *On the Origin of Species* (1859) and *The Descent of Man, and Selection in Relation to Sex* (1871), Darwin asserted that through natural selection and survival of the fittest, some individuals possess characteristics favorable for survival in certain environments and that more durable organisms would appear in succeeding generations. None of this was good for Tevya or the Jews, who were suddenly regarded as biologically unable to wipe clean the taint of Jewish blood by inheritance, assimilation, or conversion. They were stigmatized as capitalists, misers, disloyal citizens, socialists, rootless cosmopolitans, sexual predators with offensive bodily odors, or whatever else could be identified as disparaging or inferior.

This was nothing new. But, as the approaching century would demonstrate, the concept of Jews with inbred disadvantages would take on ominous implications and lead to disaster.

Across the wide Atlantic, the American Constitution and the First Amendment set the road for the future of Jewish freedoms. One of the first American-liberty activists, a Philadelphia Jew, Jonas Phillips (1736–1803), wrote a letter to George Washington on September 7, 1787, praising a constitution that banned all religious tests for national office. In nearby Newport, Rhode Island, Congregation Shearith Israel, the oldest synagogue in North America, counted patriotic Jews among its members, including its *chazzan*, Gershom Mendes Seixas (1745–1816), the first native-born Jewish religious leader. In 1790, he quoted Micah 4:3–4 at the time of Washington's inaugural, offering gratitude on behalf of the Jewish community for a "government which gives to bigotry no sanction, no assistance to persecution." The president responded, re-quoting Micah, "May the children of the stock of Abraham, who dwell in this land, continue to enjoy the good will of the other inhabitants, while everyone shall sit in safety under his own vine and fig tree and there shall be none to make him afraid."

Sometimes love shows up as love of country.

Thomas Jefferson, the "Man of the People," took office in 1801. The election was seen as a triumph of majority rule over government by the privileged class. Of a total of about five million, he became president of some two thousand Jews. A decade later, the War of 1812 broke out. English forces reached the capital, setting fire to the White House and sailing as far as Baltimore. Driven back after a desperate fight in which bombs burst in air, proof was given that our flag was still there.

Love of country was instilled by the sight of the flag.

That flag still flew for President James Madison, one of the Jews' strongest supporters, who appointed Mordechai Manuel Noah as consul to Tunis. However, when James Monroe, then secretary of state, reported that Noah's Jewish religion "would form an obstacle to the exercise of your Consular function," Noah was dismissed.

Mordechai Noah's first cousin, Commodore Uriah Phillips Levy, was the first American Jewish naval officer to hold the country's highest military rank—Commander of the Mediterranean fleet. He is recognized as the father of the law to abolish flogging and corporal punishment in the U.S. Navy. Nevertheless, the secretary of the navy held him guilty "of being of the Jewish persuasion." In 1836, Levy bought Monticello, Jefferson's debt-ridden home, which he restored and willed to the government as a gift to the American people.

Sometimes love works for American heroes.

When the Civil War erupted, approximately nine thousand Jews took up arms on both sides of the conflict—for or against the private ownership of human beings. In 1862, General Ulysses S. Grant accused the Jews in his military jurisdiction of speculating illegally in the cotton market. Calling Israelites "an intolerable nuisance," he expelled "all Jews, as a class, from the department territory ... within twenty-four hours." President Lincoln immediately rescinded the order, although many had already been forcibly ejected. (Grant later apologized.)

Sometimes love needs a champion.

Although many Eastern European Jews still found themselves on the outside looking in, entry to America remained open. Yet, their arrival in the late nineteenth century was

9. Chasing Modernity

grudgingly welcomed by their established German-American cousins, who, embarrassed by their *shtetl* behavior and Yiddish speech, kept them at arm's length (but opened their checkbooks to provide economic, health, and social benefits).

Sometimes Jews gained advantages—and qualified love.

Jewish labor literature, often written in Yiddish, concentrated on sweatshop socialist or anarchist ideologies. Rebellions against urban bosses, politicians, and fanatical rabbis were marked by militant strikes and demonstrations. The popular poet David Edelshtat (1866–1892) urged workers to meet challenges:

> How long will you bow, unable to rise,
> Debased, with no home and no right!
> Day dawns! Wake up! Oh, open your eyes!
> Discover your ironclad might.

Sometimes Jews found that love and might were possible together.

10

Tracing Modernity

In 1900, the world's population consisted of almost two billion people. Some 10.5 million of that number were Jews, most of whom at one time or another loved someone.

In 1899, Sigmund Freud (1856–1939) introduced his *The Interpretation of Dreams*, defining and interpreting the "progressive" ways in which Western man dismissed supernatural influences, repressed prurient fantasies, celebrated inhibitions of the unconscious irrational mind, and explored the primacy of sex. Modernity required, he believed, a great transformation and redefinition of traditional social interactions, relationships, and prejudices. Although he claimed to be indifferent to religion, he preserved an attachment to his Jewish ancestry and remained interested in modern Jews as subjects for psychoanalytic inquiry.

In 1914, American Jews numbered 3.5 million, the largest and most affluent Jewish population in the world. In the decades before that year changed the world, European economic and political rivalries launched the secret alliances and military buildups that laid the groundwork for the carnage of World War II.

In 1917, three pivotal events impacted Jewish life: the Bolshevik Revolution, which overthrew the Czarist authority and replaced it with the Soviet Union; the Balfour Declaration, announcing "British support for the establishment in Palestine of a national home for the Jewish People"; and the American entry into World War I. When peace—or what mimicked peace—arrived in 1918, the balance of power that had prevailed in Europe was history: four empires had disappeared—Austria-Hungary, Czarist Russia, Germany, and the Ottoman territories. The war to end all wars had grievously failed with soured egos, bleak resources, and inflexible leadership.

The brief Weimar Republic (1919–1933) existed as a test (and failure) of the viability of democracy in Germany. Jewish life in Germany was wedged between radical extremism and moderate socialism, between faith-based ethics and a lapsing humanism, between normative patriotism and a growing revanchism. The period likewise marked the end of the great wave of immigration from East to West.

In 1933, many Germans, crediting the incipient economic recovery to right-wing Aryans, blamed the subsequent economic depression on left-wing Jews. As Adolf Hitler (1889–1945) moved in, rational behavior moved out, leaving a police state bent on world aggression, the glorification of the "master race," and elimination of the Jews. Tens of millions died or were displaced during World War II, including 4 percent of Europe's population. By the time the world finally climbed out of the "just war," it met a new set of challenges: student protests, civil rights, nuclear threats, environmental hazards, communist hysteria,

10. Tracing Modernity

Cold War tensions, and Middle East swagger. But it was the trauma of the Holocaust that cast the most devastating shadow on every aspect of Jewish life and culture.

In 1947, the United Nations Partition Plan for Palestine established two states in that contested area. It also paved the way for Israel to declare its independence the following year, and that resulted in a decades-long antagonism between rival contenders for what was called the Holy Land.

The second half of the twentieth century witnessed the affluence of American Jews and their movement into previously unknown political, economic, and cultural activities. Jews accounted for about 0.2 percent of the world's population and 2 percent of the American population, but they were represented in many times those percentages in philanthropy, theatrical achievements, Nobel Prizes—and 54 percent of the world's chess champions. While no single explanation can account for these records, Judaism has historically been known as learning-based, not rite-based. Perhaps anti-Semitism forced Jews to live by their wits (and witticisms).

The transformations found men—and some women—on the horns of competing pressures of success and integration into the general society versus the guilt of disavowing or neglecting their Jewish origins. Custom had not yet lost its hold, but the hold was becoming slippery. Bagels and lox still served as identity markers. Bar and bat mitzvah children combined pop culture with Jewish studies and community social services. Synagogue facilities and learning opportunities remained widely supported and attended by all age groups. Passover and High Holiday traditions were almost universally observed. Young people visited Israel in large numbers, although religious issues in its open society alienated some. Brides veiled their faces but hardly their bosoms; bridegrooms waited for rabbinic permission to lift the veil for a first kiss, having already savored everything else.

Holocaust survivors were dying at a rapid pace. Alarmists warned Jews to create or retrieve spiritual meaning in Judaism—or face extinction. But if modernity had arrived, and it certainly had, most denominations emphasized that Jewish continuity rests on inclusion, philanthropy, support of Israel, and willingness to understand and accommodate others' rituals and preferences.

Postcard of the Rt. Honorable Alfred Balfour (1848–1930), MP and British Foreign Secretary. He facilitated the establishment of a Jewish national home in Palestine in 1917 (though not the only one) (University of Michigan Library, Special Collections Research Center).

∼ ∼ ∼

Modernity aside, medievalism still retained a claim on the contemporary imagination.

Supernatural creatures had never totally abandoned the villages of Eastern Europe. Demons, evil spirits, and transmigrated souls continued to visit every poor tailor and shoemaker, every young maiden and lovelorn fool. The Yiddish-speaking world remained traditionally cohesive, with dedicated storytellers gathering and preserving many of the naïve and wondrous tales stuck in the memories of grandparents patiently awaiting the Messiah. Still, upward financial and educational opportunities distanced some modern Jews from ghetto nostalgia. (Not always successfully: the past has a way of intruding.) Some recast their predecessors' experiences into prickly socio-historical stories of life in the contemporary world. Others remained tied to the mighty theme of love in its many moods—heroic, funny, and painful. Still others, marginally connected to their roots by commonality and culture, but not necessarily by conviction, found Jewish values in angst, erotic experiments, hedonism, or sexual preference.

Romantic life had already loosened up a bit during the previous century, with its focus on rational considerations. Still, although new courtship rules took hold, love remained melded to the conventions of feminine decorum. Nevertheless, the Enlightenment, often hypocritical or coy in its eroticism, raised questions of sexuality: What is it? Who decides what it is? What is it for?

Times were now focusing on complex or previously screened emotions, introducing new choices and dealing with gender ambiguities. Actually, these issues were not new at all. Androgynous or hermaphrodite ancestry was already visited in the two Biblical versions of creation. As indicated in the Midrash Genesis Rabbah (8:1), Adam was originally a single body with both male and female sexual members and two faces pointing in opposite directions When God split the figure in half, giving each two backs and two fronts, it became much easier to be fruitful and multiply. In the second account, God realigned the entity by removing one of the male's ribs and installing it in the female form, thus producing the two separate beings we recognize as Adam and Eve (Leviticus Rabbah 14:1). As distinct humans, they were now able to communicate with advanced styles of love and technique.

The two narratives may be of greater interest to persons whose gender identity and gender expressions are connected to their birth-genitalia. Questions challenge thoughtful consideration or deliberation: Is sexual orientation a biological, immutable condition, determined by genetic testing, or by the sex listed on birth certificates by parents? Are legal definitions of male and female affected? While scientific and medical communities are tied to intellectual and humanitarian concerns, religious institutions likewise share social and critical interests. Jewish movements teach that sexuality is a Torah issue, not only pertaining to conjugal relationships, conversion, and circumcision, but to reconciling historical Judaism with current lifestyles.

But love is nobody's intimate business except for God, Who, not being physical, transcends the whole issue.

∾ ∾ ∾

As national and local politics elbowed their way into a new age of social and sexual conversations, the transition from early to contemporary Jewish fiction challenged ambiguous, conventional, or figurative use of words and expressions. "Novels of ideas" served as links between the nineteenth-century classical period and their transmission to more flexible prose idioms in modern and post-modern formulae. Readers encountered many moods of love—feisty to faint, wry to introspective, sacred to profane, traditional to post-religious. As we shall see, authors incorporated wide sweeps of experiment and imagination. But, best of all, they never forgot that people still fall in love, albeit in a style that might have been largely unrecognizable to their elders.

Abraham Mapu (1808–1867) is acknowledged as the first poetic Hebrew novelist—and a secular one at that. The distinction of his *Ahavat Tsiyon (Love of Zion)* lies not in narrative originality, but in its use of Hebrew and vernacular language as normative literary agencies, in its dual settings and latent eroticism, in its depiction of Palestine's pristine beauty at the time of the First Temple, and in its denunciation of the corrupt "pride and wealth" of urban Israel. The Biblical romance, which appeared in editions from 1853 to 1928, unfolded the lives of realistic lovers, no longer imagined *shtetl* figures, who spurned the proprieties on which they were expected to model their behavior. Family authority and courtship rituals such as arranged marriages were rejected; relaxed love affairs and freer choice of mates were tentatively accepted. The book served as a harbinger of reason, tolerance, and the relevance of an independent Sabra culture in a sovereign Israel:

> Amnon, a handsome young shepherd in the Holy Land, is unaware that he is the son of wealthy Yoram, who, as the victim of a nefarious scheme by his presumed friend Mattan, has been expelled from Jerusalem for twenty years. Amnon is thus deprived of his rightful inheritance, as well as of Tamar, a beautiful heiress who has been pledged to him. In an attempt to install his unappealing son Ezrikom as Tamar's husband, Mattan forces Amnon's mother to flee the country with her son. Tamar resists marriage to Ezrikom, especially after she spots gallant Amnon, who saves her from a fierce lion whose fur mane, yawning jaws, and fiery red tongue carry strong sexual overtones. *[Let us hope they were not understood as such by modest young Tamar.]* As the story slowly winds its way towards its inevitable conclusion, Yoram returns to Zion, Mattan gets his just desserts, and the new era of women seeking men is acknowledged. The young lovers are happily wed through the power of libido and the demands of the Haskalah novel.

Israel Zangwill (1864–1926), the English-born son of Russian immigrants, lived a good part of his life as a "transitional" Jew who didn't want to be a Jew. What he wanted was an identity, not based on cultural uniformity, one that promoted different or opposing moral standards. To that end, he wrote a series of novels about Russian Jews who had fled persecution and were struggling for recognition on their own terms in more accommodating American lands. When his enormously successful play promoting universal faith, *The Melting-Pot*, opened in New York City in 1908, it was loudly cheered as God's crucible, the great furnace where all the races of Europe melt and re-form—Germans and Russians, Jews and Gentiles, each purified and molded in God's fire. Old hatreds fade, new relationships blossom and thrive, culturally distinct groups leave the past behind and become regular Yankees.

> The talented Jewish musician, David Quixano, recently arrived in America, has escaped the horrors of the 1903 Kishinev pogrom where his entire family was murdered. When he meets Vera Revendal, the daughter of a former Russian officer, they fall in love despite divergent political and religious histories. Will adhering to their separate identities overcome the discrepancies of birth or origins? Does the shocking knowledge that Vera's father participated in the massacre of David's family deter the star-crossed lovers? Not according to Zangwill. Vera's father admits guilt and regrets his role in the brutal killings of forty-nine Jews and many others who were wounded or raped. Is violence or a musician's violin the answer to evil? In the end, David opts for peace: "I must get a new string." His symphony, "The Crucible," is a resounding success. The lovers marry and live in contentment in the Republic of Man, the Kingdom of God, and the Glory of America.

Love succeeds, not through mindless assimilation, but through forgiveness.

The Rise of David Levinsky (1917), by Abraham Cahan (1860–1951), was one of the first and most influential American novels to address the "sleepwalk" from greenhorn to filthy rich. The immigrant experience for David begins with his bewildered identity in an unknown environment and the need to find a job and eat. Once these immediate challenges are met, he spreads his interests to include love-making in and out of a variety of beds, muddled business affairs, empty friendships, failed romances, and disreputable success in the cloak and suit business. On the road to assimilation, David sheds his side-locks as well as his Jewish folkways. He is left with a score of political and social stresses, tensions between Jews and non-Jews, class conflicts, secular versus religious attitudes, out-dating, and, of course, love and no love:

> After his passage from Talmud student in Russia to sweatshop slave in New York, David Levinsky muddles his way from the exploitation of cheap labor to million-dollar prosperity in the garment industry. Although he has sharpened his brain, reinvented his conscience, and dropped outmoded religious restrictions, he has been unsuccessful in affairs of the heart. His boyish infatuation with Matilda and his passionate entanglement with Dor have gone nowhere, as have his meaningless experiences in one brothel after another. Botched attempts by matchmakers and blurred dalliances with uninterested women offer nothing but frustration and rejection. Marriage and a comfortable Jewish home elude him. Is he nothing more than a wealthy fraud? Yes, he is, according to Cahan, having paid too high a price in the pursuit of genteel and Gentile membership, and not enough in the quest for love.

There are cases, he muses, when success is tragedy.

Cahan founded the Yiddish socialist newspaper *Forverts* (*Jewish Daily Forward*) in 1906, which eventually reached a circulation of 200,000 readers. Its *Bintel Brief* (*Bundle of Letters*) column, introduced in 1907, specialized in aid and comfort for recently arrived immigrants, warned against conversion and intermarriage, denounced men who abandoned wives and sweethearts, campaigned against sweatshops, offered compromises between immigrant values and twentieth-century misbehavior, cheered happy (seldom-realized) affairs or expressed sympathy for unhappy relationships. The column expired in 1970 because of a dearth of Yiddish readers rather than because of the intriguing ins and outs of love.

Jewish novelists were heavily represented in twentieth-century American literature. Henry Roth (1906–1995), Saul Bellow (1915–2005), Bernard Malamud (1914–1986), Cynthia Ozick (1928–), and Philip Roth (1933–2018) explored the power of words, dwelling on themes of assimilation, self-hating Jews, and Jewish anti-heroes in the aftermath of the Holocaust and the rise of the State of Israel. Challenging these perceptions, however, they suggested that many Jews return to Jewish traditions as they get older and less angry. For all that, there remains the question: is traditional Judaism still workable in a time of secular culture and frayed community bonds, when the sanctity of marriage vows may no longer obtain, and many of the Commandments are overlooked or denied? Henry Roth's 1934 quasi-autobiographic novel, *Call It Sleep*, addressed Depression-era politics, disillusion with the not-so-golden streets of America, and the sexual and emotional awakening of a boy coming to terms with love's complexities and inconsistencies:

> Unnamed fears trouble David Schearl, an impressionable and perceptive six-year-old raised in the slums of New York. He is frightened upon realizing that Luter, the family's boarder, and his mother's lover, may be his father. He notices that Luter is distracted by Genya's breasts, which suggests an Oedipal rivalry with his father and awakening his awareness that his mother is a sexual being. For three years, he is obsessed with dark fantasies, guilt and sin, or, as he represents them, lack of purity. He has grown up with a father with whom he is unable to connect and has a close and loving relationship with his mother—perhaps too close and too loving for the emotional health of either. Following disturbing sexual encounters with young girls, he is filled with disgust and fear of women—including

his mother—all tainted with chilling immorality, if not perversion. Believing he has gone astray and longing for purity, he turns to his rabbi who channels a vision of God, heavenly seraphs, and the prophet Isaiah who, obsessed by "unclean lips," is freed from guilt when one of the angels touches his mouth with a live coal from the altar [Isaiah 6:5–7].

David rushes to local car tracks where he accidentally sparks an electrical arc, causing unawareness or sleep. When he awakens, he feels mystically released from the triple spiritual decay of his father-mother-son world. Having been touched on his lips by the burning metal, David, too, has become purified, absolved from the sins that haunted him. He believes that, like Isaiah, he has been freed by God's mercy. He is now worthy of loving and being loved.

Call it sleep? Call it coming-of-age. Call it redemption.

Bernard Malamud (1914–1986) grew up in an unhappy home (who didn't?). In 1958, he published a tragic-comic fantasy, barely differentiating between the two. From his collection of short stories, *The Magic Barrel,* he introduces Leo Finkle, a serious-minded rabbinical student who, unable to attract a mate on his own, must find a suitable partner before being hired to lead a congregation. And so he turns to a matchmaker:

After rejecting pictures of unappetizing girls in the disreputable Pinye Salzman's "Magic Barrel" of prospective brides, Leo falls desperately in love with a discarded photo that Salzman carries around in his barrel. What Salzman doesn't reveal is that the object of Leo's desire is his daughter, Stella, unfortunately burdened by a misshapen body and too many years. Although Leo is not much to look at himself, he and Stella unexpectedly find love in a match made in heaven, or close to it.

But what to make of the story's last line? "Around the corner, Salzman, leaning against a wall, chanted prayers for the dead." *[According to some Jews, those who flout valued traditions, such as marrying out and deviant sexual behavior, may be regarded as dead.]* Stella, having dishonored herself and her father with bent virtue, has been disowned. Salzman knows that he has been guilty of manipulating the young people for his own devalued self and that he will have to answer for that sin to a higher authority. He has been implicit in her shame and must pray—and pay for it—by chanting prayers for his own dead self—the dead self that he carries around in the bottom of his barrel.

Steve Stern (1947–) made unsettling progress from a seventeen-year-old Ozark hippie to a middle-aged interpreter of Yiddish folklore. The ironically titled "Romance," from *The Wedding Jester* (1999), demands suspension of disbelief long enough to enjoy—and decry—the lost world of arranged marriages. Having endured a blind leap into confusion and doubt, his character Esther Bluestein will not tolerate a mistaken illusion of love to sabotage the lives of her children.

Here is a fairy tale devoid of mysticism, but not of magic:

Eli Goldfogle and Esther Bluestein, both age eighteen, having grown up miles apart in the Old Country, find themselves standing beneath a wedding canopy. Their families were already united over honey cakes and brandy, the ketubah was duly signed, and good wishes were offered for long life and many children. But what did it all have to do with the bride and groom who had never yet committed the sin of glancing at each other? Eli was a pallid, otherworldly Talmud scholar, fervently dedicated to his hourly prayers—and little else. Esther filled her time reading Yiddish romances about a dashing prince who would rescue her from Putsk and transport her to a wide-but-frightening world.

Their world, meanwhile, was trapped by the Russian tsar, who ordered Eli into the army. To avoid its virtual death sentence, he, like many Jewish boys, had been packed off to the golden shores of America where, for five years, he sat behind a sewing machine in a pillow-making sweatshop hoping to earn enough money to bring his wife to Ellis Island. For five years, he worked, studied, and—to break the monotony—occasionally visited Glikman's Tearoom, where he kept impure thoughts away. When Esther finally arrived, he whisked her off to his tiny rooms. They were too shy and embarrassed to look at each other since their hearts were not yet sufficiently pure.

But God refused to let this arrangement continue. One day Esther entered Glikman's Tearoom, seated herself at an inconspicuous table from whence she was able to gaze at a man who was shyly gazing at her. She believed he was the hero of her dreams. He believed she was the girl who could share his passion for the Torah. They fell silently in love over the teacups.

As the years passed, Eli and Esther eventually developed an intimate relationship—in the darkness of night, of course—continuing to avert their eyes, believing themselves sinfully unfaithful in their bodies while their hearts were engaged in Glickman's Tearoom. Eli sometimes looked at his dowdy housewife and shrugged. Sometimes Esther noticed her slump-shouldered, stubble-chinned husband and smiled inwardly. Things would be different for her children.

They would marry for love.

∼ ∼ ∼

The "first wave" of Jewish feminism in America dates from early twentieth-century attempts at educational and suffrage reforms that examined what women could do and what they could and couldn't be. Emma Goldman (1869–1940) was a world-famous anarchist activist involved in the Sacco-Vanzetti Defense Committee. Clara Lemlich Shavelson (1888–1982) was an unknown champion of activist women, shouting in Yiddish at a meeting of New York's shirtwaist workers, "I move that we go on strike!" Twenty thousand toilers agreed, forming the incipient labor movement in 1909 that eventually established basic decent political, social, and factory conditions. Tenants' unions, rent control actions, voting privileges, consumer boycotts, and recognition of the International Ladies' Garment Workers' Union all were among the tools that eventually made lives safer, workdays shorter, and wages higher—and that found their way into mid-twentieth-century culture.

The "second wave," emerging during the radical '60s and '70s, led to a new breed of spiritually religious and sexually expressive women, who took up their enlightened pens in the fledgling Women's Movement. Advocating gender parity, they demanded the same rights granted men as well as the same status in political and economic life. They undertook pioneer roles in reinvigorating and revitalizing belief systems. They examined traditional texts, culture, and the ethical expressions of the sixteenth-century German scholar, Cornelius Agrippa, who argued, "Woman hath that same mind that a man hath, the same reason and speech." All that was lacking, he noted, was physical strength, education, and the ability to avoid men's ill will. Modern woman has already achieved the first two of those assets. She's still working on the third.

Judith Plaskow advanced the Movement with her 1971 essay "Standing Again at Sinai: Judaism from a Feminist Perspective" and with her expanded 1990 book of the same title, raising the issue of women's roles following the experience at Sinai. She charged rabbinic tradition with marginalizing women and demanded women's full and equal participation in Jewish life. Others who engaged in the feminist struggle were Blu Greenberg, whose *On Women and Judaism* (1981) explored synagogue and family observances from an Orthodox perspective, and Rachel Adler in *Engendering Judaism* (1998), both invoking *Halachic* observance. Their narrative techniques offered new possibilities for developing women's issues, as well as for extending traditional beliefs into modern principles. Otherwise, as some suggest, ingrained nostalgia will remain as the chief engine of continuity, enabling men to maintain unchanging attitudes towards women.

The most politically active novelist of the feminist club was Grace Paley (1922–2007), the Bronx-born daughter of socialist immigrants. Among the short stories collected in *Disturbances of Men* (1959), "Goodbye and Good Luck" unfolds the amatory adventures of Aunt Rose, the brash, middle-aged Jewish doyen of working-class women.

In her uninterrupted confessional soliloquy of sexual rebellion, she introduces her family history, Yiddish theater, and her smart-ass self—"*I was popular in certain circles.*" And so she was:

> As she recites her story to her young niece, Lillie, we are introduced to Mr. Krimberg, the manager of the Russian Art Theater, who has hired her to sell tickets for Yiddish plays. She had recently been fired from a sweatshop for loudly demanding a seat near an open window and the precious luxury of fresh air. Gutsy determination was her answer to confrontation. Gutsy determination soon installs her as mistress of the leading man in the theater troupe, Volodya Vlashkin, the Valentino of Second Avenue. Rose's "shameful" behavior upsets her conventional sister (Lillie's mother), whose claim to respectability rests on a spotless kitchen, marriage to a boring husband who never washed, always smelled, and became so shriveled that she hardly realized he was gone. Rose has a message for her brother-in-law: Goodbye and Good Luck. Now fat, fifty, and "past her use," Rose overlooks Volodya's philandering as well as his inconvenient wife and children. But let no one doubt her independent spirit. With "Goodbye and Good Luck," she waves him off, not knowing that when they meet again, older and wiser, they will marry—at her insistence, of course. After all, life is short: isn't every woman entitled to a husband and financial security? Living and loving don't stop, she tells Lillie; they only sit for a minute. Keep going, have children, and be happy until you die tired.

Rose was a twentieth-century woman of parts, ready for evolving feminism and changing cultural norms, determined to accept and arrange her own circumstances and her own reality. But, for now, she must untie Lillie from her mother: "This is a different way of living."

And the best way of living is to be driven by love.

There were about 350,000 Jews in France before the First World War, most of whom were arbiters in all matters of the heart. Among those gifted persons was Marcel Proust (1871–1922), whose agitated sensibilities are developed in his seven-part novel *À la recherche du temps perdu (Remembrance of Things Past)*, published between 1913 and 1927. During his lonely life, he battled desire, jealousy, sexual inversion (which he linked to his Jewishness), pretensions of social superiority, betrayal by supposed friends, and domination by a controlling mother. "*Swann in Love,*" a novelette within the first volume, deals with painful early memories and the swift and difficult passage of lost time:

> In the role of narrator, Proust dredges up the haunting childhood recollections of a family friend who, dropping by one evening, prevented his mother's bedtime kiss—for him "a moment of utmost pain." His relationship with his mother was his closest and most important, although he had many men and women as lovers in fiction and in life, most of whom he drove away with unseemly and unrelenting demands. His insecurities controlled him; illness confined him to his bedroom for the last years of his life.

Proust's alter ego, the aesthete Charles Swann, is an assimilated Jew who is indifferent to his Jewishness, but comes to terms with his identity during the Dreyfus trials.

> His "Jewish" nose asserts itself, "the nose of an old Hebrew," reawakening "a sense of moral solidarity with the rest of the Jews, a solidarity which Swann seemed to have forgotten." He finds himself in and out of a hopeless love affair with the courtesan Odette de Crecy, who has lured him into a disastrous and misguided union. He confuses infatuation with a connection based not only on her supposed interest in the arts and culture but also on sexual desire. Unfortunately, her type of sexual desire involves a colorful assortment of men and women lovers. When he finally recognizes that she has neither taste nor refinement, his passion wilts.

What Swann failed to understand is that, in a futile search for a woman of his "type," he has fallen in love with himself. With the perception of the irrevocability of Time Lost, he recognizes too late that love and reality have escaped him.

Time Regained is not enough.

Andre Maurois (1885–1967), prolific novelist, biographer, philosopher, and investigator of the vagaries of the heart, likely shared Proust's view that there is nothing more interesting than the psychology of love, the revelation of inner emotions. He was born as Emil Herzog to a middle-class Jewish family in Normandy where, after experiencing anti–Semitism as an adolescent, he rejected his name and heritage, choosing assimilation as the best path to French identity. Nonetheless, he was quick to praise the intellectual enrichment that Jews brought to his native literature. His semi-autobiographical novel *Climates* (1928) takes place in a small French town where he attempts to unravel feelings of jealousy, caprice, and deception—and to search for his unrecognized self:

> Philippe Marcenot, a well-to-do industrialist, falls in love with and marries Odile Malet, a young woman thoroughly unsuited to his romantic ideal of a partner. They live in a state of fantasy and hope, beautiful and pleasant, but too otherworldly for reality. They spend time reading aloud to each other, but, unfortunately, they are unable to read or express what is in their hearts and minds. He characterizes himself as loving, but not being loved. Odile is frustrated because although Philippe showed no unkindness, he has no "generousness of spirit." She experiences their disconnection as too much discipline, not enough devotion, ultimately rejecting the domineering style of love, which is all he offered. When she dies, allowing him the possibility of a second marriage, he is far from enthusiastic: "Marriage is one thing; love is another." Isabelle de Cheverny now moves in, dedicating herself to him, but, she, too, is not of his dreams. This time he is loved, but he does not love. He engages in unsatisfactory erotic fantasies, revealing details of his intimate relations with his first wife to his second, which Isabelle encourages because, she says, it gives her an opportunity to understand the workings of his mind. As with Odile, there is silence between them, communication chiefly being achieved through mutual letters and diaries in which atmospheric vapors or changes in the climate control their romantic sensations. He is frustrated when love doesn't shift as easily as the weather. Happiness eludes him because neither changes in climate nor changes in the human condition can satisfy his expectations. Although he doesn't abandon Isabelle, he doesn't love her because he doesn't love himself.

Happiness and love are not here to stay. Suffering is.

Le Dernier des Justes (*The Last of the Just*) (1959), by French-born Andre Schwarz-Bart (1928–2006), was the first important novel by a survivor of World War II to document the destruction of the Polish *shtetls* where his parents were lost in the atrocities. He based the story on the Talmudic legend that God chooses 36 Just Men (*Lamed-Vovniks*) in every generation for whose sake He permits the world to continue. They must agree to take on all of mankind's traumas; to refuse would spell mankind's end. During eight centuries of Jewish martyrdom, beginning with the 1290 expulsion of English Jews, twelve generations of the Levi family have been designated to accept human suffering and defeat. It is now his turn:

> Young Ernie Levi grows up in the twentieth century hearing such stories from his grandfather—one of the Just Men—and realizes that he could be the Last. He decides to accept the challenge, but it is almost too much to bear. Relentlessly bullied and tortured as a child by so-called Christian friends, he attempts suicide; as an adult, he loses his reason to Nazi torture. He is saved by the love of Golda, who rescues him from madness and remains with him until she is captured by the Gestapo. He insists on joining her in the Drancy concentration camp, although they know that togetherness is possible for only a brief time. When they, along with hundreds of frightened children, are crammed into cattle trains on the way to death, he welcomes his destiny, comforting and consoling the orphans, urging them to breathe in the noxious gas to hasten death and be reunited with their parents in Paradise.

He transcended the limits of love. And answered the timeless question of what it takes in a damaged world to be a Just Man.

Many thousands of French Jews interned during the 1940–1944 Vichy regime suffered physical and emotional abuse, round-ups, betrayals by fellow citizens and French police, deportations to Germany, and death. Those who survived in a restructured Europe struggled with new models of cultural and intellectual life, a life in which Jews determined to be visible as functioning partners. Over time, many became involved in Israeli-Palestinian intrigues, religious fundamentalism, rebellions, civil rights, and other seemingly intractable problems. Did the French no longer fall in love? Was *l'amour* no longer *toujours*?

Apparently, not for the second generation of French Jews, who were still picking up the broken pieces. Myriam Anissimov (1943–) was born in a Swiss refugee camp to members of the French resistance movement. Like other Jews facing the unhappy past, she had difficulty coping with the survivor guilt, which rendered many others incapable of forceful resistance. The experience continued to haunt her as she revisited the trauma in her 1973 novel *Comment va Rachel? (How is Rachel?)*.

Answer: Not good.

> Rachel still mourns her father, who had died during the struggle for liberation. She obsesses over post–Holocaust Jews who remain numbed victims of industrialized mass murder. Eventually unhinged, she compares her parents' witnessing of mass persecution and extinguished hopes with her lesser troubles and narrow frustrations, fearful that her current interests, by comparison, are small-minded and limited. Can she still fulfill her dream of self-determination? Can she live with endless regret and humiliation over an empty marriage with an arrogant husband and a deceitful lover, neither of whom are able or willing to offer emotional support? Is a gas jet the answer, or is life only endurable on the forgiving side of love?

When Queen Victoria died in 1901, England was at the pinnacle of prosperity and well-being. Not so the quarter-of-a-million Jews in the squalid Whitechapel district of London's East End, who struggled against poverty and despair for upward mobility. What had been relatively orderly social and family conventions before their arrival from Eastern Europe became hopeless scenes of alienation and disintegration. Nevertheless, against all odds, the Yiddish-speaking immigrants soon upgraded England's cultural and economic life through their gifted musicians, artists, writers, and commercial achievements, becoming self-educated and politically active.

Cecily Ullmann (1855–1934), publishing under her married name, Mrs. Alfred Sidgwick, wrestled with themes of love and intermarriage in *Scenes of Jewish Life* (1904). Because of her German origins, she was well suited to compare the relatively easy attitudes of middle-class English families with those of the inflexible, anti-Semitic, money-grubbing German elites she remembered. Her stories struck uneasy chords between modernist ideas and traditional European attitudes.

Bernard Kops (1926–), Harold Pinter (1930–2008), and Tom Stoppard (1937–), whose novels examined the post-Holocaust years of disillusion and rebellion in British family life, were more psychologically attuned than romantically inclined. Too bad. We might have been rewarded with Jewish Romeos and Juliets and Elizabeths and Mr. Darcys. However, we must be satisfied with a fourth novelist of the group, Howard Jacobson (1942–). *The Finkler Question* (2010) introduces us to love and loss among three old friends, each still needing acknowledgment in diminished lives, each still sharing emotions and a tenacious grip on humor. Jacobson, who claims to be unconventionally Jewish, nevertheless credits himself with a Jewish mind and a Jewish intellect—no question about that!

> Sam Finkler, a middle-aged man in middle-age crisis, Libor Sevcik, a ninety-year-old former teacher—both widowed Jews—and Julian Treslove, a Gentile TV producer and womanizer who is determined to become Jewish—have just finished their regular male-bonding dinner. As they reminisce over the sad-glad amorous adventures of wives and lovers, they look to a spiritually empty future. Treslove is obsessed with having sinned with Finkler's deceased wife, as well as with Hephzibah, Libor's great-niece, during a Passover Seder—hilariously unlike any Seder before or since. Despite futile attempts to cope with and unravel their losses, they know that the Timekeeper is waiting outside the door, invisibly documenting Libor's impending suicide, the weakening of Jewishness, and the trauma of lost love.

The excesses of two world wars inevitably focused attention on tragedies of death and destruction, as well as on romantic memories where love (or divine direction) had once afforded quiet pleasures. Beliefs in world improvement and goodwill appeared threadbare or outdated; disenchanted idealists expressed themselves in wild joy or drug-infused hopelessness. Nevertheless, some die-hards still struggled to find meaning in love and warm fellowship. Blurred memories overlap the minutely observed boundaries of their ordinary, but extraordinary, daily lives during the war years in Alexandria—concerts, cafes, theater, beach, servants, tutors, matriarchal gatherings, and, yes, the scents of rosemary and rhododendron in the city they never knew they loved. And then came the 1956 takeover of the Suez Canal by British, French, and Israeli forces as Gamal Abdul Nasser (1918–1970) nationalized Jewish assets; introduced secret police, threatening phone calls, and forfeited citizenship; and demanded the destruction of the State of Israel "once and for all." And then came "dirty Jews," liquidated assets, smuggled-out money, dimmed lights, dark streets, illegally purchased passports, round-ups, barely-remembered Hebrew words at the cemetery, and Happy Chanukah. And then, finally, one day's notice before it was over before they fled forever from Egypt.

André Aciman (1951–), born in Egypt but raised in France and Italy, reserved his love for his wonderfully outlandish Sephardic home in cosmopolitan Alexandria. Through his memoir, *Out of Egypt* (1994), we come to know the boy and man who, even as he longs for a wider world, does not want to be driven out of his own country where fading and decaying lifestyles have destroyed three generations of his once exuberant Jewish family. With that backdrop, the narrator (with Proust in the wings) remembers the times past and present that remain frozen in his memory:

> Here is great-uncle Vili, the "strutting, daredevil, cocksure, soldier-braggart, womanizer," and onetime British spy. All of which has won him an estate—but no money—in England. Not to worry. He is now known as Dr. H. M. Spingarn, an eighty-year-old Christian auctioneer. Soon we will meet a deaf mother, four sisters, four brothers, and an assortment of in-laws. There are also two grandmothers, the Princess and the gentle, demented Saint, devoted friends and rivals. The family has learned what to remember and what to forget, who they should be and how they should love, and what they can hope for and what must be shrugged off. Now they must cope with imminent rupture. As Aunt Flora (who had no luck in love) says, "Jews lose everything twice in their lives"—first home and then country. And as Uncle Vili wonders, "Siamo o non siamo," by which he means, "Are we progressing or receding?"

The important thing was that they were still together, tied by kinship, loyalties, tenacity, dreams, and the memories of love.

~ ~ ~

Hebrew printing returned to Palestine after a hiatus of over two hundred years. Israel Bak (1797–1874) brought his presses from Ukraine in 1831, providing mechanical access to the newspapers and books that raised the country's cultural level and called attention to its literary and social history. Bak's was not the only seminal or creative voice. The idea of a Jewish arts program, with the goal of melding past and future into a fresh modern experience, was promoted by Boris Schatz (1867–1932) and seconded by Theodor Herzl in 1903.

Herzl grew up in Hungary in a vastly different family and religious environment: his indoctrination was secular; his theology, atheist. The visionary founder of political Zionism, Herzl was a journalist on temporary assignment from Vienna who, after witnessing and reporting the Dreyfus trial, determined to challenge its anti–Semitism, which denied Jews political and economic rights, and to establish them in a free democratic socialist country of their own.

In 1904, the lexicographer Eliezer Ben-Yehuda (1858–1922) introduced thousands of newly coined words and idioms in the aforementioned *Complete Dictionary of Ancient and Modern Hebrew* (completed in 1959). Although it had not been spoken as a vernacular for seventeen centuries or more, the revived Hebrew language became an essential link between Ashkenazi and Sephardi Jews who had few other ways to communicate.

The spokesman for Zionist cultural ideology was Ahad Ha-am (1856–1927), who, deploring the lack of important academic, social, and intellectual opportunities, encouraged the adoption of Hebrew in science, art, and literature. Nevertheless, serious Israeli literature awaited the influx of immigrant writers from Eastern Europe.

Mendele Mokher Sforim (1836–1917), the Israeli author known as Mendele the Bookseller, culled Aramaic phrases from the Talmud, which he transformed into contemporary "unworthy" Yiddish and "approved" Hebrew idioms. With his novel, *Fishke der Krumer* (*Fishke the Lame*) (1868–1888), he railed against mysticism and superstition. He did not satirize his *shtetl* characters, as did Shalom Aleichem, but dealt with the daily problems and troubles of the moneyless, fortuneless urban Jewish underclass and underworld:

Theodore Herzl (1860–1904), the father of modern Zionism who demanded an end to the "Jewish Problem" through the creation of a safe political homeland for the Jews. Glicée, 1903. Anonymous.

> One hot afternoon, Mendele and his friend, Alter, gossip over the miserable but remarkable existence of their Russian neighbor, Fishke the Lame. Although the ugly fellow who works in the local bathhouse went virtually unnoticed, he unaccountably surfaces as an unwilling bridegroom to a poor, half-blind widow who has been abandoned at the altar. The wedding meal has been prepared, but there is no one

to eat it because cholera invaded the sinful community when the locals profaned the holy Sabbath. The only way the dinner could be saved and the sickness purged would be by marrying the unfortunate lady to the poorest fellow in town. Who else but Fishke?

Wedding accomplished, they take to the road as itinerant beggars, skilled in the time-honored trade of panhandling and thieving. One day, they are picked up by a gang of toughs traveling with a young hunch-backed girl. Fishke promptly falls in love, promising that whatever misfortune comes their way, he will never forget her. Unfortunately, their destiny is out of his hands. His wife elopes with one of the bandits. Fishke, now an inconvenience, is abandoned. Although he eventually gets himself divorced, what touches Alter most in this sad story was the history of the young girl. Guess what? She turned out to be his long-lost daughter, the hunch-backed sweetheart Fishke never forgot.

In his short stories, Isaac Leib Peretz (1852–1915) elevated the Yiddish language to the level of modern European culture, retelling the supernatural fables that had sustained generations of pious Jews who sought God's responsive presence regardless of the doubts and scorn of emancipated Litvaks. "Oyb Nisht Noch Hekher" ("If Not Higher"), from his 1917 collection of Hasidic mystical tales, pays tribute to a rabbi's dedication to the command of loving one's neighbor.

> Where is the pious Rabbi of Nemirov this midnight when the congregation is gathered to recite Selichot during the ten penitential days before Yom Kippur? No one has seen him since last night. Could he be in High Heaven soliciting God to protect them from Satan, who knows their sins and unfeelingly reveals them? So they believe—until a Litvak mocks their innocence, saying, "Why, not even Moses had reached that high!" There is no point in arguing with a Litvak who is not at all impressed with mystical happenings. Nevertheless, the mystery is worth examining. The Litvak hides under the Rabbi's bed, watching and waiting until dawn when his quarry awakens, performs his ablutions, recites the morning prayers, dresses himself as a humble peasant, pockets a rope, and tucks an ax under his belt! A mystery indeed.
>
> Trailed by the Litvak, the Rabbi leaves the house, stops by a small tree, chops it down, and gathers its small sticks. Soon he arrives at a tumbledown shack and knocks on the door. Not wishing to frighten the sick old woman inside, the Rabbi has disguised himself. He provides her with a fire from his bundle of wood, and he sings the required prayers with joy and passion. No matter that she hasn't the six cents to pay for his services. With his blessing and the assurance that God doesn't exact payment, the Rabbi leaves.
>
> The Litvak no longer laughs when asked if the Rabbi ascends to Heaven.
>
> He adds quietly, "If not higher."

Theodor Herzl's novel *Altneuland (The Old-New-Land)*, published in 1902, is a dream of what might be accomplished, a dream of amity between Jew and Arab that he did not live to see. The book, the language of which is more like a political monograph than a romance, suggests that a diverse and dedicated people can achieve compatibility in an open society:

> Responding to an ad for an educated, desperate young man willing to undertake a final experiment with his life, Doctor Friedrich Loewenberg attaches himself for twenty years to Mr. Kingcourt, a wealthy Gentile businessman who has forsaken civilization for peace on an uninhabited island in the South Seas. Friedrich, seeing no worthwhile future at his Jewish home, decides to join him. Before leaving, he encounters a child, David Littwak, who begs for a pittance to help his starving parents and sister. Friedrich gives him enough for their rent and immediate necessaries. David promises to repay the debt when God gives him strength in the Land of Israel.
>
> The adventurers stop off in the decayed town of Jaffa before proceeding to Jerusalem, which, desolate as it is, convinces them that a viable Jewish nation exists beneath the rubble. They look forward to the day when Jews will recreate a new and vibrant commonwealth there. It is 1902.

Twenty years pass. They had seen no newspapers, knew nothing of the lost decades. They return to Palestine to take another look. A miracle has happened. Magnificent cities had been built in their absence, places with high levels of industrial and commercial development, religious culture, and art—including the reconstructed Temple.

But who is this sunburned, black-bearded man who falls on Friedrich's neck? None other than David Littwak, who, having prospered beyond his expectations, has kept his promise to restore Palestine. He is president of the Nationalist Party in which Arab, Christian, and Jew coexist in love, friendship, and peace, and in which women are respected, salaries are allotted for skill and merit, and systematic planning makes everything work. Kingscourt and Friedrich decide to join the Zionist dream.

Herzl invented the ultimate love story—love between the Jews and the Land of their inheritance. For those who appreciate fairy tales sprinkled with romance, we welcome the courtship between Friedrich and David's sister, Miriam. We do not learn if they marry, but we certainly hope so.

Sholem Asch (1880–1957) adopted a peasant lifestyle in Poland, teaching children Jewish ritual and teaching himself the art of storytelling. He was a quick learner. His play, *God of Vengeance* (*Gott fun Nekoma*) (1907), created a theatrical frenzy on opening night in New York City by suggesting that lesbian love was as tenable as heterosexuality. (His fellow author and mentor, I. L. Peretz, had urged him to burn the manuscript.)

> Can Yankel, a pious brothel owner who draws his profit from illicit sin, remain a good Jew? Is payment for sexual favors compatible with religion? Looking down from his apartment above the whorehouse he owns, Yankel does his unholy best to reconcile the exploitation of women with the strict ethical demands of Judaism. He is assured that redemption is possible by commissioning a Holy Torah: God will surely reward him with a respectable Jewish son-in-law for his beloved daughter Rifkele—and cancel his sin.
>
> It doesn't work.
>
> Rifkele's first concern is for a romantic lover; she dreads the prospect of an arranged marriage with a materialistic husband. Yankel's first concern is that she remain pure and virginal. Lonely and inexperienced, she contrives a forbidden connection with Manke, a prostitute who conducts her profession in the cellar of the building. Manke, trapped in a life of pretense and shame, needs love as much as Rifkele—and finds it by arousing sexual desire in her friend.
>
> "Let your body touch mine," she urges. "Your breasts are so soft and white…. It's nice, Rifkele, isn't it?"
>
> They hunger for a fanciful world in which there is no social stigma to their relationship, where rebellion is no sin, in which there is no angry father to demand obedience and no mother (herself a reformed prostitute) to coax Rifkele home. Of course, she returns, having no alternative in the real world. Half mad with anger and shame, Yankel roughly throws his daughter—and the commissioned Torah—to the brothel below. "The devil has won her. Take away the Holy Scroll. I don't need it anymore!"

When the play opened in 1923, the producers and cast were arrested and convicted on charges of obscenity following on-stage caresses and kisses between Rifkele and Manke. After an extended legal battle, the defendants won the case in the New York State Court of Appeals.

Isaac Bashevis Singer (1904–1991), the acknowledged dean of modern Yiddish folklore, filled the world with pious Jews who never heard of—or wished to hear of—modern literary Jewish fiction. His eccentric tales were spun into action by an almighty Deity who loved His children (or didn't) because, as Esther Rosa remarks in his 1970 story, *Die Nuddle (The Needle)*, everything depends on luck.

> We are here in a world of love-shmuv, where Esther Rosa presides over the local matrimonial bureau. No ordinary busybody, she is the doyen of good taste and sound judgment. Her only son, Benze, is as learned, attractive, and stylish as his mother allows. In spite of the pimples on his forehead, she devotes her remarkable talents to matching him, not with the richest girl in town, but with one whose nobility of character meets her own high standards. Which she does, because Esther Rosa never makes a mistake.
>
> Esther Rosa and her friend Zeldele are going to Zamosc to find a suitable bride for Benze because there are no such paragons in all of Hubyeshow. As they enter Berish Lubliner's dry-goods emporium, they encounter his daughter, Itte.
>
> "We would like to see a needle with a large eye."
>
> The girl is annoyed. "If you can't see well, get a pair of eyeglasses."
>
> Out they go. Next stop, Reb Zelig Izbitzer's store, presided over by his daughter, Frieda Gittel. "Do you have a needle with a large eye?"
>
> "Certainly. I'll move the stool to the door where there is more light."
>
> Announces Esther Rosa: "You will be my daughter-in-law, God willing."

Frieda and Benze lived and loved like doves because Esther Rosa never makes a mistake.

But what about rude Itte? She languished and began to fail. When she tried to thread a needle, she imagined she swallowed it. Doctors were at a loss. The truth is that everything—including sewing and matchmaking—is fated by heaven.

Samuel Josef Agnon (1888–1970), pioneer of modern Hebrew literature, was born in Galicia to an upper-middle-class but pious Jewish family. Having studied Talmud as well as secular works, he emigrated to Palestine in 1907, to Berlin in 1913, and finally to Jerusalem in 1924. The range of his imagination extended from the theology of Spinoza and the mysticism of Kabbalah to estrangement in the contemporary world. In *HaRofe Ugerushato (The Doctor and Divorce)* (1941), he describes a failed marriage in which the inability to communicate or confront problems leads to separation without hope of repeal or repair. The decaying Viennese atmosphere of the 1930s is already palpable. Its breakdown mirrors the lives of an unbending man of science and a pathologically overemotional woman unable to accommodate each other's needs:

> The doctor cannot forgive his wife's affair with a young clerk before their marriage. Nothing can erase his obsession; nothing can restore the balance of love. There, the situation might have festered had not fate brought the young clerk to the hospital as his patient. The doctor treats him with professional courtesy and barely controlled hostility as he fantasizes over the sexual capers of the clerk and his wife. Repelled by his fixation on the past, his wife initiates their estrangement, avoiding the sentiments that somehow linger in spite of herself. The doctor ultimately and sadly realizes that what he and his patients need—and what he is not able to supply—is his wife's warmth and compassion. It is too late for recriminations, too late to sensitize his emotions, too late to restore the balance of love.

We may seek perfection, but imperfection stands in the way.

Amos Oz (1939–2018) opened his fiercely Zionist soul and post-religious idealism in his 2004 autobiographical novel, *A Tale of Love and Darkness,* writing, "I secretly dreamed that … my life too would become a new song, a life as pure and straightforward and simple as a glass of water on a hot day." It was not to be. His mother's depression and suicide when he was twelve years old led to a deep melancholy—"all secrets are the same—love, hatred, fear, and loneliness." With time, however, he immersed himself in leftist politics, arguing eloquently (but with naïveté or treason depending on one's viewpoint) for a two-state accord between Arabs and Jews in the Holy Land, a solution that for almost one hundred years has frustrated and eluded both man and God.

Reminiscent of his parents' unhappy marriage and his mother's tragic end, his novel, *My Michael* (1968), explores the discontent and alienation of the scientist, Michael, and his gentle wife, Hannah, whose vulnerable natures and mutual obsessions push him into remoteness and her into darkness. Two fully human characters, unbalanced between the real and the surreal and attempting to interact in plausible human terms, discover that love is not an illusion to win and hold, but a flawed uncertainty. (The theme suggests parity in the Arab-Jewish conflict, in which two political entities attempting to interact in plausible human terms discover that a peaceful solution is a flawed uncertainty.)

> Hannah and Michael meet by chance when she is a young student at Hebrew University, and he is attending a third-year geology program. They fall in love, although their conflicting psyches create difficulty in establishing a relationship. He is calm and serious about his work. She lives in awe of his scholarship, but, as the title suggests, is too possessive of his personal identity. Motherhood, which might have created mutual interests and dependence, results instead in numbness and decay. As Michael acquires professional success (and an extra-marital affair), Hannah struggles with withdrawal and a diminished self-image. Both perceive themselves in fantasies that render them incapable of breathing new life into an ominous situation. Hannah, wracked by uncertain desires and spiritual emptiness, lapses into madness.

A. B. Yehoshua (1936–) was born to a Sephardi family, grew up in Jerusalem, and served as a paratrooper during the Six-Day War before beginning his career in left-wing politics. He is one of the experimental "New Wave" Israeli writers (along with Agnon and Oz) who viewed the progression of life through unforeseen or different stages of development. His 1987 novel *Molkho* (*Five Seasons*) examines the uneasy wanderings of a middle-aged widower who draws a blank with five women in his yearlong search to reconnect with the living:

> At precisely 4:00 a.m., Molkho's wife died after a seven-year battle with breast cancer. He had cared for her with unwavering devotion as she faded away. Now, unsure how to navigate freedom without her ever-accurate compass, he assumes full responsibility for his family. None of that shuts out his reawakened urges, since, at her insistence, they had abstained from sex during her illness. He is beginning to worry over his fortyish bulges and thinning hair but nevertheless is determined to fall in love or, at least, connect with a romantic partner. Aching memories are never far from his consciousness. It is not going to be easy.
>
> Winter is lonely. He considers the possibility of a tryst with a legal adviser on a business trip to Berlin. It doesn't help that she spends most of the time in drugged sleep. Strike one.
>
> Spring may lighten things up. He goes to Galilee on a business trip to investigate possible government fraud. His frenzied imagination fixes on a dark-skinned eleven-year-old Indian girl with exotic eyes, spindly legs, and a firm little bouncing buttock. Strike two.
>
> Summer in Jerusalem is brutally hot, and it is high time to fall in love before his longings destroy him. An old classmate and his wife turn up after thirty-four years, during which their marriage had been tragically childless. Would he be willing to impregnate her and share any offspring? After a few desultory efforts, he returns her to her husband. Strike three.
>
> Autumn arrives. He escorts a plump little friend back to Russia but doesn't connect physically. He tries and fails to locate his wife's former home, but he cannot bring back their past, and he cannot bring back their love. Still, he refuses to strike out.

There is work to be done.

Dorit Rabinyan (1972–), like other politically conscious twenty-first-century novelists and artists, relates to strong-willed men and women adrift in a polarized society. Her semi-autobiographical novel, *All the Rivers* (2017), is the story of Liat, an Israeli translator temporarily studying in New York, and Hilmi, a Palestinian Muslim on a visa. Both focus on love, resistance to love, the inappropriateness of love, and the impossibility of love in the disputed homeland of twenty-first-century Israel. Yet there remains the aching need for love:

> Liat and Hilmi meet one chilly autumn afternoon in a Greenwich Village cafe and are immediately drawn to each other. Why not? She is pretty. He has curly hair and an enchanting smile. And so, they wander the city, realizing that none of their dreams could come true. Too late for warnings or restraint, their love is cast. But another feeling intrudes—guilt. What would his family and friends say? Can he reject his widowed mother and his brothers and sisters? Does he understand the difference between the Israeli Defense Army and Hamas in the midst of changing demographics? She insists he's not the Palestinian people. He's one person. Nevertheless, he's an Arab from the Territories where geographic isolation threatens two people who share the same land.

Is love or loathing all there is? Are boundaries inevitable and unyielding? Do only reality and tragedy endure and survive? Nevertheless, as Rabinyan and Ecclesiastes remind us: *All the rivers eventually flow into the sea, yet the sea is not full; to the place from where the rivers come there they will return again.* (1:7)

(In 2016, the Likud government banned the "lefty" novel from high school studies on the grounds that it encouraged interfaith marriage. Prominent writers—Amos Oz., A. B. Yehoshua, and others—successfully challenged the verdict.)

Aharon Appelfeld (1932–2018), born to a middle-class family in what is now Ukraine, wrote of being "uprooted from our house and driven into the ghettos. There I noticed that all the doors and windows of our non-Jewish neighbors were suddenly shut, and we walked alone in the empty streets…. It is from there that I spin threads." Haunted by the Holocaust, he spoke of self-deluded "clownish victims of misfortune," as well as of the depraved instigators of death. But, despite his fears, there was the prospect for hope in his 2014 novel, *Suddenly, Love*:

> Ernst is a grouchy seventy-year-old frustrated novelist slowly and painfully recovering from surgery. He regularly growls at Irena, his devoted young helper, who is the unmarried daughter of Holocaust survivors. While she tends to his daily routine, she quietly and shyly becomes a faithful companion, cherishing her role as audience to his endless readings. Harsh as he seems, he is struggling against depression and the fear that his unpublished history as an obedient, high-ranking, anti-Jewish communist will remain an unfinished novel. With increasing weakness, he gradually fades, but Irena forces him to seek a satisfying direction for his work. What they find is that love of God and love of people are the same thing. What they magically find is that age and youth can find deep comfort in sudden love.

In 1942, Anne Frank, along with seven family members and friends, began a two-year concealment behind a secret wall in a building in German-occupied Amsterdam. On her thirteenth birthday, Anne began the handwritten diary that was to be her "great comfort and support." In her journal, she details her fears, her isolation and loneliness, her antagonisms, and her attraction to Peter, the fifteen-year-old son of the Van Daan family who shares their hiding place and with whom she explores emerging sexualities and unrealized love. Finally betrayed to the Nazis, she died of typhus in the Bergen-Belsen concentration camp; Peter succumbed soon after in the Mauthausen camp. Anne's father, Otto, the only member of the family to survive, retrieved the scattered pages of her journal from the ransacked annex after his return from Auschwitz. It has been translated into more than sixty languages and seen by millions in stage and film versions.

Het Achterhuis (The Annex) was published in 1947 in Dutch and in 1952 in English as *The Diary of a Young Girl*:

> How wonderful it is that nobody need waste a single moment before starting to improve the world.... In spite of everything, I still believe that people are really good.... Everyone has inside of him a piece of good news ... how much you can love.... If God lets me live, I will not remain unknown. I will work in the world for people.... I see the world being slowly transformed into a wilderness. I hear the approaching thunder that, one day, will destroy us.

All was far from well in twenty-first-century Judaism. The quest for meaning is often viewed as a disturbing void with assimilation, high intermarriage rates, and the diminishing religious and traditional involvement of most Jews (other than the Orthodox community) threatening its vital principles. Arab and Jewish hostility festers in Israel. Threats of bloodshed and terrorism are daily reminders that all sides know how to wage war; strategies for waging peace are less certain. Muslims and Jews live side by side but hardly as friendly neighbors. Fratricidal hatred roils between Biblical brothers. Jews of different religious denominations confront and affront each other. Henry J. Friedman, professor of psychiatry at Harvard Medical School, writes in *The New York Times*, December 9, 2018 (*Letters column*), that without vigilance and devotion to its traditional tenets, atheism or agnosticism may soon be the comfortable or necessary identity for many American Jews. He suggests that the country may be in danger of losing some of its overt "Jewish" content although Jews continue to adjust to change and ambivalence and to foster their artistic and literary capacities in radically new ways. Some of their dreams may prove empty and ephemeral; perhaps they have always been unrealistic.

Nevertheless, post-modern Zionism—sophisticated, universal, and pluralistic—is opening new concepts in aesthetics and systems of belief that demand expression, if not universal acceptance. While poverty, bigotry, or illness cannot be eliminated, care for those who cannot care for themselves is possible. Two thousand years of Jewish history still lends credence to a religion of dignity and pride expressed through the pursuit of justice through broadened interest in Jewish lore and living, through hope, and through love of friends and family.

God does not give up on love.

11

How God Coped with Sex

It was only the First Day, but God had already created the heavens and the earth, darkness and light, day and night, as His spirit hovered over the waters. It was good. But because He was pretty new at this, He waited until the Second Day to place a firmament above and below the waters, calling it Heaven. On Day Three, He gathered the waters into seas, exposing dry land or earth. Having a pretty secure grip on this waterscape, but wishing to shape everything into a sustainable and diverse landscape, He began to pollinate the ground with grasses, seed-bearing herbs and fruit trees. Clearly a good day, but too early to rest, as He was busy working hard and fast on additional wonders. On Day Four He introduced heavenly lights, a sun and a moon dividing day and night, seasons and years. Good. Did He now sit back among the clouds self-satisfied? No, He didn't. Day Five was a challenge—designing and setting into motion great sea creatures as well as birds according to their kind. Having been blessed, they were admonished to be fruitful and multiply and populate the earth. Since the land had space to spare, additional animals were brought in—domestic cattle, beasts, and creeping things. Yes, everything was good. But something unprecedented and unexampled was still missing. Good heavens, it is already Day Six! The process is admirably succeeding; God is nothing if not diligent. Time now to form man in His own image. Having finished His great work, He declared it to be *very* good. Justifiably satisfied, He rested on the Seventh Day and made it holy.

On the Eighth Day, God, now relaxed and refreshed, pulled together His cabinet. The Angel of State was charged with organizing Abraham's and Sarah's vast progeny; the Angel of Agriculture made sure that there were at least two trees and enough fruit for everyone to multiply. The Angel of Commerce saw to it that the Ark, once emptied of its cargo, could ferry manufactured goods to the world's ports; the Attorney-General looked after His legal decisions, including the razing of objectionable sites; the Angel of the Interior monitored men's personal religious beliefs, especially those who declared for One Creator; the Angel of the Treasury provided the wherewithal for graft and bribery, beginning with Jacob and still ongoing; the newly appointed Angel of Psychotherapy was instructed to read up on the literature of love and sex. All of which was good.

What is going on? We are told that at the very beginning of time, a mist watered the land, and that man was able to till the ground. Having been formed from the dust of the earth with the breath of life in his nostrils, he had become a living being. For his enjoyment, God planted a garden in Eden in which He placed two trees—one of Life and one of the Knowledge of Good and Evil. God warned man not to eat of the tree of good and evil, lest he die. (Couldn't He have placed it somewhere else? But that would have ruined the rest of the story.) To compensate man for that draconian message, God generated a woman from his rib so that he would not be lonely. The surgery was performed while the man slept, after which the man, now called Adam, acknowledged the loss, saying, *"This is now bone of my bones and flesh of my flesh. She shall be called Woman because she was taken out of Man."* Man, we are instructed, will leave the parental home, cleave to his wife, become one flesh unashamed in nudity.

Are these Genesis verses only about anatomy and sex? What about love? There is nothing inconsistent. The two yearned to unite, to cling and be faithful to each other with physical sex for passion and pleasure and spiritual love, for steady attachment and wholeness. Because man and woman are no longer lonely and incomplete, they will unite in spiritual fulfillment, physical desire, and the consummation of conjugal love as the height of human attainment. Any questions? Yes. To what extent do erotic elements help create a firm foundation for family life? Are sex and love synchronous, operating simultaneously? Do they speak in unison or with separate voices? We learn from the Bible that the ultimate basis for physical love is faith in God. Be satisfied with the answer. The Jewish tradition of sex suggests that the prelude to loving relationships is the motivation to serve one's partner's needs rather than concentrating on one's own, that sex and love are something other than self.

Well, anyhow, there's sex, a scientifically-charged term for a process in which germ cells unite for fertilization—and then there is Sex which overreaches biology, gasping or weeping at every tone of voice or inviting glance. Within Jewish law, sex and Sex are neither unholy nor shameful but *mitzvahs* when combined with commitment and responsibility. They deal with a wide variety of marital relations, family purity and modesty, typically ranging from puritanical to wildly liberal, titillating or thrilling. While other cultures have viewed sex as inherently sinful, God invented companionship, compatibility, tenderness and passion in Biblically approved libido. By and large, the Sages found little or nothing scandalous in prescribed sexual behavior (hopefully even experiencing a bit of naughty love themselves). As Charles Schulz's *Peanuts* observed, love is great, but a little chocolate now and then doesn't hurt.

Among the 613 commandments related to Moses, 65 are concerned with spiritual and sexual behavior. The Bible, it must be remembered, does not outlaw desire. That is not a sin. Nevertheless, certain practices and postures are considered abominations: no sex act is permissible that involves destruction, wasting, or blocking of the seed, ejaculation outside of the vagina, or abortion for non-medical reasons. Birth control is forbidden except in cases of threat to mother or child. Masturbation, outside of marital intercourse, is prohibited. The Talmudic tractate Niddah (13a) stipulates, "The hand that reaches below the navel should be chopped off." It does not say how all those handless people will be able to till the ground or write the Scriptures. Leviticus (18: 22–23) prohibits homosexuality between men on pain of death (20:13). No such restrictions affect women, although they are instructed to observe what passes for sexual modesty. Adultery, forbidden by the Seventh Commandment (Exodus 20:13), is only practiced by fools who would destroy themselves—at least that is what it says in Proverbs 6:32—and adultery is cited as well as one of the reasons for the destruction of the First Temple. Other abominations involve incest and sexual relations between close relatives. (Cain's relationship with his sister doesn't count; there were no other girls available.) Noah and his family had to resort to inbreeding; otherwise, the rainbow would have been created for naught. Lot's daughters were guilty of incest presumably because they believed it was the only option for extending the human race. Fortunately, the sin could be expiated by repentance or by diligently studying the Law, and we believe that it was.

All types of promiscuity, indiscriminate sexual intercourse, and sex for payment are outlawed. Leviticus (19:29) and Deuteronomy (23:17) make it clear that no Israelite woman shall be a prostitute. (Unless, of course, God decides otherwise. See below.) However, because the practice could not be suppressed, the men and women who indulged in "shameful" behavior were relegated to the lowest level of society. Brothels, accommodating the demand, were regulated frequently on the outskirts of the towns, but infrequently removed. Although prostitution was prevalent in certain times and places, it never became universal in Jewish life. The pioneering German sexologist Dr. Ivan Bloch (1872–1922) noted in *Die Prostitution* that it was the Romans, not the Jews, who, following the destruction of the Second Temple, were among the first to force women into brothels. Not until the fourteenth century did Jewish prostitution become a relevant social issue when lax Spanish and Italian communities overlooked the temptations of young Jewish men. In 1347, Queen Joanna of Naples ruled that any Jewish man found in a bordello would be subjected to public lashing or official punishments. Over time, the "burning shame" associated with "scandalous behavior" deterred the activities of the relatively small number of Jewish procurers or brothel owners; nevertheless, those who were engaged in the "evil in our midst" thrived in every populous city of Europe and America. Sexual purity (often overlooked in the breach) was central to Jewish identity ever since the Israelites first arrived in Canaan.

> The Talmud records, with surprising leniency, a story about a pious man who was so scrupulous about his tzitzit that he guarded them even when visiting a famously beautiful courtesan. As he was about to pleasure himself, four of the fringes slapped him in the face. Taking this as a warning sign, he immediately desisted. His reverence for God so moved the young lady that she not only returned the payment for her favors but also became a sincere convert seeking redemption. She applied to Rabbi Chiya for advice. "Go and enjoy yourselves," he told them. "But first I will perform a proper marriage ceremony" [Menachot 44a].

In Genesis 38, prostitution is excused because it was for the worthy cause of securing a legitimate heir. Judah was unaware that Tamar was his son's widow when she dressed herself as a harlot, covering her face in order to seduce him so that their issue would inherit the family name and fortune. True, Tamar was not a professional prostitute, but why was Judah messing around with paid pleasure?

By ordering Hosea (3:1) to marry Gomer, the harlot, God exemplified the broken, but renewed, relationship between Himself and Israel through forgiveness and redemption. Samson's misbehaviors in Judges 16 were overlooked through punishment and repentance. While the usual penalty was strangulation, King David was exempted from this fate; perhaps God couldn't bring Himself to do away with His favorite sinner. The Talmud and *Halachah*, having established the limits of Biblical morality, decided who sinned and who were excused.

The second chapter of the book of Joshua relates that, with the help of a prostitute, the children of Israel prevailed over their enemy, especially as God had once again orchestrated the proceedings. When Joshua sent two spies to report on the hostile powers, the king recruited the local madam, Rahab, to ferret out treasonous information, but instead of cooperating, she facilitated their escape by hiding them on her roof. In return, she asked them to spare her family when they attacked. Which they did. "I know the Lord has given you this land," she said, "I have saved you because your God is in heaven above and on earth beneath." God then destroyed the city, men and women, young and old, oxen, sheep, and donkeys, keeping only the valuables for the house of the Lord. That is how Rehab, one of the

11. How God Coped with Sex

Judah and Tamar. Biblical Tamar posed as a prostitute hoping that Judah would give her a son. Etching, c. 1620. By Pieter Lastman (Metropolitan Museum of Art).

great beauties of all time according to the rabbis, became one of Israel's brave and revered heroines, and—according to some—Mrs. Joshua.

≈ ≈ ≈

The ultra-Orthodox hold extremely restrictive attitudes towards male-female interaction. They disapprove of practices with sexual overtones such as watching unauthorized television or movies with members of the opposite sex or using computers to connect with forbidden ideas. While they have been accused of narrow-minded provincialism and die-hard reactionary morality, they have been credited with promoting zealous commitment to Scriptures. Rescuing mid-twentieth-century American Judaism from what they perceive as materialism and spiritual vacuity, they cling to the legacies of physical and aesthetic segregation between men and women basic to Orthodoxy. The physical barrier separating the sexes in the synagogue prevents men from eying the ladies who sit out of sight in the women's section. According to the Talmud, women may not sing when they can be overheard by men as a woman's voice leads to sexual thoughts. Males must cover as much of their faces or bodies as is reasonable in order to overcome whatever erotic thoughts may occur. It is another of God's miracles that the sexes get together at all.

Other activities among the Orthodox, such as separate camping, sports, and games, may be permitted under proper supervision. Education is generally confined to *Halachic* teachings. Dress codes are mandatory. Yiddish is the daily language for most ultra-Orthodox and Chassidic sects. *Haredi* Jews make every effort to avoid assimilation into the majority culture, opting to live among fervent members like themselves. They read books that reflect or define their own lifestyles, recite stories or myths about their perceived history, and school their children according to their moral values. Secular education for professional training may be permitted, but the liberal arts are discouraged. Women often take paying jobs because of economic necessity or to free husbands for daily study in yeshivot and raise children where they are not exposed to the hazards of *Olam Hazeh (this world)*, but are cheered with expectations in the *Olam Habah (the World to Come)*. While there is no escaping surrounding technology and culture, they have gained strength from Holocaust survivors, European refugees, and returners to the "righteous path" who are determined to reignite strict traditional observance.

While the *Haredi* community publishes vast numbers of self-help books, appropriate child and adult literature, and holiday cookbooks, some members have surreptitiously taken up sleazy reading material, hedonism, and other forbidden preferences. They are accommodated by previously inaccessible books dealing with loosened relationships in which partners mingle freely or illicitly. Although *Haredi* publishers struggle to keep readership confined to the recommended positive spiritual and ethical works, secular books are widely accessible to anyone with rebellious instincts, the pursuit of novelty, and a valid library card.

Haredi publishers of sexual guides on the "intimate aspects of marriage" avoid explicit information, except for details of family purity. Popular novels express moral issues often didactic in style, arguing against assimilation, intermarriage, "improper" conversion, and most aspects of Western or secular culture. That said, there remain books that convey forbidden sex. No self-help book can avoid the subject, drawing readers to suggestive material with biologically charged terms. None can adequately capture the scent of bodies or the shivering of muscles or the clutch of the heart when the lusty hero or busty heroine appears in their pages. The following stories admit to the passions of the flesh as well as sharing some of the spiritual journeys *Haredi* readers have taken along their chosen paths.

The American writer Nathan Englander (1970–) (not a *Haredi*) covered the well-trodden ground of ultra-Orthodox religious identity in an interview in the January/February 2018 issue of *Moment* magazine. He discusses themes that cut across generations of Jewish literature, explaining that his logic is "Talmudic" and that he is aware that imbalance of power undermines the possibility for men and women to meet each other's wants and needs. Neither men nor women want rejection; both need the capacity for shared feelings and the understanding that sexuality is fragile and that the abuse of intimacy erodes self-worth. Englander's 1999 short story, *For the Relief of Unbearable Urges*, emphasizes that both sexes grapple with tensions between tradition and modernity and must adjust their behavior and emotions before disaster strikes. And strike it does:

11. How God Coped with Sex

Dov Binyamin is tormented by his wife Chava Bayla's refusal to make love on Sabbath evening, insisting that her months-long menstrual cycle forbids intimacy. And so, he visits his Rebbe for consolation and advice. "I want her, but I don't have the strength to keep away." The wise scholar gives him a dispensation to save his marriage with a prostitute. It's a tall order, but Dov is desperate. A taxi driver directs him to an accommodating young woman who assures him that she knows how to treat a black hat. He rejects a condom because "it's a sin to spill seed in vain" [Genesis 38]. Time passes. Why does he avoid Chava's now belated overtures? Guilt is one thing, but he is suffering from a lot more than shame. As tears stream from his eyes, he sees himself on an examination table with the doctor's terrible diagnosis: The fire inside is not lust. It is syphilis.

Rachel Pomerantz (1948) is the penname of Malka Schaps, the first female *Haredi* dean of Bar-Ilan University's Faculty of Exact Sciences. Having written about logarithmic growth of systole of arithmetic Riemann surfaces, she penned the best-selling adult novel, *Peetom Alta Hashemesh (Suddenly the Sun Rose)*. The protagonist Mina, partially grounded on the author's life, takes on the combined roles of school teacher, mother to eight children, care-taker of a sick mother, and wife of a husband who pursues Torah learning to the exclusion of gainful employment. Mina accepts the situation, but unhappily. She is an emancipated woman, attempting to bring her secular academic duties into balance with religious observance and her unanswered physical and emotional needs. She is critical of some *Haredi* demands, yet faithfully adheres to the Torah commandments in which spiritual benefits and sexual happiness are equated with observance of mitzvot. It is hardly necessary to point out that Pomerantz does not portray overt sexual activity—the bedroom door is closed. So, what can Mina do?

Twentieth-century Orthodox writers who attempted to understand the masculine and feminine psyches remained at a disadvantage until they were willing to break the taboos, until they admitted the hidden sensualities of the characters they wrote about but hardly knew outside the immediate family. Explicit sexual expression was occasionally tucked in among "kosher" or permissible descriptions of romantic trysts, dating, and courtship hints. Sexual desires of the aging were carefully avoided.

As the unacceptable slowly became unavoidable, however, secular and religious leaders were faced with old and new questions: What is now permitted, allowable, or lenient? Is bodily foreplay encouraged? Is sex only for procreation, a means to populate the world for the sake of Heaven, or a route to Heaven on earth? Old answers, as well as new, are increasingly relevant, as indifferent sex may be an invitation to boredom or, unhappily, emotional damage. Husbands are still mandated to satisfy their wives according to physical ability and work schedules. Her conjugal rights are still established before he goes on a journey. Wives need not have sex with a husband they find repulsive. Physical relations may be indulged in only by mutual consent (Mishneh Torah, Hilkhot Ishut 14.8). Women's status remains positive in traditional Jewish culture. Positive, but not conclusive. The "separate but equal" designation is rejected by liberal Judaism. Orthodoxy does not permit women to join a *minyan* or to become a rabbi or cantor. (Some accommodation to this rule has recently allowed alternative feminine titles such as *rabbanit*, although they still differ in allowed duties.) Still problematic are the *agunot*, the "chained women" who cannot secure divorces from men who refuse to provide the necessary "get," or who are constrained from remarriage if husbands disappear or may be dead.

(Women's status, according to Christianity's St. Paul, differs. Can one touch a woman other than a close family member? No. Celibacy among the unmarried or widowed? Yes, because it is a higher calling than marriage. The husband's authority over his wife's body?

Yes. Divorce an option? No. If the man cannot exercise self-control, as a concession, it is better to marry than to burn with desire [1Corinthians 7:1–19].)

For some Orthodox people, such problems are irrelevant. Faith and prayer alone see them through difficulties and losses. Many accept that although love and life are puzzles, there are answers; it's just that we're not privy to them at this time. God has been willing to cover whatever disparities exist, just not now: "I am God, in its time I will hasten the changes" (Isaiah 60:22). He has already decided that Jewish society should not remain a male meritocracy, that women are no longer to be subject to men, that love and lovemaking can bloom whenever the participants yield to sex for satisfaction or mutual pleasure. He has approved of sex for recreation or a pick-me-up, acknowledging its psychological as well as biological values. And that translates Jewishly as *shalom bayit*, a peaceful, happy home.

Happy and peaceful homes were also at the forefront of the people that we and the world call Jewish. But trite sayings don't address the radical changes that are taking place across the wide geographic twenty-first-century Jewish world. For one, the ancient Bukharian culture in Uzbekistan is being obliterated because of the dearth of young people to populate it. It formerly boasted two synagogues, a Hebrew school, and family associations. Its cemetery, which has 10,000 graves, is making room for the last few Jews, most of whom no longer follow Jewish tradition, although the older people resolutely hang on to preserve the Jewish presence that they believe dates back to the exile of the Lost Tribes in the eighth century BCE. Nevertheless, a traditional Jewish wedding was held in the old country in 2000, although it has been increasingly difficult to find proper spouses.

Radical change likewise affected the few, but vocal, writers who were largely influenced by the Anglo-Jewish emancipation efforts. Their spokesman, Israel Zangwill, drew a large following with his living images of "melting pot" culture, but because Jews were neither wholly welcomed nor rejected in the post–World War I period, many are still reeling from the breakdown of the East End culture. Holding ambivalent or mixed feelings about Judaism, or even its ultimate significance, the prominent Scottish-Jewish writer Muriel Spark addressed the topics of alienation and conversion: the daughter of Jewish parents and mother of an estranged son who was meaningfully Jewish, she converted to Catholicism, referring to herself as a Gentile Jewess. Ruth Prawer Jhabvala, German-Jewish by birth, was married to an Indian Parsi husband. Her family had fled Nazi Germany, later becoming British citizens. Working in America, she won two Academy Awards for screenwriting. Although her father had committed suicide after losing forty family members to the Holocaust, her fictional characters carry no trace of Jewishness. By universalizing Jewish attitudes to conform to English conservative culture, she left little room for the aesthetics of love and romance. Her "universal" political and social philosophies pointed towards negativity about Jewish "otherness" and less towards comfortable personal identities. These writers' fiction rejects broader boundaries to include the ins and outs of love, sex, fairy tales, and fantasy.

On the other hand, many French Jews, representing one of the oldest and largest Jewish communities in the Western world, seem to view Jewish life through sharper political and social lenses. Their numbers are augmented by the large number of immigrants from Sephardic North Africa who have revived Judaism through the growth of kosher restaurants and refurbished synagogues. By the nineteen eighties, post-Shoah French Jews found new ways of being Jewish writers and artists, celebrating, rather than disavowing, their religious identity. Love, sex, fairy tales, and fantasy do not seem to be featured, as they once were. Cecile Wajsbrot's 1997 autobiographical novel, *La Trahison (Betrayal)*, points out that "France doesn't know how to face reality." France certainly always knew how to face bodily urges.

Something changed. Wajsbrot focused on political history, having become detached from the present, unable to "feel at home in a nation in which she had been born ... and from which she has a fierce desire to turn the eyes away, to look elsewhere." The daughter of Polish Jews, she confronts the past through the story of Louis Merian, the seventy-five-year-old retired radio host who, caught amid silence, exile, and suffering, remembers almost nothing about the war he reported. It is through Ariune, a young journalist who eventually draws him out, that he calls up the memory of Sarah, a Jewish woman he loved but, heartbrokenly, was unable to save.

Mid-nineteenth-century American women's rights advocates pioneered movements for social change during and after the Civil War. That goal was introduced by non-Jewish women activists such as Susan B. Anthony and Lucy Stone, who railed against second- and third-class relationships of blacks and poor whites. It was picked up by Ernestine Rose (1810–1892) and other Jewish women in the first wave of feminist activity. Originally focused on legal and health issues and the women's suffrage movement, Jewish women such as Emma Goldman (1869–1940) and Rose Schneiderman (1882–1920) opposed the religious laws and social attitudes that had guided their mothers and from which they believed they had escaped. Many were moved by the Jewish tradition of social justice as articulated in labor, socialist, anarchist, communist, and voting-rights movements. Others found their voices fulminating against Orthodox laws preventing women's participation in the *minyan*, exclusion from saying the *kaddish* (mourner's prayer) at gender-restricted times, and limitations of secular education.

As new political and courtship rules took hold, romantic love styles did not always cling to the prescribed conventions of feminine modesty. The "second wave" of the late nineteen sixties and the post-modernist liberal feminist movement raised new questions: what did women need to be liberated from and why?

Patterns of female solidarity soon emerged in meetings of women who discussed oppression, assaults, harassment, misogyny, and injustices at home, at work, and in the bedroom—all, of course—in a largely patriarchal world. Entrenched authority and cultural norms were newly identified and redefined. "Consciousness-raising" programs addressed feminist issues and offered moral and legal support. Jewish "liberationists" Bella Abzug (1920–1998), Betty Friedan (1921–2006), Gloria Steinem (1934–), Letty Cottin Pogrebin (1934–), Anne Forer Pyne, (1945–1918) and Shulamith Firestone (1945–2012) concentrated on improving vocational and economic opportunities, political access, reproductive rights,

Ernestine Rose (1810–1892) was a Jewish suffragette who also focused on women's health and legal issues. Photograph published by S. B. Anthony, Rochester, NY.

and maternity leave, as well as exploring gender-bending roles and homoerotic identification. Sexuality, in terms of male aggression and rape, was more vocally addressed by younger feminists. Pornography, lewd speech, and references to bodily functions, unheard of in their grandmas' day, were casual conversational subjects.

In his 1947 book, *Sex in Our Changing World*, John McPartland describes in frank detail the social changes in American life. He contends that sexual mores shifted from timid or reserved behavior to the pursuit of pleasure as the chief good, from moral choices to persuasive sensual appetites, from traditional family values to weakened marriage and divorce attitudes. It is not a recent discovery, he assures us: "There have been carnal people before and they were the ancestors of most of us." There will be carnal people again. The academic journal, *Porn Studies,* founded in 2014, and a documentary, *Hot Girls*, produced as a Netflix series in South Florida a year later exemplify the growing interest in adult films and online porn that are now major avenues of education for teenagers of all backgrounds and religious persuasions who arrive with limited backgrounds, lack of partner support, and continuing poverty. Sexual counseling, becoming trendy, often lacks reliable practitioners with reliable credentials and motives. Television and the Internet replace qualified people—not with love, but with kinky sex.

The Orthodox Jewish world, in other respects slower to publicly address birth control and other women's issues, has adopted some "fertility awareness" programs, including the rhythm method and abstinence until marriage. These have proved of only limited effectiveness, particularly to low-income and religious women who must deal with taboo health and reproductive choices. Nevertheless, pertinent information is taught to young people in some Jewish day schools where educators and health care providers offer access to chastity and contraception information, including condoms, pills, and implant devices. Most of these options are not available to Jews who retain traditional elements of modesty, who avoid offensive language, or who abstain from discussions of bodily functions or gender issues.

Which brings us in a roundabout way to the wider topic of *Jewrotic* culture, surely an important element of God's focus on sex, although He probably didn't have in mind the graphic descriptions of violence, obscenity, pornography, or hybrid identities that are now available. He has created a long Jewish road from reticence (or just plain ignorance) to the realities of a liberated society in which topics like eroticism in contemporary culture have shaped modern sexuality. According to a March 26, 2007, *New York Times* editorial, porn is watched daily by tens of millions of adult media visitors; it is successful in reaching out to those for whom it has become an explicit form of sex education.

Philip Roth (1933–2018) broke the rules. In his famous (infamous) book, *Portnoy's Complaint* (1969), he fearlessly served up toxic masculinity with amazing clinical detail, examining his real life, as well as that of his alter ego. Taken to an outer limit of obscenity, with plenty of wracking lust and hardly a fillip of shame, we have Roth's comic-tribute to what some critics have called Jewish self-hating love; others called it smut; *The New Yorker* in 2009 called it one of the dirtiest books ever published. But, for many, his enormous gift as a storyteller overrides the bleak or hollow emotional shadows of his tale.

> In a windy, witty, monologue by a young Jewish man to his silent psychoanalyst, Alexander Portnoy delves into guilt and shame, which he attributes, among other things, to his mother's viewing him as an "erotic plaything," his ineffectual father's presumed virility, and his own unsatisfactory sex with himself and non–Jewish women. He believes that his life is little more than a Jewish joke, which has rendered him impotent. His "disorder" translates into an uninterrupted wordy repugnance of

himself and of assimilated Jews, which prevents him, and them, from integration into his version of the American way. He wants to know how to "be bad—and enjoy it," how to survive the confines of middle-class American culture, how to deal with an overbearing, guilt-inducing mother, how to celebrate a need for sex with shiksas—how to leave behind, and yet cling to, his conflicted Jewish origins. His generous libido accommodates an affair between a tumescent man and his overworked penis; it was probably not exactly what God or Freud had in mind—Portnoy's amorous connection with a piece of raw liver that his mother later served for dinner.

Legions of fascinated readers, who confessed to their own acquaintance with masturbation, have probably never before—or since—thought about it with such insistence and devotion. Portnoy hasn't found out who, or what, he is, or why confiding to a psychotherapist is not a substitute for having friends. Given his "perverse nature," the question at the end is: can he ever overcome his past and emerge as a Jew and a reasonably decent human being?

In 1973, Erica Jong (1942–) published her semi-autobiographical novel, *Fear of Flying*. The book immediately became the ultimate mantra of the Jewish feminist movement, shattering the myth of the Jewish woman as a weak sexual vessel, while creating the myth of the Jewish woman as a hot-blooded sex goddess. We learn of the incredible sexual encounters of Isadora Wing, a young, bold, and bawdy Jewish poet trapped in a frustrated five-year marriage. She attends a psychoanalysts' conference in Vienna in an effort to renew her erotic memories, inspect her inner complexities, and follow her unspoken longings into the dark recesses of body and mind. "If you don't own your body," she reflects, "you don't own your mind." (Perhaps she was confused, not recognizing that if you don't own your mind, you don't own your body.) Accordingly, she decides to "fly free," pushing sex for itself—"zipless fuck"—a de-romanticized courtship and lust with a partner she hardly knows, of whom she is barely aware. In brevity and anonymity, with no remorse or guilt, she belatedly learns that fantasy and liberation don't equate with happiness. Nevertheless, she pursues the elusive goal of freedom from the male's dominant role, the goal of making her own sexual choices rather than those imposed on women in their ongoing battle with men. Flaubert, Tolstoy, D. H. Lawrence, and Henry Miller had previously mined the dilemma between pure sex, porn, and feminism. Sex always sells, or, as Ogden Nash reminded every novelist, "purity is obscurity."

Nevertheless, Roth and Jong both understood the sociology of the American/Jewish experience, its juxtaposition between two worlds. Detail, frankness, yearning, bravery, panache, and humor accord with *good* sexual mores—*not good* habits are interpreted as narcissistic ego trips, i.e., looking out for number one. Within that definition, *bad* sexual mores remain socially and politically explosive subjects:

> Isadora fears air travel, and almost everything else. She fears loneliness and the absence of love in rotating relationships that evolve into meaningless experiences. Yet her restless insistence on torrid, titillating sex controls her code of behavior—sleeping with someone simply because she wants to. She hooks up with a handsome young psychiatrist, Adrian Goodlove (I kid you not), and runs off with him to for a two-week European tour of passionate sex for its own sake, outrageous, seamy, no questions asked, no future demanded: indifferent zipless fuck—orgasm, the purest thing there is, rarer than a unicorn. Unhappily, Isadora (or Erica) admits, she never had one. In the end, she returns home, soaks in a warm bath, and muses on her naked body. Will she or won't she stay?

She does. But she still wants everything and more that she had promised herself. She will not be able to dampen her inner torment. She will struggle with the feminine consciousness and the need for self-expression, self-ownership, and women friends.

Relationships with no-strings-attached encounters become power struggles, intimidation, non-consensual badgering, or harassment. All of these may be perilous or exhausting. Many husbands and wives, according to some psychologists, are devoted to each other and prefer being intimate with each other, but may no longer be tied to monogamy because the desire for sex may wane with their hormones, aging problems, lack of interest, or because it's kinder to stay silent. Some men, restless, guilty, resentful, or desperate for closeness and affection admit that they are no longer sexual acrobats. What to do? Patricia Schiller (1914–2018), a Jewish sex educator and therapist, stresses that "sex is not an end in itself, but a function of being human. When all there is between people is sex, it is time to split." While physical desire may be met by a pill, she warns, "its goal is to become warmer, more caring."

Judy Blume (1938–) is an American-Jewish writer specializing in children's stories and realistic fiction for young adults. The title of her 2004 novel, *Wifey*, has been termed demeaning to upper-class Jewish women:

> Sandy Pressman has recovered from a variety of illnesses with the help of her devoted mother, something her good-natured, dull husband Norman is not capable of providing. She combats loneliness and boredom with parties for her children, shopping afternoons at Loehmann's, or at the club. Weekly nail and hairdressing sessions, golf lessons, tennis lessons, and vacations to Jamaica have convinced her she was created for better things. Smashing a dish across the kitchen is her answer to virtual adulthood. Unimaginative and predictable three- to five-minute sex with Norman hasn't solved her dilemma. Masturbating like crazy is hot and helpful, but not something she is comfortable talking about with her gynecologist, although everybody is doing it. Before long, she is having sex with golf pros, her gynecologist, and a variety of strangers. Breaking from the role of responsible wife and mother, she uses sex as an obligatory adventure. Desperate, she decides to experiment after buying a sexual encyclopedia, but Norman tells her she is not a whore.
>
> She tries again. "Norman, do you love me?"
>
> "I'm here, aren't I?"
>
> So, where did things go so wrong? Soon she is making out with her brother-in-law. True, it's against the Tenth Commandment, but she didn't covet him—she just fucked him. It's not her fault. All men want those things.
>
> Her life changes when she bumps into Shep, a sweetheart from eight years ago. He has a wife, but they begin all over again. She hopes he will get a divorce. He won't. Eventually, she tires of the endless combinations and permutations of bodily orifices, movements, and positions. (Perhaps some of Blume's readers do, too.) She discovers a canceled check and a hidden packet of love letters written to Norman by Brenda Partington Yvelenski, a girl he once loved and who loved him but who ran away and married a more "dependable" man. Besides, she was a shiksa. And that's not all. Sandy has discovered she has gonorrhea, for which Norman might be responsible. Nothing to do but accept each other as best they can. Alone, she inserts her diaphragm. She comes twice. Tomorrow the kids will be coming home from camp. She'll be busy again.

Blume describes every agony of adulthood: the social differences between spouses, the increasing financial independence of women, and heedless intimacy tinged with fear. Has marriage like Sandy's, once considered desirable or mandatory, fallen out of favor? Economists report that in 2017, fewer Americans married, and when they took the leap, socioeconomic or cultural issues were more crucial elements in their decisions than romance.

Popular advice columns on men's and women's issues were probably originated by John Dunton, a seventeenth-century London bookseller and publisher whose magazine printed questions submitted by readers and answers by "experts," *i.e.*, his friends, who fielded thousands of queries, many of which were not meant for tender eyes. (Is it acceptable to masturbate? Definitely not.) In 1895, Elizabeth Gilmer (Dorothy Dix) was among the early pioneers on the genre, offering such tidbits as how to conceal one's "weirdness."

Self-help gurus promised to be useful but were—and are—largely entertainers. Were they or their copyists professionally qualified? Mostly not. Anyone with a typewriter and a copy of Dale Carnegie's *How to Win Friends and Influence People* could dispense advice on how to live and love. In the forties, columnists Esther Lederer (1918–2002) and Pauline Philips (1918–2013), Jewish twins better known as Ann Landers and Abigail Van Buren, successfully took up the challenge. Other prolific contributors, such as Helen Gurley Brown in her 1962 blockbuster book, *Sex and the Single Girl*, shocked untold million on websites and social media.

Hardly two generations later, news of workplace harassment and assault of women by high profile actors and performers, lecherous doctors, predatory clergymen, rotten relatives, and abusive husbands and boyfriends made the front pages and urged women to talk freely and openly about unpleasant experiences without fear, shame, or stigma. The international #MeToo movement, a grassroots campaign dating from 2017, responded to women who demanded the right to decide what they wish, or do not wish, to enjoy or tolerate while insisting on their right to have their grievances treated with respect and sensitivity and to hold perpetrators responsible for unwanted behavior. Sociologists, psychologists, and other experts in the early years of the twenty-first century have found that young people are marrying and having children later in life than previous generations, taking six years or longer between first sight and "Here Comes the Bride." Platonic friendships can grow into courtships, evolve into "friendly benefits" (friendship with casual sex), and collapse into committed lifelong relationships, hopefully with securely tied knots. Perhaps rules of love and marriage that were normative or acceptable in the twentieth century, or more simmering in the twenty-first, will augur benefits in the twenty-second.

Or maybe not.

If, from time to time, unbearable urges in the upper bodily organs become as demanding as those in the lower, if rumblings in the stomach speak as loudly as other avenues of desire, if hunger for food and drink remind us that man does not live by sex alone—and if sometimes, other needs become overwhelming, and the taste for chopped herring will not be denied—turn the page and indulge in some of Judaism's choicest delectables. And my mother's *halishkes*. Try it. You'll love it.

Or maybe not.

Part II

The Way Jews Loved Tradition

12

Essen un Fressen

Before we get started, straight from Zlochov, Austria-Hungary, and dictated by my mother, here is:

Neshe's Halishkes (Sweet and Sour Stuffed Cabbage)
- 1 large cabbage
- 3 large onions
- 1 egg
- 1 lb. ground beef
- 1 cup rice, half cooked
- 2 cans tomato sauce
- 2 green apples, grated
- Brown sugar, a little honey, garlic, red wine, raisins (how much or how many—use your taste or let your kishkas decide.)

In a large pot, cover cabbage with hot water. Boil about fifteen minutes or until soft. Slowly take leaves apart, cutting away hard core. Slice 2 onions into the pot, adding enough water until the pot is about half full. Add 1 can of tomato sauce, 3 tablespoons brown sugar, 2 tablespoons honey, 1 grated apple, some raisins, and 1 clove scraped garlic. Add bits of leftover cabbage and red wine. Filling: mix ground meat, rice, egg, 1 grated apple, 1 can tomato sauce, a little brown sugar and chopped onion. Fill and roll leaves envelope style. Place slowly in pot, cover and simmer about 1 hour. Prepare the day before you serve it.

As you read through these recipes, exact equivalents and measurements are not important. The food will be delicious because its secret ingredient is love. Food is a path to love when shared with the needy, allied with comfort to a friend, and when joined with others in religious and festive celebrations. Food is a path to love because it tastes good and doesn't talk back.

∾ ∾ ∾

The moment Man opened his eyes and took his first breath, he knew he was hungry. There before him were the agricultural grasses and herbs and fruit trees that God had thoughtfully prepared for him as early as the Third Day. Deuteronomy (8:8) lists the seven types of produce that were already available: wheat, barley, grapes, figs, pomegranates, olives and honey. He looked around and knew that it would be good. With every comfort arranged for his pleasure, it was no hardship to avoid eating from the Tree of Knowledge of Good and Evil. He had already experienced Good; he knew nothing about Evil. Soon he would learn. His wife caused all the trouble (as wives are wont to do). They ate the forbidden fruit, and that's how their troubles—and God's—began. He realized that if they also ate from the Tree of Life, He would be stuck with them for eternity. Better to move them elsewhere where they could learn to cook and make babies.

God tried again. He told Noah to build an ark with enough food for his animals and family to survive for forty days and nights. The menu was adequate, but He had forgotten the wine list. After the troupe exited the ark, Noah remedied the situation by planting a vineyard that yielded a delicious liquid. He passed out drunk, but that was not his fault. No one was around to warn him of the effects of liquor.

God tried again. By Genesis 9:2-3, He had given man permission to add meat to his diet—"every creature that lives shall be yours to eat." Good news for Abraham and Sarah, who were tired of being vegans. When three hungry, thirsty, and unkempt strangers arrived at their tent, Sarah hastened to prepare an appetizing meal of lamb stew and cakes flavored with butter and milk. (They were actually angels for whom it was permissible to skirt *kashrut* laws.) (According to some sources, Abraham served the butter, milk, and meat to people whom he believed to be traveling Gentiles [there were no other Jews back then] and were obviously under no dietary obligations. He saw no reason that his personal stringencies should diminish the enjoyment of his guests.)

As we have seen, Abraham's niece, Rebecca, knew what to do when she saw her uncle's thirsty servant, Eliezer. She let down her pitcher for him and his camels to drink. He immediately recognized her as the proper bride for Isaac when she offered food and comfortable sleeping arrangements. When her brother Laban accepted Eliezer's proffered nose ring and bracelets, and with the further distribution of jewelry and clothes, she took off for the "accidental" meeting with Isaac, becoming his wife and comfort after Sara's death. In time, they had two children—Esau, a hunter whom Isaac loved because he prepared savory game, and Jacob, a milder (but devious) man who was his mother's favorite, possibly because he resembled her way of getting things done. Jacob cooked up a delicious *cholent* (see below) in order to cheat Esau out of his birthright. Then, with the connivance of Rebecca, Jacob tricked his father into granting him the blessing that was due to his brother: "*May God give you of the dew of the heaven, of the fatness of the earth, and abundance of grain and wine*" (Genesis 27:28). Have you noticed that God's blessing focused on food? What about the Torah? Food was still on God's mind at Jacob's and Rachel's wedding. He made sure that her father prepared a grand feast because He knew that good food connects people.

Joseph, Jacob's son, saved the Egyptian economy by storing seven years' worth of plentiful food, but it was not enough to stave off the following seven years of famine, which brought his wicked brothers from Canaan to buy grain. We will hear about them elsewhere, but, for now, we look ahead several generations to hungry Israelites who, having run out of the unleavened bread they had brought from Egypt, are upset with Moses. Moses doesn't have Joseph's enormous food resources, but he does know that God will provide sweet dews or cakes of *manna* on which they will miraculously subsist for forty years and be satisfied. Or, claimed they were. Nevertheless, according to Numbers (11:4-6 and 21:5), they continued to fantasize about the succulent meat, fish, cucumbers, melons, leeks, onions, and garlic, which they never had in Egypt. Perhaps their importunate nagging to return was responsible for the long delay before their arrival at Canaan.

Nevertheless, after four decades of wandering, they were finally settled in Palestine, hoping for a more interesting *table d'hote*. Psalm 102 assured them that their prayers were heard. Now they could partake of the tasty showbreads (*challah?*) apportioned for each of the designated twelve tribes of Israel (Exodus 25:30). Priests, of course, ate in comfortable ease before inviting the common folk to join them at the altar of the Jerusalem Temple. The sages knew there is no joy without good company and good food. That's why they were sages. They knew that eating evokes pleasure through sight, smell, and taste. If the fare lacked meat, they remembered that God, in His nutritionist wisdom, had provided plant foods high in protein, fiber, and iron. Vegetables were good then and are good now. Ask any vegetarian.

∽ ∽ ∽

Modern professional-style cookery was invented in 1896 when Fannie Farmer's *The Boston Cooking-School Cook Book* taught American women to adopt precise measurements for best results in food preparation. Fannie wasn't lucky enough to be Jewish. Honors for the earliest known Jewish cookbook go to *The Jewish Manual*, 1826, "edited by A Lady" (Judith Cohen Montefiore). London took the prize for that. The first American entry was by Mrs. Esther Levy in 1871, notable for not including a single mention of *gefilte fish*! *Cholent* fared better—a stew of meat and bones, potatoes, beans and whatever else fits into a large pot of seasoned boiling water and tastes good and keeps hot over low heat on the Sabbath.

Heinrich Heine added a poetic note:

> Dearest, smoking is forbidden
> For today is the Sabbath.
> But, at noon, as compensation,
> There shall steam for thee a dish
> That is in very truth divine—
> Thou shalt eat today of cholent.

Cholent is one thing, but not the main thing. For observant Jews, *kashrut* is a great deal more. They comply because the Torah says so. Restrictions for food preparation and consumption, primarily derived from Leviticus and Deuteronomy, are ritually demanded as aspects of spirituality, morality, and holiness. *Kashrut* gives meaning to the concept that what goes into our mouths is more important than the drivel that comes out. Eating is inherent in our animal nature; we are what we eat. We express compassion by abstaining from meat taken from live, injured, or dead animals. We show concern for livestock by requiring painless and humane slaughter methods. We show care for tradition in the separation of meat and dairy utensils and products. We profess soulfulness by draining life-giving blood from meat and poultry. These practices offer daily reminders for the gifts of sensitivity and for providing mankind with suitable or appropriate food.

There are a variety of explanations regarding Jewish dietary laws. No one knows their reasons or rationale. The three times that the Hebrew word *kosher* shows up in the Bible (Esther 8:5, Ecclesiastes 10:10; 11:6), the term is not related to food. Some suggest that the Divine statutes are motivated by hygienic principles or that the rules were meant to set Jews apart from the Gentile world. Others refer to their connection with pagan idolatry, the special qualities of holy peoplehood, the morality of the human spirit, the control of brutish appetites, or the wholesomeness of allowed foods, including fruit, grains, honey, eggs, spices, nuts, and items derived from them. Whatever their origins, they are certainly very ancient. Israelite settlements from 1200 BCE are easily distinguished by archaeologists from contemporary Canaanite settlements because of the lack of pig bones.

God provided many foods high in fats, protein, iron, and fiber, as well as nuts and minerals for energy and to maintain life and growth. While food is a universal necessity, talking and thinking about it became Jewish cultural markers, part of Jewish identity reminding them who they were and who they are. What other group adopted the mantra "They tried to kill us. We won. Let's eat"?

∽ ∽ ∽

The Bible associates *kashrut* with *kadosh*, or holiness, because its origins are connected to the ancient laws of purity. The Hebrew word *kadosh* infers not only personal holiness but also diversity. It may be difficult to define, but Jews know it when they see it. Fish with fins and scales may be eaten, as well as most domesticated fowl. Meat from animals with split hooves who chew their cud is acceptable. No pork products or shellfish. Meat and fowl must be slaughtered by a trained *shochet* and must be soaked and salted in the prescribed manner. Bread and wine have their own rules that govern usage. Different traditions offer unique foods for Sabbath and holiday meals. Purim invokes *hamantaschen*—pastries in the shape of Haman's hat or pockets. Passover mandates matzah and ritually prepared foods for the Seder meal. Chanukah suggests latkes and doughnuts fried in oil—*soufganiot* in Israel. Rosh Hashanah calls for honey for a sweet and buoyant new year. Dairy products celebrate Shavuoth, the spring harvest and the giving of the Torah at Mount Sinai. Sukkot goodies commemorate the seven-day pilgrimage festival. Simchat Torah celebrates the completion of the annual cycle of reading the Torah with round apples and candy coins. Ashkenazim or occidental traditions begin with braided egg bread *challah*, golden chicken soup and matzah balls, *kugel*, and fish (fish is suggested in the Talmud, although we miss its incarnation as *gefilte*).

Potato latkes apparently originated as peasant food in Eastern Europe—Germany, Austria, Poland, Russia—where potatoes were plentiful and cheap. Because oil is a main ingredient, it is associated with Chanukah, the holiday remembered for the rededication of the Second Temple when the allotted oil for one night miraculously burned for eight:

Potato Latkes

- 2 large russet potatoes
- 1 large onion
- 2 large eggs
- ½ cup flour
- 1 tsp. baking powder
- Oil

Grate or process potatoes. With a dishtowel, squeeze and wring out the liquid. Add eggs, flour, baking powder, and a little salt. In a flat pan, pour about ¼ inch of oil. Heat until hot. Drop a heaping

Matzah Gnebflich (Matzo Balls). Etching, 1890. By Alfonse Levy.

spoon of batter into the oil. Flatten into disks with a spatula. Cook about five minutes until edges are brown and crispy. Flip and cook another five minutes until deeply browned. Drain on paper towels. Serve with sour cream or apple sauce.

Litvak or Lithuanian Jews, with roots originating from border areas of Poland, Russia, and Ukraine, have their own specialties, which are better suited to northern climates. Their cuisine features peas, barley, potatoes, beets, greens, cabbage, sour pickles, and chopped meat sausages. Other favorites are fresh-water fish, cheeses and dairy products, dark rye bread, horseradish, mushrooms, berries, pears, and plums.

Herring and Apple Salad

- 2 cups finely diced Granny Smith apples
- 2 cups chopped hard-cooked eggs
- ¾ cup chopped onions
- 12 oz. jar herring in wine sauce, fish drained and cut into small pieces
- Diced beets, sugar and dill to taste

Mix, cover, and chill. Cover with 1 cup thinly sliced cucumbers. Serve with brown beer, rye bread, and dill sprigs.

Foods characterized as Sephardi, Mizrachi, or oriental offer cereals, spices, olive oil, lamb, beans and rice, grape leaves, leeks, and eggplants.

Kosher meat was slow-cooked before the Sabbath, eaten after twilight, and served uncooked Saturday afternoons. Meals were secretly served during special rituals or holidays that remained on festival tables until neighbors, who smelled the delicious aromas that wafted down the alleys, outed them. Nevertheless, many recipes survived with the Sephardi Jews who forcibly left homes but carried their traditional food into more welcoming cultures.

In the Ottoman Empire, Sephardi fish dishes were served over couscous along with beef-stuffed potatoes in tomato sauce. Turkish *burek* pastries were filled with feta cheese or spinach. Romanians enjoyed fresh fish, zucchini, broccoli, and pineapple, along with *ghiveci*, a favorite vegetable stew. When Sephardim couldn't afford expensive meats or chicken, they invented vegetarian chopped liver, herring-flavored eggplant salad covered with green onions, dill, and mayonnaise, grilled chicken livers drenched in a spicy tahini sauce, and *adafina*, a braised beef *cholent* simmered with chickpeas, fats, red wine, hard-cooked eggs in their shells, garlic and onions. *Prasa*, leeks simmered with garlic in tomato sauce, and *pashtida*, a crustless vegetable pie mixed with eggs and flour and baked to toasted perfection, are favorites.

In the Beginning, before the earth was formed, God prepared some appetizers to pique the interests of His future guests and to display His gastronomic creativity. He has been good enough to share some of His choice items with us: He made no rules about mixing ingredients up. Leaf through these recipes—you will love them.

Babka

- ¾ cup warm milk
- ½ cup sugar
- 3 tsp. active dry yeast
- 3¼ cups flour

- 2 large eggs
- 1 large egg yolk
- 1 tsp. vanilla
- ¾ tsp. salt

Mix ingredients until dough is shiny, soft, and sticky. Let it rest 2 hours. Punch down and roll into 2 loaves—each 8 × 10 inches. Spread each with egg yolk and a little milk. Let loaves rest 2 hours. Bake at 375 degrees until golden brown.

Bagel

Mix 3 cups of flour with 2 teaspoons of yeast and 1 tablespoon of sugar. Knead dough until smooth, elastic, and stiff. Let rest for 30 minutes. Form into balls. Let rest 10 minutes. Punch hole in center. Drop balls into salted boiling water until they float to top. Place on greased sheet and bake at 375 degrees until golden brown.

Helzl

Stuff chicken neck skin with crumbs and seasonings and bake at 375 degrees.

Pitchah

Boil calves' feet in water with garlic, seasonings, and carrots until natural gelatin is released. Strain, add lemon juice and a little wine.

Cheese Puffs

- 1 cup boiled milk
- ¼ cup butter
- Salt and pepper
- 1 cup flour
- 4 beaten eggs, added one at a time
- 1 cup shredded cheese

Dump flour into milk, stirring until mixture leaves sides of pan. Form 8 mounds touching each other on greased baking sheet. Using a little "stolen" dough from the mounds, form a small round ball and place on top of each. Sprinkle with cheese. Bake at 350 degrees for an hour until light brown and crisp.

Shakshuka (Egg Mishmash)

- 1 cup feta cheese
- 6 eggs
- 2 tsps. tomato paste
- ¼ cup oil
- 5 chopped garlic cloves
- 2 lbs. tomatoes unpeeled, cut up
- 1 tsp. salt

Simmer and stir all ingredients, except eggs, in large greased frying pan until thick. Break eggs over mixture and cook until eggs are set. Sprinkle with paprika and parsley. Or, you might try thin layers of eggplant, sliced hard-boiled egg, and tomato on pita, topped with hummus, shredded cabbage, mango, and savory condiments.

It is customary to start Jewish meals with soup made with meat stock and/or meat bones, vegetables, seasonings, and water. If the beginning is good, "the end will be great," as Job assures us (Job 8:7). Its first mention in the Bible is a pot of red lentil soup. With it, Jacob bought his brother Esau's firstborn right and blessing. Not a good thing for Esau, but a great hot dish on a cold winter night:

Red Lentil Soup

- 2 medium onions
- 1 box of sliced mushrooms
- 12 oz. red lentils
- 1 6-oz. can of tomato paste
- 12 cups water
- 2½ Tbs. consommé mix
- 2 Tbs. oil
- Seasonings

Dice and sauté onions in oil. Add mushrooms and cook until tender. Add remaining ingredients. Bring to a boil, then simmer covered for an hour, stirring occasionally.

Chicken Soup

[Recommended by Maimonides as a cure for whatever ails you. A Yiddish saying: If a pauper dines on a chicken, either he is sick or the chicken was.]

- 1 chicken—all parts
- 10 cups water
- 2 onions in quarters
- 2 carrots, cut or chopped
- 2 stalks celery, cut or chopped
- Parsley, dill, bay leaf, salt, garlic

Simmer all ingredients uncovered for one hour. Skim surface to remove fat and unwanted vegetables. Strain soup while hot.

Rose Michaels' Borsht

- 4 unpeeled and washed beets with tops
- Separate stems from leaves, discard stems, wash leaves and chop.
- Shred beets and 1 medium onion

Boil in eight cups of water until beets are tender. Add salt, lemon juice, a little sugar, and fresh dill to taste sweet and sour. Serve with sour cream and/or boiled potato.

Next come the entrees. We can hardly wait.

Gefilte Fish

Its origin is unknown, but its place on the holiday table is familiar to all celebrants. It may have originated in Germany, Holland, Russia, or Poland, or anywhere else in Europe where Jews were too poor to buy anything of higher quality. The following recipe is included because friendships that lasted decades have been known to break apart because your version is no good. Nevertheless, here it is in a basic style that should satisfy almost anyone who wants to remain a member in good standing of the gefilte fish club.

12. Essen un Fressen

- Filet and chop 3 lbs. of any firm-fleshed fish, preferably whitefish and carps.
- 2 large ground onions
- 2 eggs
- Seasonings, bread crumbs, or soaked and squeezed white bread

Form balls and place in cold water to cover. Boil slowly for 1–2 hours, chill liquid, serve with sliced carrot and horseradish.

You're on your own. But here are a few things to add if you have a reputation to keep: grated carrot, diced celery, parsnip, green pepper, parsley, ground almonds, salt, a bit of sugar, 1 tablespoon of flour, lemon juice, garlic.

Side Partners

Carrot Tsimmes (A Fuss Over Carrots)

Heat oil in a pan over medium-high heat. Add sliced carrots, pineapple, apple and/or prunes. Add raisins, orange juice, honey, brown sugar, cinnamon, salt and pepper Bring to a boil. Reduce heat, cover, and simmer until carrots are tender.

Noodle Pudding (Lukshen Kugel)

- 1 lb. packaged egg noodles
- 1 lb. sour cream
- 1 lb. small curd cottage cheese
- 4 large eggs, whisked
- 20-oz. can pineapple with juice
- 1 cup sugar (more if you prefer sweeter taste)
- ½ cup raisins
- 1 tsp. vanilla
- 2 sticks of butter, melted (one for pan)

Heat oven to 350 degrees. Grease 8 × 12 inch pan. Cook noodles according to package directions. Drain. Whisk remaining ingredients. Add to noodles. Pour into pan, dot with remaining butter. Bake 30 minutes, rotate pan, and bake another 30 minutes, until golden brown and until no liquid remains. Cut into serving portions. Best served chilled after overnight in refrigerator. Serves 24. (This could anchor or sink a small boat, except there will be none left over. Enjoy what's rich. We're poor too soon.)

Corn Meal Pudding

- 8 oz. sweet butter
- 3 large eggs
- ⅔ cup sugar
- ½ cup milk
- ½ cup cornmeal
- ½ cup flour
- 2 tsps. baking powder
- 1½ lbs. ricotta or farmer cheese

Heat oven to 350 degrees. Grease 8-inch baking pan with butter. Mix remaining butter, ⅓ cup sugar, and milk. Slowly add corn meal, flour, baking powder, and a little salt. Mix well. Mix remaining ingredients separately. Spoon half of mixture into pan, cover with all of cheese mixture, spread remaining corn meal mixture on top. Bake until golden brown and set. Serve with fruit.

Some meat dishes present challenges. Because chuck, flank, rib and shoulder cuts are less tender, they require special care. Flank steak was a Jewish favorite in the Old Country, where expensive rib roasts were unheard of, unseen, and, sadly, uneaten. (Meat is the prince of all food.)

Flanken

- Cut meat one inch thick, ½ lb. per person.
- In hot frying pan sear on both sides, turning quickly, but be careful to prevent escape of juices.
- Add thinly sliced onion.
- Add minced garlic.
- Sprinkle with flour, salt, pepper, and paprika.

Cover and cook over reduced heat for 3–5 minutes. If it comes out tender, the cook marches in pride up and down the main street of the shtetl.

Great Brisket

- 4–5 lb. brisket
- 2 onions, sliced
- 2 cloves garlic, minced
- 1 cup ketchup
- 2 Tbs. seedless raspberry jam
- ¼ cup water
- 2 Tbs. mustard

Preheat oven to 325 degrees. Mix ingredients. Pour over meat. Cover pan and roast slowly for 3–4 hours. Chill before cutting against the grain.

Sally Feldman's Stuffing

- Celery and onions, chopped
- 2 sticks of butter
- 2 loaves of bread, toasted and cubed
- 2 eggs
- Parsley (lots)
- Seasonings—salt and pepper, sage (not too much), thyme, tarragon, nutmeg (½ teaspoon or more)

Sauté celery in butter for about 2 minutes. Add onions and sauté some more. Pour mixture over bread. Add an egg, and then add another one. Add a third egg if necessary. Add seasonings. Add ½ cup or more of water and mush around. (How much of everything is up to you. After a few experiments it will be great, says son, Michael.)

12. Essen un Fressen

Passover Seder traditions date back thousands of years in hundreds of communities. Matzah is the star, replacing forbidden leavened bread. It is eaten during the eight-day holiday until the body cries out for a bagel or a slice of *challah*. Ashkenazim exclude rice; Sephardim permit it. Either way, the Seder is a raucous as well as a religious performance, geared for the delight of children who are encouraged to ask the Four Questions and to stay awake long enough to "ransom" a piece of matzah for which they will get a prize.

Close, distant, or unknown family members and friends gather every year around the Seder table to recite and sing the stories in the Haggadah that accompanies the service. Each participant recalls the Exodus from Egypt, where his ancestors were slaves burdened with hard work and little to eat until Moses convinced Pharaoh to let his people go. In their memory, ceremonial foods are placed on a central platter. The meaning of each item is questioned by the youngest person—from age six to sixty or more—and explained by the leader. In recent times, a contentious man protested that a woman no more belongs on a traditional synagogue pulpit than an orange belongs on a Seder plate. So, some families now add an orange to the plate, representing the women's movement. Traditions must be expandable. That's how they eventually become traditions.

The standard Seder plate consists of bitter herbs, together with a bit of parsley or lettuce dipped in saltwater, to commemorate the tears that were—and still are—shed for those who suffered in Egypt; a hard-boiled egg to represent the continuity of life despite the recognition that it is ephemeral; a roasted shank bone to evoke the sacrifice that was offered in the Temple; horseradish to recall the bitter lives of the slaves; and *charoseth*, a mixture that suggests the bricks and mortar which the slaves made for the construction of the pyramids.

Charoseth

Chop almonds, walnuts, toasted pine nuts, raisins, dried fruit, tart apples, and cinnamon in any order or amount. Mix with Kosher for Passover sweet wine. Make enough! This concoction should taste awful because it is combined with a hefty dose of horseradish, but sans the latter is one of the most delectable foods

An illustrated Haggadah showing four seated figures inviting "all those who are hungry to enter and eat" at a Passover Seder. Woodcut, c. 1490.

ever invented. Some cooks pride themselves—or outdo their neighbors—with imaginative versions of this splendiferous dish. You'll enjoy it with:

Matzah Apple Kugel

- 6 matzahs
- 6 eggs
- 1 cup sugar
- 1 tsp. vanilla
- 2 tsp. soft butter or margarine
- 1 cup soaked raisins
- 2 Granny Smith apples, grated

Heat oven to 400 degrees. Cover broken matzah with hot water. Drain and then add beaten eggs, vanilla, butter or margarine, raisins, and apples. Pour into a 3-quart casserole. Bake 30 minutes, rotate pan. Bake another 30 minutes until golden brown and no liquid remains. Sprinkle with cinnamon and sugar. Bake ten minutes. Lower heat to 300 degrees and bake another 20 minutes.

What is dinner without a sweet, especially on Passover?

Easy Honey Cake Cookies

- 1 egg
- 2 Tbs. oil
- Passover honey cake mix
- ⅓ cup orange or raspberry juice
- ½ cup chopped nuts

Mix and bake on greased baking sheet in 350-degree oven for 12 minutes. Cool and cut into squares.

Meet the millions of immigrants who became part of the world landscape and introduced unfamiliar food, vernacular languages, and eccentric social cultures. Beginning in the 1980s, professional chefs across the globe adopted "exotic" groceries. Everything that had once been distinct or unique to specialty shops now showed up at your neighbor's dinner party or Passover Seder: French cheeses, *crème fraiche*, jade-green kiwi fruit, cilantro, Asian pears, papayas, star fruit, extra-virgin olive oil, balsamic vinegar, sun-dried tomatoes, radicchio, white chocolate, sushi rolls, falafel, kebabs, and flavored coffees and teas.

Of course, holiday treats involve a lot more than fun and nutrition. They come with environmental costs because so much eventually ends up in landfills. Restaurants, packaging, and transportation seriously contribute to food waste. World populations, growing faster than affordable, deal with inequitable market access, lack of pesticide regulations, and reliable food labeling. Poverty, droughts, air and water pollution, crop failures, and climate change significantly reduce agricultural and meat production.

"Peasant food," starchy dishes, and less desired cuts of meat once disdained are enjoyed today. As Joan Nathan, Jewish cookbook historian, informs us, cultural gastronomy results from diaspora and adaptation: Jewish food fairs in America, date from the end of the Civil War: chopped liver became popular in the eleventh century in what is now

Alsace-Lorraine. Chicken soup became a tasty Jewish dish when a meat shortage following the Black Death led to a chicken-raising culture in Ashkenazi Europe. Jewish physicians helped overcome Roman fear of tomatoes and eggplants in the 1700s. A variety of good foodstuffs served as lines of communication between wandering Jews for centuries; the world developed their own cuisines from them as well. Foods that were not "Jewish" at one time are now part of Jewish identity.

Did you know that locusts or grasshoppers were forbidden by rabbinical authorities, who had forgotten that four species of the insects were kosher according to Leviticus 11:21–22? They were a staple of the Yemenite Jewish diet. In his *Jewish Communities in Exotic Places* (2000), Ken Blady describes the techniques of lighting bonfires near known nests to collect multitudes of these bugs:

> Before dawn ... when the locusts were covered with frost dew, entire families carrying sacks ... would ascend the hills in the direction of the bonfires. The docile insects were collected until the sacks were full. When multitudes of locusts were in the trees, one person would climb up and shake the branches while those below hastily scooped them up for dessert or as a main course in times of drought.

Yemenite Locusts

Dry locusts after removing legs, wings, and heads. Mix and add salt, black pepper, butter, and ground cumin. Roast until crisp. Locusts can also be ground into paste, kneaded with flour, or mixed with milk, boiled or sautéed as unsweetened wafers or biscuits. Save leftovers for leaner times, for when locusts swarm in vast numbers, one can safely predict drought and famine.

Armenian Chicken with Applesauce

- 1 chicken
- 1 lb. apples
- 1 cup rice
- 2 cups chicken broth
- 5 Tbs. oil
- 2 tsps. sugar, potato starch, cinnamon, and lemon juice

Boil chicken until soft. Cut up and fry pieces in oil. Drizzle with lemon juice. Slice unpeeled apples, cover with water. Simmer until very soft. Add sugar and cinnamon. Mix starch with 2 Tbs. cold water, add to chicken broth and mix for 2 minutes. Boil rice in broth. Combine and serve.

Russian Galushki

- ½ cup semolina
- ½ cup corn flour
- ½ cup all-purpose flour
- 2 quarts water
- Salt, sugar, oil, bread crumbs
- Pitted plums

Boil water, salt, and sugar. Slowly add and stir in semolina and corn flour and simmer 15 minutes. Add flour, simmer 10 minutes more. Cool dough, flatten into small pieces, put plum in middle, roll up the galushki, roll in bread crumbs, and place on cookie sheet. Warm in oven, sprinkle with sugar. Good served with honey.

Moroccan Moufleta

- 8 cups all-purpose flour
- 1 Tbs. sugar
- 1 tsp. salt
- 1 tsp. instant dry yeast
- 1 cup vegetable or canola oil
- Butter and honey for serving

Mix first four ingredients. Add 3½ cups warm water until a light, elastic dough is formed. Cover bowl and let rest for half an hour. With oiled hands, make about 20 balls, dip each in oil, place on oiled baking sheet, let rest for 15 minutes. On oiled work surface, with oiled fingers, flatten each ball one at a time, and stretch into thin uneven 7-inch circles. Place each on a large oiled skillet over medium-low heat. Cook quickly until underside has light brown spots. Turn over, and then place another pancake on top of first one. When bottom side has spots, flip both over and cook the new one. Repeat until there are 7 or 8 piles. Except for the first one, they are cooked only on one side. Cover with a towel to keep moist. Serve immediately with butter and honey. *Very sticky, very good.*

German Cookies

- 1 cup powdered sugar
- 1 cup honey
- 2½ cups flour
- 2 eggs
- 2 tsps. baking soda
- ½ cup walnuts or almonds
- 1 tsp. cinnamon and cloves

Boil honey and mix with sugar. When cool, add remaining ingredients and let rest for 2 hours or more. Roll out thin. Cut and bake at 375 degrees on greased cookie sheet.

∽ ∽ ∽

The *Holocaust Survivor Cookbook* calls itself "the most important cookbook you will ever own." And it's probably right. Collected from around the world are stories you will never forget and recipes you will always enjoy. The book was conceived in 2003 as a volunteer support program for the Carmel Ha'ir Soup Kitchen and Community Center in Jerusalem, which feeds and counsels hundreds of Israelis who pay if they can or when they can. The cooks and bakers memorialize the six million journeys from near starvation to economic plenty. Their testimonies to hope, prayer, and tenacity, as well as their legacies and recipes (adapted for general use), remain to remind us never to forget:

Ruggaleh Dough Remembered from Sighet, Romania

- 5 cups flour
- 1 lb. butter
- ¾ lb. sour cream
- 1 egg
- 3 tsps. baking powder
- ¼ cup sugar

Roll out dough, cut in triangles, fill with jam, poppy seeds, nuts and cinnamon. Roll from wide side, bake at 375 degrees for about one hour.

Kreplach Dough Remembered from Smooch, Poland

- 2 jumbo eggs
- 4 cups flour
- 1½ cups water
- 3 lbs. chopped meat
- Fried onion, salt and seasonings

Make a dough and roll it thin, cutting it into 2-inch squares. Place a teaspoon of meat in each square, fold in triangle, and pinch sides. Cook in salted, boiled water for 10 minutes or until done.

Asparagus Tart Remembered from South Africa

- Puff pastry sheets
- 2 cans cut and drained asparagus
- 8 sliced mushrooms
- 12 oz. heavy cream
- 2 jumbo eggs
- Seasonings
- Shredded cheese

Line pan with puff pastry. Place fried, seasoned vegetables over pastry. Whip cream and eggs, pour over vegetables. Sprinkle with cheese, dot with butter. Bake at 375 degrees until golden brown.

Mandel Broit Remembered from Lebow, Latvia

- ¾ cup sugar
- 2 eggs
- 2 tsps. baking powder
- Salt
- ¼ cup orange or tangerine juice
- ¾ cup oil
- 3 cups flour
- Chocolate chips or chopped nuts

Mix all ingredients and bake in long pan at 400 degrees. When brown, slice and brown again.

Fruit Cake Remembered from Occupied Paris

- 1 cup cut-up dried fruit
- ¾ cup sugar
- 1 Tbs. baking soda
- ½ cup egg whites
- ½ cup oil
- 2 Tbs. vanilla
- 2 cups flour

Preheat oven to 350 degrees. Mix all ingredients except flour. Mix again with flour. Pour into greased pan. Cover with cut-up fruit. Bake until outer edges are brown.

Cheese Spread Remembered from Kolosvar, Hungary
- 8 oz. whipped cream cheese
- 4 oz. margarine or butter
- 1½ Tbs. chopped onion
- Anchovy paste to taste
- Paprika

Mix all ingredients. Serve on crackers or toasted bread.

But whenever and wherever you eat, don't forget the proper blessings.
God is listening.

13

Artisanship and Crafts

Surviving material from Biblical times indicates that artists were already occupied in the production of useful Jewish crafts. As early as 70 CE, following the destruction of the Second Temple, religious sacrifice gave way to the study of sacred texts, illustrated Hebrew Bibles, Haggadot, and, later, works by Rashi and Maimonides (as well as later beloved communal items such as menorahs, *kiddush* cups, and wedding rings). Most of these items were produced by highly trained Gentiles under the direction of knowledgeable Jews who developed unpretentious but no less significant items, often ignored or overlooked by connoisseurs of the "finer" arts.

Over time, a wide variety of religious and symbolic objects were produced as ties to religious ceremonies as well as of necessity, created by artists wherever they lived and prayed. While they were considered commercial in nature, many were more or less ritualistic, drawing admonitions in praise of craftsmanship, as noted by Professor Mark Wischnitzer. Jewish customers sustained Jewish artisans. The magnificent gateways and decorations of Solomon's Temple were admired by royalty, merchants, and locals. Children's toys were among the best-loved handiwork of the potters who catered to fond parents. Parents, of course, loved their own toys—anklets, pendants, nose rings, and gorgeous woven dyed garments.

The Palestinian Rabbi Simon ben Yohai honored labor because it honors the worker. (Nedarim49b). Vocational training of youth was implemented by fathers who taught their sons regular handcrafts. The second-century Rabbi Ishmael interpreted the term *choose life* to mean *choose a craft*. Clearly, artisans were well respected, if not loved, in the seventeenth- and eighteenth-century guild communities. Rabbis decided the labor policies in Palestinian Patriarchate town councils, hopefully with the approval of their congregants. Possibly the most beloved members of communities were the craftsmen who provided their most precious articles: tailors, launderers, weavers, and dyers of the blue fringes of *tzitzits*, embroiderers of Temple items, and leather craftsmen. By the Middle Ages, bookbinding, the illumination of manuscripts, and the making of playing cards became popular crafts. When towns needed artisans—including some women—in order to function, they must have been loved, or, at least, honored. (According to some, these attributes happily coexist.) "Individuals and whole communities turned to them for advice and guidance in religious, legal, educational and economic matters," reports Wischnitzer. The response of rabbinical authorities "constituted one of the main sources of information." If that doesn't breed love, what does?

Mariano del Buono (1433–1504), a Jewish decorator of an Italian-rite prayer book, produced fine Haggadot and the liturgy for Chanukah and Purim. A Jewish northern Italian artist, known as the Master of the Barbo Missal (c. 1457), was recognized for his illustrations of Maimonides' *Mishneh Torah*. While simultaneously functioning as middlemen or agents between Jews and their non-Jewish neighbors, self-taught amateurs contributed to a broader understanding of diverse customs and rituals. However, as Church and state economies grew, Jews were limited in their ability to challenge the competition in marketing and mercantilism.

But let us return to the very beginning of artisanship. Although skilled workers—tanners, weavers, dyers, glassblowers, and instrument makers—were among the earliest craftsmen—Adam and Eve were the first tailors (but not the most fashionable) to cover their nether regions with fig leaves. Jubal enlivened the Garden atmosphere with tuneful musical programs on harp and flute. God must have been pleased indeed that His artisans provided appropriate instruments for the singers and dancers of the Temples, instruments which He had commissioned in Numbers 10:10. We hear of Miriam praising God with song, while Psalmists honored Him with tambourines, lutes, harps, stringed instruments, flutes, trumpets, and clashing cymbals in glorious explosions of sound. King David made merry with lyres, drums, pipes, and rattles, while young maidens—much to the mortification of his wife—got eyefuls of his manly charms (II Samuel 6:5, Chronicles 13:8).

However, after the destruction of the Temples, instrumental music was prohibited on the Sabbath and holidays—and still is in communities that adhere to Talmudic law (perhaps to be renegotiated with the coming of the Messiah). While singing remains integral to synagogue services, eliciting "prayers of the heart," the female voice, according to the Orthodox tradition, is regarded as an erotic temptation. Liberal synagogues take a more relaxed view, permitting the use of mixed-gender choirs and an accompanying guitar. Reform services offer a variety of musical refreshments, including the organ.

☙ ☙ ☙

Tubal-Cain, a sixth-generation descendant of Cain, is remembered in Genesis (4:22) as a craftsman of bronze and iron-cutting instruments (which furnished mankind with the metal-ware and tools used in the first act of murder). Evidently, artifacts of various uses were already embedded in daily life when God commissioned Bezalel and Oholiab to create a "permanent sanctuary as a dwelling place for His delight and glory," employing the "wisdom, understanding, and knowledge to do all manner of dexterous work" (Exodus 35:30–35). Some three hundred years later, the Phoenician king, Hiram of Tyre, provided Solomon with cedar and pine lumber from Lebanon, after which a labor force of thousands built the House of the Forest of Lebanon with courtyards, a hall for the throne, and a Hall of Judgment. Finally, Solomon hired Hiram, a craftsman, to create bronze pillars, a molten bronze sea or basin standing on the backs of twelve bronze oxen, as well as a golden table, candlesticks, carved figures, and other furnishings for the decoration of the holy Jerusalem Temple (I Kings 7:15–51).

Carpenters and masons, who figure in the third chapter of Ezra, "built the altar of the God of Israel to offer burnt offerings" in preparation for the restoration of the Temple. In Ecclesiastes, Koheleth, sometimes identified as Solomon in his old age, describes the great pleasure he had working with his hands (2: 4–11):

> I made my work great. I built myself houses and planted vineyards. I made myself gardens and orchards, and I planted all kinds of fruit trees in them. I made myself water pools from which to water the growing trees of the grove…. I also gathered for myself silver and gold and the special treasures of kings and of the provinces…. Whatever my eyes desired, I did not keep from them. I did not hold my heart from any pleasure, for my heart rejoiced in all my labor. And this was my reward from

all my labor: that I looked upon all the works that my hands had done and on the labor in which I had toiled.

Before long, a variety of goods, unknown even to Koheleth (King Solomon), was prepared for anyone requiring decorative ceremonial objects. Certainly, the *Hiddur Mitzvah* injunction affirmed Jewish sensibilities through the making of handsome ritual artifacts: "*Make a beautiful sukkah, a beautiful lulav, a beautiful shofar, and beautiful tzitzith.*" (Sabbath133b). And they did. Artistic silver Torah accessories, ceramic *Seder* plates, and embroidered silk *matzah* and *challah* covers added beauty and meaning to synagogue and home décor. As provincial communities grew into urban towns, local artisans became master craftsmen turning out ever-finer wares—leather-tooled book bindings, lace nettings, gold and silver embroideries, and gem-cut stones. Silk weavings were particularly sought. Their manufacture depended upon silkworms that fed on mulberry leaves, forming cocoons of gummy or jelly-like fibers, which, when unraveled and wound on spools, were spun into thin or thick silk threads. Ezekiel tells us they were woven into splendid silk garments worn by splendid ladies (16: 10,13). Medieval Jewish weavers brought the silk culture to Egypt, as it passed through Bukhara, Samarkand, China, Muslim Spain, Southern Italy, Greece, and elsewhere on the way to Europe and Judea.

In addition to luxury merchandise, locksmithing, cobbling, tobacco-dressing, seal engraving, uniform tailoring, glass manufacturing, and soap- and candle-making offered broad opportunities for burgeoning industries. But let us not forget that Jews also shopped for beauty treatments, designer gowns, unnecessary frippery, and necessary baubles for mistresses and wives. They supported musicians, comedians, dancers, acrobats, seers, and rabbis—all dedicated to the improvement and pleasure of body and mind. However, to no one's surprise, distasteful occupations—tanning and dying, repairing damaged goods, cleaning toilets, sweeping roads of animal droppings, serving as public executioners, and discarding the rotting bodies of criminals and paupers—all eschewed by Christians and Muslims—were delegated to Jews.

Numbers (15:37–41) explains that Moses instructed Jews to make blue dye for the tassels or fringes stitched to the corners of the *tallit* or prayer shawl. Blue or purple coloring matter was drawn from the mucus of spiny sea snails or mollusks, after which fabrics were soaked until the material reached the proper intensity or stain. Dyeing was largely a Jewish trade, one in which Jewish merchants and guilds imported and exported dye ingredients from northern Africa to southern Italy and points north, as well as to Greece, Israel, and the Ottoman Empire. American colonies, as well, played an important role in the development of dye products, particularly by planting indigo.

Ecclesiasticus, the *Wisdom of Sirach*, or *Ben Sira*, is a second-century BCE book by a Hellenistic Jewish scribe who recorded the social status of artisans—dye makers, silk weavers, engravers, smiths, bakers, glassblowers, butchers and technicians—who were necessary as suppliers for wide markets. "Without them," he noted, "a city cannot be inhabited.... Wherever they dwell, they do not hunger" (38:27–32). With them, embryonic guilds were formed with workers operating out of their own homes. Almost everyone, from unskilled farmers to the sages of the Mishnah, pitched in to do mundane and holy work. Among those sages, Hillel was a woodcutter and vintner; Nechuniah ben Hakana, a cistern builder; Yochanan, a sandal maker; Nehemiah, a potter; Hanina and Oshaya, shoemakers. All contributed to a growing prosperity of the Second Commonwealth period.

As we look back over time, beginning from the third century CE to the recent present, we become aware that the significance of Jewish craftsmanship can hardly be exaggerated.

A synagogue, excavated in the Roman garrison town of Dura-Europos, created a storm of interest; originally built in 245 CE on the Euphrates in present-day Syria, and unearthed in the 1920s and 1930s, its thirty surviving painted panels were found wonderfully preserved and included Biblical scenes and human figures as well as *menorahs, lulavs,* and *etrogs.* Nothing else of its scale has since been found, attesting to the presence of handcrafted ceremonial objects shortly after the destruction of the Second Temple in 70 CE. When King Cyrus the Great of Persia (600–530 BCE) was prompted by God to repatriate Jews who wished to aid in the Temple rebuilding, he not only permitted their return but generously provided funds for the recall and repair of their holy vessels (Isaiah 45:1–3).

Early illustrations of Jewish crafts, dating from the third- and fourth-century synagogues in Hammat, Tiberias, were excavated in 1920 and 1961–63. Depictions of synagogue objects fill the upper areas of the mosaic floor of a sixth-century synagogue in the Israeli kibbutz of Beth Alpha, unearthed in 1929. However, from the seventh to the ninth centuries, there is a break in the chronology, and few examples of Jewish artisanship survive other than clay pottery and textile garments. Because Jews needed a settled and stable environment to produce significant artifacts, it was a long time before they made important contributions. Although they were still turning out crafts for general use, at times they still farmed out orders to Christian artisans. But as Jewish life recovered, Jewish artisans took advantage of relative liberties, moving westward to new areas in Sicily, Spain, Southern France, and later, in the Italian city-states, where they joined Christian or Muslim guilds, establishing their own workshops.

Jews—and the rest of the world—were startled by the find of hundreds of thousands of shredded Hebrew, Aramaic, and Judeo-Arabic secular and religious illustrated manuscript fragments bearing God's name in the storerooms or *geniza* of the Ben Ezra Synagogue in Fustat (Old Cairo), lying untouched for almost a thousand years. Brought to the attention of Professor Solomon Schechter (1847–1915), the collection, which includes Maimonides' handwritten *responsa* and designs embodying verses from Isaiah, has been documented and preserved.

What made it possible to reproduce such material was the new method in Europe of mechanically printed hand-written texts. An enterprising Jewish dyer, Davin de Caderousse, may have anticipated by about ten years the famous 1455 Bible by Johann Gutenberg (1394?–1468), whose business, incidentally, was bankrolled with loans by Johann Fust, a wealthy Jewish businessman and goldsmith. When Gutenberg was unable to repay the debt, his type and the incomplete Bible were surrendered and completed by Fust and his son-in-law, Peter Schoffer.

Although relative late-comers to skilled occupations, by the fifteenth century in Mediterranean communities and Eastern Europe, a large artisan class developed as towns grew and prospered through Jewish cross-disciplinary knowledge and proficiency because their skills were highly valued. King John III of Navarre (1469–1516), who, for a short period in the 1490s, gave open and legal sanctuary to Jews until forced by the Portuguese Inquisition to desist, declared that it was "for the convenience of the country folk that he permitted Jewish workmen to offer their services…." A few other rulers in Portugal, Aragon, and Castile followed his lead, recognizing the need for artisans, even if they were Jews, who introduced innovative methods such as piecework, assembly-line production, and well-organized production systems. These skilled artisans, whose work was of superior quality, succeeded in improving their social standing, raising possibilities of conditional acceptance in many communities where Jewish artists were predominant.

13. Artisanship and Crafts

Spanish Jews had monopolized the manufacture of leather goods and some ceremonial items for the Church until 1415 when Pope Benedict XIII prohibited the craft. However, Polish law allowed Jews to organize shops in which metalwork—pewter for the poor, copper or silver for the rich—was created for home and ritual use. Permissive Moorish rule in the Near East and North Africa found Jews engaged in paper-making, coin-minting, stone masonry, woodcarving, glassmaking, dyeing, and embroidering. Although religious restrictions and municipal authorities hampered Jewish craftsmanship, periodically destroying material during expulsions, pogroms and wars, much remains, conjuring up an entire culture and history. Expressed in the verses of the Yom Kippur service God Himself molds Jewish artisanship *"like clay in the hand of the potter, stone in the hand of the cutter, iron in the hand of the blacksmith, glass in the hand of the blower, fabric in the hand of the embroiderer, silver in the hand of the silversmith."*

Rabbi Solomon ibn Adret of Barcelona (1235–1310) recognized that every trade that requires an organization or a guild is a city unto itself and does not need the consent of the outer community. Among his *responsa* are allusions to dyers' guilds. This self-proclaimed autonomy of Jewish guilds, however, did not prevent Spanish guilds from guarding their own interests through persecutions, massacres, and expulsions of Jews in towns across the length and breadth of Spain in 1391. When Jewish traders and moneylenders traveled the countryside, they were charged with immorality, unfair competition, and consorting with Christian ladies—punishable by death. Declared Solomon Alami (1370–1420), the Portuguese author of *Iggeret Mussar (Ethical Epistles)* who witnessed the accusations, it was the Jewish upper classes that were responsible for "the ruin of their people" because they were among the first to intermarry and convert.

Jewish pawnbrokers, shoemakers, tailors, blacksmiths, saddlers, and weavers supplied the vital crafts that enabled royal courts, clergy, and secular communities to function smoothly. Despite the bigotry in the Iberian Peninsula, Sicily, Sardinia, and other areas in southern Italy and southern France, about a third of the Jewish population was able to engage in such tasks. With economic growth, however, mass production began to replace individual or family output. With the advent of technology, Jews lost work in traditional homemaking trades such as furriery, tailoring, and the making of hats, caps, and shoes. Unwholesome and dangerously crowded factories, irksome hand- and mind-numbing toil, shorter work hours, and the exploitation of women and children soon eroded any possibilities of improved lifestyles. In his analysis of labor policies in *A History of Jewish Crafts and Guilds* (1965), Mark Wischnitzer outlined the economic factors that controlled Jewish occupations: (a) protection by the Crown; (b) opposition to the guild monopolies; (c) the multi-ethnic composition of the working class; (d) the existence of sizable numbers of non-organized work among the various ethnic groups; and (e) the resistance of the Jewish artisans to hostile acts of the guilds.

Jewish guild interests in Eastern Europe often collided with official Jewish community leaders over taxation and other issues, including punishments for perceived infractions in their jurisdictions. Nevertheless, towards the end of the sixteenth or the beginning of the seventeenth century, Jewish guilds widened their scope, not only overseeing health, religious, and working conditions but also attempting to keep peace with fellow employees and outside authorities. When peaceful means failed, opposing groups promoted adversarial and antagonistic positions. None of this suggested warm relationships with the Christian world, which only reaffirmed its anti-Jewish and "racial" perceptions of the Jewish artisan classes.

During the seventeenth and eighteenth centuries under the Austrian Hapsburg monarchs, provincial Jewish artists were able to prosper, having received permission to work for the Christian trade during the Thirty Years' War (1618–1648), when enormous costs made Jewish contributions to government exchequers welcome. In return, Jewish craftsmen were allowed to sell their wares at prices often below those set by guilds. Nevertheless, impoverished Jewish populations, having rapidly increased with immigration from war-torn areas and expulsions, were barely able to support themselves in new trades: furniture making, gilding, plumbing, the crafting of musical instruments and carpenters' tools, and by delivering second-hand or damaged goods at cheap prices. In underselling merchandise to both Christian and Jewish clients and by being self-employed or in family businesses, they almost managed to survive. But with growing reports of sexual adventures between Jewish men and Christian women, whatever marginal acceptance they earned soon turned to expulsions enforced by the guilds.

In response, Jews set up their own guilds, which included bachelors in opposition to Christian rules which limited membership in some areas to married men. Jews elected wardens to supervise their guild activities, super-wardens to supervise elected wardens, and rabbis to supervise both and to keep their eyes on anyone who might overstep his authority or embezzle community funds.

After registering with the appropriate authorities and paying certain taxes, guild workers started out with one apprentice entitled to room and board. Apprentices trained for two or three years before becoming journeymen. After a further three years, they could try for a master's title. Working time was fixed at twelve hours a day with thirty minute breaks for improving reading and writing skills and attending religious services.

Other than in Eastern Europe, few Jewish artisans are known in the early seventeenth century. Amsterdam, which had accepted some Sephardic refugees from Iberia, earned the reputation of being "good" to Jews, although that status was tenuous. True, they were able to move freely about the country and enjoy religious liberty, but they were barred from most guilds, which meant that many were reduced to pawnbroking, money-lending, tobacco-dressing, refurbishing used clothing, cleaning shoes, selling combs and spectacles, and tailoring.

Another area in which they were active was book printing in Hebrew and Yiddish, as well as in other languages. Under the auspices of Rabbi Manasseh ben Israel, who employed both Jewish and Christian printers and illustrators (including engravings by Rembrandt), Jews enjoyed a dominant place in intercultural connections. Manasseh, however, as well as those in the Jewish medical, legal, and pharmaceutical professions, was refused guild membership.

England's Sephardic Jews were readmitted in the 1650s, thanks to the efforts of Manasseh and courtesy of Oliver Cromwell, but were too few in numbers and had not been around long enough to be troublesome. They brought with them their traditional trades—brokering, butchering, tailoring, and baking, but not fine artisanship except for a silversmith or two who provided an occasional ceremonial object. The settlement, nevertheless, was mostly free of intolerance, and Jews were allowed the establishment of a cemetery. In 1690, Ashkenazi Jews dedicated their own synagogue. (In 1941, it was destroyed by German bombs.) The main Sephardic synagogue, Bevis Marks, would not open for services until 1701, when chandeliers, woodwork, ornamentation, and other embellishments modeled on its prototype in Amsterdam were installed. The building stands in London today, much as it originally appeared, with the addition of a beautiful gilded chair reserved for Cromwell should he ever return.

13. Artisanship and Crafts

Jewish Moneylender. Woodcut, 1486. By Erhard Reuwich. From *Peregrinatio in Terram Sanctam* (Travels in the Holy Land) by Dean Bernhard von Breydenbach.

French Revolution liberties and Napoleon permitted Jews to practice their typical trades or crafts in freedom—except when Christian masters blocked their way. Some adventurous Jews from Alsace-Lorraine, denied the expected opportunities, took off for French colonies in the West Indies where a lucky few successfully braved the challenges of the New World and made a fortune—or at least a living—without the forbidding presence of authorities to ensure class distinctions. Germany, actually a group of fractious principalities bound together more by common language than by politics, was dominated by Prussia, where the Christian guilds protected their tradesmen through inflexible policies that lasted until the nineteenth century. Jews could not engage in any artisanship in which privileged associations or guilds were established. Fortunately, seal engraving, jewelry cutting, and the grinding of optical glasses were exempt from these restrictions. In Berlin, which attracted expert Polish and Lithuanian Jews skilled in lacemaking and fur dyeing, Jews were allowed to produce goods for the luxury market. Embroidery was encouraged in Bohemia and Saxe-Weimer because their Christian ladies would not be denied; some guilds, however, required Jewish artisans to cater exclusively to Jewish customers. The one craft open to Jews without conditions was engraving, necessary for printing financial materials for military and civic use, as well as for portraiture before the advent of the camera. The Edict of Tolerance, issued by the Austrian emperor Joseph II in 1782, encouraged Jewish craftsmen and helped eliminate medieval restrictions in Vienna—and soon throughout greater Europe. On this cheerful note, we refrain from looking ahead to the German disasters a hundred and fifty years in the future.

As Jewish guild organizations expanded their memberships, the eighteenth-century Enlightenment found a third of the Jewish population engaged in artisanship. Production in homes still competed with finished goods in the open market. The introduction of sweatshops, with some modern equipment and vocational training, slowly changed the history of the artisan class. Socialist and Marxist ideologies, established at the beginning of the 1870s, encouraged workers to participate in proletarian walkouts against management. With the growth of the economies and the populations of the towns, guilds were disappearing. Socioeconomic philosophies were introduced, industrialization was accelerated, trade between towns grew with the development of factories and fast railway travel, job actions and hostile strikes replaced negotiated resistance, and modern urban life was born. At this point, the story of artisanship becomes the history of European immigration, the modern labor movement, and the disappearance of large numbers of Jewish craftsmen (and Jews) after the Holocaust. Middle-class society and growing prosperity have limited interest in craftsmanship while elevating participation in finance, professions, services, industrial and electronic development, and organization. While the Jewish artist is celebrated, the Jewish artisan, as remembered, may be a relic of the past.

Jews are able to choose and buy artifacts produced in almost every town and village they visit. And buy they do—some to impress the neighbors, some for home decoration, some to renew memories, some to evoke symbolic occasions and their claim on Jewish continuity, some to indulge their fancies for as long as their credit cards hold out.

Savor these cherished symbols. Buy old and contemporary treasures. You will love them:

Besamim Container, holds aromatic spices signifying pleasant aromas for the coming week. It may include a braided candle which, when lighted, marks the closing of the Havdalah service of the Sabbath.

Candlesticks, often fitted with enough tapers to represent each beloved family member, are lighted before the beginning of the Sabbath and other holidays. Blessings are recited to welcome the Sabbath Queen.

Besamim container (spice box); double acorn design with legs, sterling silver, 1901 (University of Michigan Library, Special Collections Research Center).

Shabbat candlesticks used to sanctify the Sabbath (Jewish Heritage Collection, University of Michigan).

Chai, the Hebrew word for life, is a pendant or charm, often worn as good-luck jewelry. It is formed of the letters *chet*— the eighth letter of the alphabet—and *yud*, the tenth, which add up to the number 18, which represents a spiritual value for long life.

Two letters from the Hebrew alphabet spelling "life."

Challah, egg bread traditionally eaten on the Sabbath, holidays, and ceremonial occasions.

Dreidel, a spinning top played as a children's game with goodies for the winners, associated with the Chanukah holiday. Known in Hebrew as Sevivan, its four sides carry the letters nun, gimel, hei, and shin, an acronym for *A Great Miracle Happened There*. (In Israel, Happened Here.)

Dreidels, spinning toys used especially by children celebrating Hanukkah.

Grogger, a revolving noisemaker, spun during the reading of the Purim *megillah* whenever the name of Wicked Haman is mentioned.

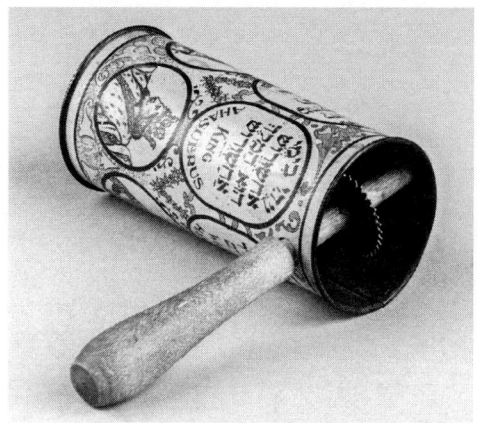

Grogger (noisemaker) for Purim, late 19th century (University of Michigan Library, Special Collections Research Center).

Hamsa, a palm-sized hand used in some Middle Eastern and North African Jewish cultures as a magical or superstitious protection against the Evil Eye. The "Hand of God" may be worn or displayed up (for luck) or down (as a fertility amulet). Its five fingers may represent the five books of the Torah as well as suggesting the five human senses.

Hamsa, a palm-shaped amulet, late 19th century (University of Michigan Library, Special Collections Research Center).

Havdallah, the prayer for ending the Sabbath with a cup of wine.

Havdalah, the service that concludes the Sabbath. Etching, 1902. By Hermann Struck.

Ketubba, a marriage contract that describes obligations of and benefits due to the bride and groom in the marriage.

A traditional illustrated Ketubah (Jewish marriage contract) (Beinecke Rare Book & Manuscript Library, Yale University).

Lulav, a closed frond consisting of four species—palm, willow, myrtle, and citron, gathered together during the Sukkot festival and shaken in all directions to signify the unity of the Jewish people; **Etrog**, a citrus fruit signifying the harvest.

Child with Lulav. Oil on canvas, date unknown. By Isidor Kaufmann. Palm fronds used during the Holiday of Succoth.

Marriage ring, a ring signifying that the person is married.

Community Jewish ring, c. 1885 (University of Michigan Library, Special Collections Research Center).

Matzah cover, cloth holder for Passover matzah, used at the Passover Seder.

Matzoh cover for the Passover seder, early 20th century (University of Michigan Library, Special Collections Research Center).

Menorah, the oldest symbol described in the Bible, a seven-branched candelabrum in the Tabernacle in Jerusalem (Exodus 25:31–40). Fresh, pure oil was burned daily, with the center lamp left burning at all times. For the Chanukah holiday, it has eight branches and an additional socket, which serves as a *Shamash* to light the other seven. It represents Israel as a Divine Light unto the Nations (Isaiah 42:6). It is the coat of arms of the modern State of Israel.

Yarmulke and Menorah. From the Harry S. Truman collection. President Truman was the first world leader to recognize Israel as a new nation.

Mezuzah, a device made from a rolled-up parchment inserted in a decorative case. It contains the *Shema* from the Torah: *You shall write the words on the doorposts of your house and on your gates* (Deuteronomy 6:4–9; 11). Traditionally handwritten by an authorized scribe, it is affixed to doorposts designating a connection to God and a reminder to obey His law; it is not a good luck charm. *Shadai*, Guardian of Israel, appears on the outside of the case. Printed examples are invalid according to Orthodox law.

Mezuzah at the entrance of the Museum am Judenplatz, Vienna. The mezuzah case is tilted and features the Hebrew letter ש (Shin), as is common in these mezuzahs.

Passover Plate, a plate with space for each of the Passover food symbols used at the Seder.

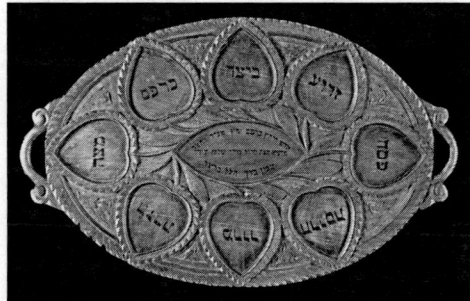

Seder Plate for Passover; wooden, 23" × 14", finely carved in a floral and leaf motif with handles, c. 1900 (University of Michigan Library, Special Collections Research Center).

Shofar, traditionally a ram's horn blown in the synagogue on Rosh Hashanah and at the end of Yom Kippur and on other important occasions. It symbolizes the breath of life and calls for repentance and atonement for past deeds and inspiration for the future.

Ram's horn used ritually in connection with the Jewish New Year.

Star of David, a six-pointed star made from two equilateral triangles, used as a Jewish symbol since the seventeenth century, particularly by the Jews of Prague. It has been used as a decorative motif in other cultures since antiquity and appears on the Israeli flag. Some claim that the top triangle points to God, the bottom to the real world.

Star of David in the flag of Israel.

Tallit, a four-cornered prayer shawl used during the morning service and for synagogue prayer. Its religious significance lies in the **Tzitzit**, or fringes, that are tied to each corner in accordance with Biblical commandments to prepare the mind and heart for prayer (Numbers 15:38–40) (Deuteronomy 22:12). They should have seven white strands, one of blue.

Tallit, or prayer shawl, used as a wrap during certain prayer services.

Tefillin, small leather boxes containing Torah verses, worn with straps on the head and arm during certain prayers. They

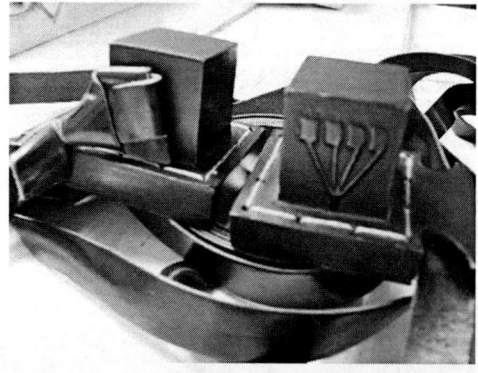

Tefillin are prayer devices worn on the head and arm to remind the user about their connection to God.

represent man's service to God through body and mind.

Tefillin Bag, a holder of the tefillin, usually decorated with a Star of David or another religious symbol.

The front of this tefillin bag shows the Western Wall of the Temple Mount together with the Temple and Midrash Shlomo (The School of Solomon). The major motif on the reverse is a wreath of flowers above which is the following inscription: "Jerusalem, the h[oly] c[ity], may it [be rebuilt speedily]." Within the wreath is the name of the owner, Moses/ s[on of] Samuel/HaLevi. These bags were usually made by brides for their fiancés. Many were modeled after contemporary 19th century prints.

Torah Cover, a cloth jacket surrounding the Torah, often highly decorated.

Torah cover from Theresienstadt concentration camp, now in Kiryat Tivon, Israel (photo by Dafna Gruber/Wikimedia Commons).

Tzedakah Box, a container to hold money for the needy. Charity is considered an obligation, not a choice. In Jewish terms, it signifies justice or righteousness.

Tzedakah box, where family members put in cash to be used for charity.

Yad, a symbolic hand at the tip of a Torah pointer used to keep one's place while reading and to avoid touching the scroll. It can be a simple metal or wooden pointer or a highly decorated jeweled object.

Ritual pointer to indicate a location to read in the Torah scroll.

Yarmulke, Yiddish for Hebrew *kippah*, a skullcap worn at all times by traditional and observant Jews to fulfill the requirement that heads be covered in deference to the One above.

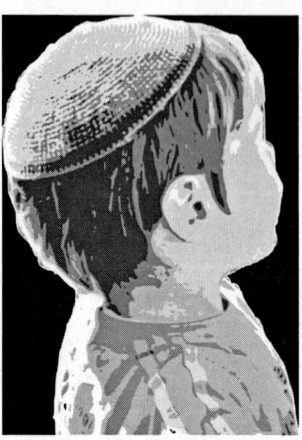

Boy wearing a Yarmulke (kippah), a sign of respect when in the presence of God.

And so it went in the past. And so it goes today with these treasured resources inspiring devotion in the synagogue and home. As you enjoy and cherish your collection, please raise high a cup filled with kosher wine:

> Praise to You, Eternal God, King of the World, Creator of the fruit of the vine,
> Who has sustained us and brought us to this day.

14

Laughing at Love

There is funny, and then there is clever. Many of the cleverest Jewish tales were told by the rabbis of the Talmud as they analyzed what was or wasn't appropriate. You may not be able to top the fourth-century Rava, who addressed the Passover problem in Pesachim 10b:

> Suppose a mouse entered a room, which had already been searched for leaven, with a piece of bread in its mouth, and a mouse then came out of the room with a piece of bread in its mouth. Can one assume that the mouse and the bread that came out are the same mouse and bread that went in? Or, is it perhaps a different mouse? What if a white mouse went in with bread in its mouth, and a black mouse came out with bread in its mouth? Must one assume that it is a different piece of bread, or can one suppose that it is the same piece of bread, one which the first mouse threw away and the second mouse picked up? Perhaps you will say, "Mice do not take food from each other." In that case, what if a mouse went in with a piece of bread in its mouth, and a weasel came out with a piece of bread in its mouth? Can one assume that the weasel took the bread away from the mouse, or could it be another piece of bread because a weasel would have the mouse itself in its mouth? Suppose then that the weasel had the mouse and the bread in its mouth. But surely, if it were the same piece of bread, the weasel would have the mouse in its mouth, and the bread would still be in the mouse's mouth. But perhaps the mouse dropped the bread in its fear, and the weasel picked up the mouse and the bread separately?

The problem was left unsolved, but it would have been a treat to see the smiles on the rabbis' faces when Rava finally sat down. The rabbis know nonsense from good sense. Hence this fragment from Bava Bathra 23b:

> If a fledgling bird is found within fifty cubits of a man's property, it belongs to the owner of the property. If it is found outside the limits of fifty cubits, it belongs to the person who finds it. Rabbi Jeremiah asked the question: "If one foot of the fledgling bird is within the limit of fifty cubits, and one foot is outside it, what is the law?" It was for this question that Rabbi Jeremiah was thrown out of the house of study.

The English humorist A. P. Herbert (1890–1971) cautioned his listeners: *"Don't stop me if you've already heard this one. There is no reason why a joke should not be appreciated more than once."* Have you heard these jokes before? In various languages? You probably have, if you're Jewish with a certain distinct identity, particularly if descended from Eastern European culture and Yiddish speech. According to Elliot Oring in *The First Book of Jewish Jokes* (2018), a collection of witty notions from Jews was published in 1812 by Lippmann Moses Buschenthal, a former synagogue leader. A translation from an earlier collection, *Anecdotes, Pranks, and Notions of the Children of Israel,* was published by an unknown author under the pseudonym Judas Asher.

They probably didn't know the one about the Jewish mother who checked to see if all the leaven had been removed from her son's room before Passover. She sees some white powder on his desk. Horrified, she shrieks, "What is this?"

"I'm snorting coke," he admits.

Mother: "Oh, thank God, I thought it was flour."

Jewish jokes typically relate to so-called Jewish issues: holidays, food, family, conflict, work, anti-Semitism, logic, money or the lack of it, making it in a *goyish* world, or simply a smart, self-deprecating punch line. Jeremy Dauber, in his 2017 *Jewish Comedy*, lists seven major conceptual rubrics or types of Jewish humor: *(1) Response to persecution and anti-Semitism. (2) Satirical gaze at social and communal norms. (3) Bookish, witty, intellectual play. (4) Vulgar, raunchy, and body-obsessed. (5) Mordant, ironic, and metaphysically oriented. (6) Folksy, everyday Jews. (7) Blurred and ambiguous nature of Jewishness.*

But none of that explains what exactly a joke is. Definitions vary with the humorist. As succinct as any is offered by Leo Rosten in his *Giant Book of Laughter* (1989): "A joke is a very short short-story, carefully structured, a very brief narrative designed to reach a comedic climax through skillful cues, deliberate miscues, and sudden surprise.... It's a trigger of laughter ... the distribution of tantalizing leads, the planting of totally deceptive expectations." Or, as Devorah Baum suggests in *The Jewish Joke* (2018), "It has a finger on the pulse of not only the present moment but the historical one.... It's a feel for the audience's narrative expectations and the ability to confound these with a sudden reversal or change of direction: what is known in the gag trade as a switcheroo. So, when we're expecting a gift, we get a sale, where we're expecting romance, we get realism, where we're expecting a positive, we get a second negative."

While humor is the universal agent to humanize the scuffing elements of life, there are good jokes, and there are lame jokes. God was the very first humorist, laughing at what He made—a world too illogical and implausible to be the revealed truth. Was it good, very good, or just unprecedented? Omnipotent or not, He would find out in time. He broke into a smile when He told a cluster of angels that He created man in His own image, but He was unsure whether the man laughed—or was upset when he looked in a mirror. God also knew that some of His jokes were on the wrong side of funny, as recounted by Michael Krasny in *Let There Be Laughter* (2016), quoting his friend Douglas Jerrold:

> God's plan got off to a happy beginning
> But Adam ruined it by sinning!
> I hope the whole story
> Will end in God's glory
> But right now, the wrong side is winning.

As an underachiever, He did the best He could. He actually was aware of the joke that when Eve first looked at Adam and saw that he was naked, she told him he needed to get his suit pressed. And speaking of looking, the comic Red Buttons (1919–2006) once overheard her twitting Adam, *"What do you mean, the boys don't look like you?"*

Or, take Sarah, whose childbearing years were long gone and whose husband was pushing one hundred. Although told she could expect a child, she wasn't exactly looking forward to sex. Abraham, however, assured that his masculinity was still viable, could hardly wait. God hadn't told them about miracles, but nine months later, Isaac was born. His Hebrew name translates as "laughter" because she laughed at her gynecologist all the way to the hospital.

Consider the following, also from Red Buttons:

> The great psychoanalyst Freud,
> Had the upper class very anneud,
> Preaching, "You cannot be rid
> Of the damn lustful Id,
> So, it might as well be enjeud."

And speaking of Freud, his book, *Jokes and Their Relation to the Unconscious* (1905), is a serious discussion of Biblical anxiety, sexual repression, and inhibitions going back to stories in the Talmud and the Midrash, but more often to the East European Ashkenazim. Shtetl life was a source of life-saving humor to the folks who needed something or somebody to joke with in order to survive:

> "Sam, why are you sitting there naked with your shoes on?"
> "I'm all alone; nobody comes to see me."
> "So, why the shoes?"
> "Maybe someone will come."

Here is Freud's position on self-criticism or masochism, unique among Jews: Are there many other instances of a people making fun of themselves to a similar degree? Probably not. Jack Benny made a fortune being stingy. And here is the self-lacerating comedian Woody Allen, who admitted that after he was born, the obstetrician slapped his mother. And the joke about the wise men of Chelm, an actual city in Poland:

> A Jew from Chelm visits Warsaw. He hears the shammes ask a riddle: "Who is my father's son but not my brother?" "It's me," the shammes says. The Chelm Jew is impressed. He returns home and asks, "Who is my father's son but not my brother?" No one knows. So, the Chelmite answers, "The shammes in Warsaw."

Humor is different from jokes. The word, originally applied to bodily fluids, was related to temperaments and dispositions. It eventually took on the issues of drollery, unreasonable behavior, the balance between irrational or immoral conduct. For the joke to be stereotypically Jewish, it should express Jewish characteristics and susceptibility, instantly recognizable to Jews of every level of intelligence, every level of religious observance, every twisted suggestion of authority, morality or neurosis.

Lenny Bruce (1925–1966) defined mid-twentieth-century Jewish comedy—not as telling jokes, but as telling the truth. Only forty-one when he tragically died from a drug overdose, his definitions of Jewish and Goyish characteristics have become classics: *Count Basie is Jewish. Ray Charles is Jewish. Eddie Cantor is Goyish. B'nai Brith is Goyish; Hadassah, Jewish. Kool-Aid is Goyish. Evaporated milk is Goyish. Chocolate is Jewish; Fudge is Goyish. Fruit Salad is Jewish. Lime Jello is Goyish. White bread is Goyish; pumpernickel, Jewish. Instant potatoes, Goyish. Black cherry soda, very Jewish. Bosoms are Jewish. Baton-twirling very Goyish.*

And remember—urban neurosis and agony are at the root of much Jewish humor:

> Hans Goldstein, an elderly Jew, appeared at Nazi headquarters to answer to an ad in the local paper.
> "Are you aware that this ad calls for a young, strong Aryan?"
> "Ja," answers Goldstein.
> "But you must be seventy years old!"
> "Seventy-two," says Goldstein.
> "You're as skinny as a rail!"
> "Skinnier!" answers Goldstein.
> "Aryan? You are obviously a Jew." Goldstein agrees. "Then why the hell did you come here?" fumes the officer.
> Goldstein: "I just want you to know that on me you shouldn't depend."

And another:

> A man's watch breaks. He goes to a store where he sees an enormous watch in the window. The Jewish clerk behind the counter tells him, "I don't fix watches. I perform circumcisions."
> "Then why do you have a large watch in your window?"
> "What else should I display in my window?"

What is Comedy? One variety is light entertainment or an amusing sketch based on pop stereotypes, the ridiculous complaints of unsophisticated, whimsical, or erratic individuals. American Jewish humor was created in large part by Jewish comics who poked fun at the immigrant experience, as well as at the frustrations of everyday life on the golden sidewalks of the big cities.

> "My husband thinks he's a refrigerator," moans Mrs. Klein to her psychiatrist.
> "What evidence do you have of that?" Dr. Steele asks.
> "He sleeps with his mouth open."
> "Why does that bother you?"
> Mrs. Klein: "I can't get any sleep with that little light on all night."

What is Wit? It suggests intellectual quickness, cleverness without feeling, a flash of impersonal mental or satirical skill, a talent for exhibiting seemingly incongruous or dissimilar things. It implies swift or spirited conversational repartee:

> "May I ask which is your synagogue?"
> "I'm a long-time member of B'nai Joseph."
> "What a coincidence! I have been the rabbi there for seven years, and I've never seen you there."
> "Well, rabbi, I never said I was a fanatic!"

Irony conveys discrepancies between literal meaning and its opposite, deliberately contrary to what is expressed. As a Yiddish saying goes, "A man isn't honest just because he never had a chance to steal."

> How about the two minks about to be killed for their fur: "Next week is Yom Tov. See you in shul."

God is still chuckling as He remembers how Noah struggled to squeeze two elephants and two giraffes into the ark. It was hard enough to find room for their long noses and long necks, to say nothing of the protuberances of other ill-assorted pairs of bipeds, quadrupeds, and winged and crawling creatures. Space also had to be found for a couple of flies whose buzzing and humming and biting was driving the crew to distraction. Which conveniently reminds me of a story that has very little to do with Noah and his troubles, but is definitely amusing:

> The Emperor of Japan, having reached the limits of tolerance for annoying flies, offers a large reward to any samurai who could rid him of the pests. Three warriors show up, each brandishing a sharp and shiny sword. Number 1 swings at a fly; it falls in two pieces! The emperor is impressed. What can Number 2 do? He swings his sword and lo! The fly drops in four pieces! Steps up Number 3, a Jewish warrior. He swings his sword and whoosh. The fly is still moving overhead at record speed! The emperor is disappointed. Explains Number 3, "Cutting a fly in half is difficult, your Honor, cutting it in quarters is more so I admit, but—circumcision?"

Would you like another Oriental joke?

> A Jewish man acknowledged that the Chinese are very wise. The Chinese man said it was because their culture is over four thousand years old. The Jewish man replied that his culture is over five thousand years old. "That's impossible! Where did the Jews eat for a thousand years?"

Or this one?

"The problem with Jewish food is that two days later you're hungry again."

Restaurant jokes?

Two men enter a Jewish diner. Both order coffee. One tells the waiter to make sure his cup is clean. The waiter returns with both cups: "Who asked for the clean cup?"

Or this one?

A man insists his waiter should taste his chicken soup. Waiter: "Is something wrong? It's the same soup you have been having here for ten years. But if you insist, I'll taste it. Where is the spoon?" Customer: "Aha!"

Then there are stories about professional and academic success, highly prized accomplishments in Jewish circles. Ask any Jew what he is proudest of, and he will say *nachas* from his children. He might casually mention the celebrated thesis of his psychiatrist daughter or his disappointment that his son accepted a cabinet position in Washington when he could have become a doctor on Madison Avenue:

A Jewish mother at the beach: "Help! Help! My son, the clinical orthopedist, is drowning!"

Or this one ...

A doctor, a physical chemist, and a lawyer argue about whose profession is the oldest. The doctor: "There must have been a doctor in the Garden of Eden to sew up Adam's rib."
"No," replies the physical chemist, "God needed assistance to change chaos into the order of the universe."
The lawyer has the final word. "You're both wrong. There must have been a lawyer there first to create the chaos."

A good legal system began when God gave the Ten Commandments to Moses with a mandate to change a chaotic society into a civilized culture with balancing values—liberty and law. Now, that is funny.

Here is a story about the Jewish wholesalers who run the garment industry and dress America:

Sam and Irv are having a terrible time producing saleable styles and fabrics. Sam decides to end it all and climbs to the roof of the twenty-story building. As he hurtles past their competitors' shops on his way down, he sizes up their inventory. "Cut velvet!" he yells as he drops past his own window.

Then there are ribald stories.

A person is without honor in three places: in prison, in the bathhouse, and in the outhouse.

Or this one?

A traveling salesman came to the door of Dave Katz's bungalow in the Catskills. "My car is out of gas. It's too far to walk to the station. Do you have a room I could sleep in tonight?"
"The only room I have is my son's. You'll have to sleep with him."
The salesman blanched, "My God, I'm in the wrong joke!"

And last—for now.

Two men from Mars greet each other, sensing each other's ultrasonic vibrations. "By the way, what's your name?"
"67M648. And yours?"
"539Z24."
"That's funny," the first Martian says, "You don't look Jewish."

The popularity of vaudeville in the early years of the twentieth century boded well for immigrant eastern European entertainers who were tolerated as a minority group alongside blackface minstrelsy and Italian slapstick because audiences enjoyed laughing at cultures they viewed as inferior to their own. Accents and mimicry, slang, physical and bawdy humor became hallmarks of a new breed of Jewish citified character comics, different from the earlier folksy styles of non-Jewish satirists, such as Mark Twain and Will Rogers. Jews honed their skills in the Borsht Belt Catskill Mountain resorts, graduating from stock Yiddish jokes to stock movies, to stock Las Vegas routines, to stock ethnic television, to social and political counterculture, to scripts extolling the confusion and changing nature of daily Jewish-American life.

There must be something fascinating about Jewish humor because so many volumes about it have been produced. What other people would be so eager to laugh at offensive jokes about themselves, treat their deepest religious feelings with irreverence, find so much amusement in their bodily parts, trivialize anti-Semitic material, or parade intimate reproductive functions and personal sexual experiences? There must be something fascinating about Jewish relationships as they deal with self-deprecation, neuroticism, and overbearing mothers. Jews fearlessly adopt material their grandmothers (but perhaps not their mothers) would find offensive.

That is the price of Modernity.

Joseph Telushkin, in his *Jewish Humor* (1992), bravely undertakes to review and analyze the roadmap stereotypes of how Jews got to be so funny. Genes? Guilt? Religion? Family? Vocations? Intelligence? Yes, all these and more. But as there is no *one* great point of origin or source, we will start with conversion humor, which at one time was popular because Jews believed it paved the way for acceptance into Gentile culture. Often it did not, because most Jews remained Jews—sinning or unspiritual perhaps—but still knowing who they are or who they were. Some Jews, seeking non-fundamentalist denominations, became Quakers or Unitarians or Buddhists. Some intermarried, choosing one, both, or neither faith. Some chose a greater dose of spiritualism, turning to the mysticism of Kabbalah, the ritual world of Hasidism, or nonsense:

> An American millionaire was Jewish by birth but had converted to Christianity. Walking with a hunchbacked friend when they passed a synagogue, he opined, "You know, I used to be a Jew."
> "And I used to be a hunchback," his friend replied.

And another:

> A Jew converted to Christianity. The next day his wife sees him praying in Hebrew with his tefillin.
> "Oliver," she says, "You're a Christian now"
> "Oy!" he says, slapping his forehead, "My Goyishe kop."

Or another:

> Two Jews decide to take advantage of a hundred-dollar reward for anyone willing to convert. Sam asks his friend Max to wait for him while he goes through the process.
> "Did you get the money?" asks Max when Sam returns.
> Answers Sam: "Why is money the first thing you Jews think about?"

Or this one:

> Did you hear about the Jewish man who looked up all the Cohens in the computer to check if any might be related to him? He emails a Mr. Cohen, who responds, "What makes you think I'm Jewish? I am Episcopalian, my father was Episcopalian, and my grandfather, olav ha-shalom, was Episcopalian."

14. Laughing at Love

Then there is the aggravation from the children. Don't ask.

Parent-children relations are as old as Kiddushin 31b, in which Rabbi Yochanan comments, *"Happy is he who has never seen his parents."* Sam Levenson remarked, *"Insanity is hereditary, you get it from your children"*—which is another way of saying that your mother doesn't drink in front of her children—and when she's away, she doesn't need to.

Every child has heard the mother's lament, *"Someday, you'll be a parent, and you'll know what it's like."* Then there's the one about the aged couple who want a divorce but who waited seventy-nine years until the children died.

There are jokes about children:

> The teacher asked the students to mention their age and favorite hobby. Andy: "I'm ten. I like to swim."
> Jimmy: "I'm nine and a half. I collect stamps."
> Morris: "I'm ten, and I pledge five dollars."

The Bar Mitzvah speech:

> "Today I am a man. Tomorrow I go back to the seventh grade."

And another:

> "Doctor, is a nine-year-old boy qualified to perform an appendectomy?"
> "Certainly not."
> "Okay, Melvin. You heard the doctor. Now go put it back."

And Jewish mothers:

> A Jewish mother, defined as a passive-aggressive Jewish peril, is determined to keep her children tied to her. She buys her son two Cadillacs. *He visits her, driving over in one of them.* "What's wrong? You don't like the other one?"
> What is the difference between a Jewish mother and a Rottweiler? "Eventually the Rottweiler lets go."

Sarcasm belongs to every ethnic group, although much of it has a distinctly Jewish flavor:

> "One day, Cohen and Levine were going..." begins Max to a friend.
> "Always Cohen and Levine!" interrupts his friend. "Why don't you tell about the Chinese for once?"
> "You're right," says Max. "One day, Soo Lung and Mao Tsu were going to Soo Lung's nephew's Bar Mitzvah..."

Groucho Marx wanted to join a country club in Los Angeles but was told that Jews were not admitted. (True. The Jews retaliated by building the Hillcrest Club, which rarely admitted Gentiles.) Marx, whose wife was Gentile, inquired, *"My son is half-Jewish. Do you think they'd let him go into the pool up to his knees?"*

Sex is always good for a laugh:

Asks the comic, Henny Youngman—*"Do you know what it means to come home every night to a woman who will give you a little affection, a lot of tenderness, and an ocean of love? It means you went to the wrong house, that's what it means."*

Mrs. Kranz, chair of the Jewish ladies' club, invited a famous lecturer to speak on proper etiquette. *"For instance, please explain that our rules forbid bridge players to discuss sex. What was—was."*

Tzedakah remains one of the most affirming and honored obligations of Jewish values, equal to all other commandments combined (Bava Bathra 9a). Sometimes jokes rely more on the honor the giver receives than on his warm heart or good deed.

Abner, a wealthy secular Jew, agrees to fund a Jewish elementary school on condition that no students wear yarmulkas and that his name and his wife's name, Sandy, appear prominently on the building. At the school's dedication ceremony, a large plaque was hung: **Abraham's and Sarah's School for Girls.**

Greed or overriding concentration on money also works:

A newly wealthy Jew has his silver bowl inscribed in gold: Nouveau is better than no riche at all.

Another wealthy man turns down a beggar, reciting laments about sick parents, out-of-work sons, unmarried daughters, and various incommoded others: *"If I won't give them any money, why should I give some to you?"*

A regular customer, wishing to buy a pair of shoes, asks the salesman for the price. *"For you, fifty dollars."* Noting that the customer is willing, the salesman, eager to make an extra profit, adds, *"With or without the laces?"*

"I'll take the laces."

"One shoe or both?"

And finally—

I love a Jewish joke. I really, really do.

Especially from an author who's really, really through.

Dayeinu—Enough is Enough.

Glossary

Afikomen. Matzah eaten as dessert at the end of the Passover Seder.

Aggadah. Talmudic or Midrashic stories, legends, anecdotes, or sayings.

Agunah. Desertion of a husband or lack of knowledge of his death; the wife is not allowed to remarry according to Jewish law.

Ashkenazi. Jews with heritage from Central and Eastern Europe.

Chazan. Jewish musician who helps in leading religious services.

Conservative Judaism. A form of Judaism, developed in the twentieth century, that takes a flexible approach to ritual and tradition.

Conversos. Spanish and Portuguese converted Jews.

Crypto-Jews. Jews that outwardly maintain Christianity, while secretly maintaining Jewish traditions.

Diaspora. Jews living outside the land of Israel.

Eruv. An artificial boundary surrounding a religious Jewish community permitting certain practices within it.

Gemara. Exegesis and comments on the Mishnah. The Gemara is many times larger and more detailed than the Mishnah.

Get. Bill of divorce.

Goy, Goyish. Not Jewish.

Hagaddah. Prayers and stories recited on Passover.

Halakhah. Rabbinic rulings concerned with legal matters, incumbent on Jews.

Halizah. Ceremony performed if a man refuses to marry his brother's childless widow, described in Deuteronomy 25:9–10.

Hanukkah. Eight-day holiday celebrating the victory of Judah Maccabee over Greek forces.

Haredi. Orthodox Judaism rejecting modern secular culture.

Hasidism. Orthodox Jewish traditions encompassing mystical and other tenets.

Haskalah. Secular Jewish Enlightenment movement in the nineteenth century bringing the European Enlightenment to Jews.

Holocaust. Organized persecution and destruction of European Jewry by Nazi Germany during World War II.

Hosen. Bridegroom. **Calleh**, bride.

Kabbalah. Jewish mystical tradition.

Ketubbah. Marriage document.

Kiddushin or **Erusin.** Betrothal.

Glossary

Kosher, kashrut. Food ritually prepared according to dietary laws.
Ladino. Language of Sephardic Jews, based on Spanish.
Litvak. Lithuanian Jews.
Maranos. Descendants of Spanish and Portuguese crypto-Jews who still practiced Judaism.
Matzah. Unleavened bread, eaten during Passover.
Megillah. Scroll of Esther, read during Purim.
Midrash. Morality stories and interpretations based on sacred literature.
Mikvah. Ritual bath.
Minhag. Tradition or custom.
Minyan. The minimum number of people (traditionally ten Jewish men) required for a communal prayer service.
Mishneh. Oral tradition describing Jewish law, written in the second and third centuries.
Nachas. Joy from children.
Niddah. Menstruating woman.
Orthodoxy. A form of Judaism that takes a strict approach to ritual and tradition.
Passover. Spring holiday commemorating the Exodus of Jews from Egypt.
Purim. Festival commemorating the delivery of Jews from the Persians in the time of Queen Esther.
Reform Judaism. A form of Judaism, developed in the nineteenth century, that takes a more relaxed approach to following ritual and tradition.
Rosh Hashanah. Holiday commemorating the beginning of the Jewish New Year.
Sabra. Native-born Israeli.
Seder. Traditional Passover meal
Sephardi. Jews with heritage from Spain and Portugal, together with their descendants, particularly from North Africa, Iberia, and the Middle East.
Shalom Bayit. Family harmony.
Shammes. Sexton responsible for the care of the synagogue.
Shevuot. Harvest festival commemorating the giving of the Torah on Mount Sinai.
Shiksa. Non-Jewish woman or girl. Sometimes derogatory.
Shivah. Seven days of mourning following the death of a loved one.
Shtetl. Small Jewish community or village in Eastern Europe before World War II.
Shulchan Aruch. Code of Jewish law written by Joseph Karo in the sixteenth century.
Simchat Torah. Last day of Shevuot, marking the completion of receipt of the Torah.
Sukkot. Autumn festival celebrating the harvest season after the Exodus from Egypt by living in foliage-covered huts.
Tallit. Prayer shawl.
Talmud. Jewish legal framework, consisting of the Mishnah and the Gemarah.
Torah. Scroll containing the Five Books of Moses, read in the synagogue during services.
Wimple. Torah binder.
Yichus. Family status.
Yiddish. The language spoken by Ashkenazi Jews.
Yom Kippur. Day of Atonement, ten days after Rosh Hashanah.

Selected Bibliography

Adelman, Howard Tzvi. "Law and Love: The Jewish Family in Early Modern Italy." *Continuity and Change* 16, no. 2, 2001, 283–303.
Adler, Rachel. *Engendering Judaism*. Philadelphia: Jewish Publication Society, 1998.
Alexander, Tamar. *The Heart Is My Mirror: The Sephardic Folktale*. Detroit: Wayne State University Press, 2007.
Armistead, Samuel G., and Joseph H. Silverman. *Folk Literature of the Sephardic Jews*. Berkeley: University of California Press, 1986.
Bark, Sandra, ed. *Beautiful as the Moon, Radiant as the Stars: Jewish Women in Yiddish Stories*. New York: Warner Books, 2003.
Baum, Devorah. *The Jewish Joke*. New York: Pegasus, 2018.
Bayme, Steven. *Understanding Jewish History*. KTAV, New York, 1997.
Ben-Amos, Dan, ed. *Folktales of the Jews*, Vols. I and II. Philadelphia: Jewish Publication Society, 2006.
Ben-Amos, Dan, and Jerome R. Mintz, eds. *In Praise of the Baal Shem Tov*. Lanham, MD: Roman & Littlefield, 1993.
Berger, Joseph. *The Pious Ones: The World of Hasidism and Their Battles with America*. New York: Harper Perennial, 2014.
Berger, Peter L. *The Desecularization of the World*. Grand Rapids: Eerdsman, 1999.
Biale, David. *Eros and the Jews*. New York: Basic Books, 1997.
Bin Gurion, Micha Joseph. *Mimekor Yisroel*. Edited by Emanuel bin Gorian. Bloomington: Indiana University Press, 1976.
Blady, Ken. *Jewish Communities in Exotic Places*. Northvale, NJ: Jason Aronson, 2000.
Bloch, Ivan. *Die Prostitution*. Berlin: Markus, 1912.
Brenner, Michael. *A Short History of the Jews*. Princeton: Princeton University Press, 2002.
Bristow, Edward J. *Prostitution and Prejudice*. New York: Schocken Books, 1983.
Calvino, Italo. *Italian Folktales*. Translated by George Martin. New York: Harcourt, Brace. Jovanovich, 1980.
Dauber, Jeremy. *Jewish Comedy*. New York: W.W. Norton, 2014.
Dimont, Max I. *Jews, God and History*. 2nd Edition. New York: New American Library, 1994.
Douglas, Mary. *Jacob's Tears*. Oxford: Oxford University Press, 2004.
Dreyfus, Alfred. *Five Years of My Life*. New York: McClure, Phillips and Co., 1901.
Finkelman, Yoel. *Strictly Kosher Reading*. Boston: Academic Studies Press, 2011.
Frankel, Ellen, ed. *The Jewish Spirit: A Celebration in Stories & Art*. New York: Stewart, Tabori & Chang, 1997.
Fuchs, Anne, and Florian Krobb, eds. *Ghetto Writing*. Columbia, SC: Camden House, 1999.
Gampel, Benjamin R., ed. *Crisis and Creativity in the Sephardic World, 1301–1648*. New York: Columbia University Press, 1999.
Gaster, Moses. *Ma'aseh Book: Book of Jewish Tales and Legends* (in English). Philadelphia: Jewish Publication Society, 1934.
Gerber, Jane S. *The Jews of Spain*. New York: Simon & Schuster, 1992.
Ginsberg, Louis. *The Legends of the Jews*. Philadelphia: Jewish Publication Society, 1909–1938.
Goldin, Farideh. *Wedding Song*. Hanover, NH: Brandeis University Press, 2003.
Graetz, Heinrich. *History of the Jews*. Philadelphia: Jewish Publication Society, 1891.
Greenberg, Blu. *On Women and Judaism*. Philadelphia: Jewish Publication Society, 1981.
Greenblatt, Stephen. *Will in the World: How Shakespeare Became Shakespeare*. New York: W.W. Norton, 2016.
Harris, Constance. *The Way Jews Lived: Five Hundred Years of Printed Words and Images*. Jefferson, NC: McFarland, 2009.
Hartman, Geoffrey H., and Sanford Budick, eds. *Midrash and Literature*. New Haven: Yale University Press, 1986.
Heer, Friedrich. *The Medieval World*. New York: World, 1986.
Hess, Jonathan M., Maurice Samuels, and Nadia Valmam. *Nineteenth-Century Jewish Literature*. Stanford: Stanford University Press, 2013.
Holocaust Survivor Cookbook: Collected From Around the World. Port St. Lucie, FL: Caras & Associates, 2007.
Jewish Literature: A Reader. Stanford: Stanford University Press, 2013.

Journal of Jewish Identities 8, no. 1, January 2015, pp. 23–47.
Kass, Leon R. *The Beginning of Wisdom: Reading Genesis*. New York: Simon & Schuster, 2003.
Kirchheimer, Gloria. *Devidas, Goodbye Evil Eyes: Stories*. New York: Holmes & Meier, 2000.
Kirzane, Jessica. "Ambivalent Attitudes Toward Intermarriage in the Forverts, 1905–1920." *Journal of Jewish Identitiesn* 8, no. 1, January 2015, pp. 23–47.
Krasny, Michael. *Let There Be Laughter*. New York: HarperCollins, 2016.
Kugel, James L. *The God of Old*. New York: The Free Press, 2003.
Kugel, James L. *How to Read the Bible*. New York: The Free Press, 2007.
Lamm, Maurice. *The Jewish Way in Love and Marriage*. Middle Village, NY: Jonathon David, 1991.
Lehrer, Jonah. *A Book About Love*. New York: Simon & Schuster, 2016.
Leonard, Leah W. *Jewish Cookery*. New York: Crown, 1949.
Lim, Timothy H. *The Formation of the Jewish Canon*. New Haven: Yale University Press, 2012.
Liska, Vivian, and Thomas Nolden, eds. *Contemporary Jewish Writing in Europe*. Bloomington: Indiana University Press, 2008.
Malinovich, Nadia. *French and Jewish Culture and the Politics of Identity in Early Twentieth Century*. Oxford: The Littman Library of Jewish Civilization, 2007.
Marcus, Jacob R. *The Jew in the Medieval World*. Cincinnati: Union of American Hebrew Congregations, 1938.
McGinity, Karen R. *Still Jewish: A History of Women and Intermarriage in America*. New York: New York University Press, 2009.
Miron, Dan. *From Continuity to Contiguity*. Stanford: Stanford University Press, 2010.
Moddor, Frank Montagum. *The Jew in the Literature of England*. New York: Jewish Publication Society, 1939.
Nathan, Joan. *King Solomon's Table*. New York: Alfred A. Knopf, 2017.
Navon, Chaim. *Genesis and Jewish Thought*. Brooklyn: KTAV Press, 2008.
Nolden, Thomas. *In Lieu of Memory: Contemporary Jewish Writing in France*. Syracuse: Syracuse University Press, 2006.
Oring, Elliot, ed. *The First Book of Jewish Jokes*. Bloomington: Indiana University Press, 2018.
Pagnini, Deanna L., and S. Philip Morgan. "Intermarriage and Social Distance Among U.S. Immigrants at the Turn of the Century." *American Journal of Sociology* 96, no. 2, September 1990, 405–432.
Palmer, R.R., and Joel Colton. *A History of the Modern World*. New York: Alfred A. Knopf, 1965.
Penslar, Derek J. *Shylock's Children: Economics and Jewish Identity in Modern Europe*. Oakland: University of California Press, 2001.
Peters, Sim. *Learning to Read Midrash*. Brooklyn: Lambda, 2004.
Petrovsky-Shtern, Yohanan. *The Golden Age of the Shtetl*. Princeton: Princeton University Press, 2014.
Plaskow, Judith. *Standing Again at Sinai*. San Francisco: Harper, 1990.
Prell, Riv-Ellen. *Fighting to Become American Jews: Gender and the Anxiety of Assimilation*. Boston: Beacon Press, 2000.
Rosten, Leo. *Giant Book of Laughter*. New York: Crown, 1985.
Sabar, Yona. *Folk Literature of the Kurdistani Jews*. New Haven: Yale University Press, 1982.
Sacher, Howard M. *A History of the Jews in the Modern World*. New York: Alfred A. Knopf, 2005.
Sacks, Jonathan. *Covenant and Conversation*. Jerusalem: Koren, 2009.
Samuels, Maurice. *Inventing the Israelite: Jewish Fiction in Nineteenth Century France*. Stanford: Stanford University Press, 2010.
Sasso, Sandy Eisenberg, and Peninnah Schram. *Jewish Stories of Love and Marriage*. Lanham, MD: Rowman & Littlefield, 2015.
Schwartz, Howard. *Jewish Tales of the Supernatural*. New York: Harper & Row, 1987.
Seidman, Naomi. *The Marriage Plot*. Stanford: Stanford University Press, 2016.
Shama, Simon. *The Story of the Jews*. London: Random House, 2013.
Shulvass, Moses A. *The Jews in the World of the Renaissance*. Leiden: E.J. Brill and Spertus College of Judaica Press, 1973.
Sicher, Ephraim. *Beyond Marginality: Anglo-Jewish Literature After the Holocaust*. Albany: State University of New York Press, 1986.
Telushkin, Joseph. *Jewish Humor*. New York: William Morrow, 1992.
Trachtenberg, Joshua. *Jewish Magic and Superstition*. Eastford, CT: Martino Press, 2013.
Tye, Larry. *Home Lands*. New York: Henry Holt, 2001.
Vidal, David. *A People Apart*. Oxford: Oxford University Press, 1999.
Waxman, Meyer. *A History of Jewish Literature*. New York: Bloch, 1930.
Weinberger. Leon J. *Twilight of a Golden Age: Selected Poems by Abraham Ibn Ezra*. Tuscaloosa: University of Alabama Press, 1977.
Weinreich, Beatrice Silverman, ed. *Yiddish Folktales*. New York: Yivo Institute for Jewish Research, 1988.
Westheimer, Ruth K., and Mark Jonathon. *Heavenly Sex*. New York: New York University Press, 1995.
Wirth-Nesher, Hana, ed. *What Is Jewish Literature?* Philadelphia: Jewish Publication Society, 1994.
Wischnitzer, Mark. *A History of Jewish Crafts and Guilds*. Middle Village, NY: Jonathon David, 1965.
Yudkin, Leon Israel. *Jewish Writing and Identity in the Twentieth Century*. London: Croom Helm, 1982.
Zinberg, Israel. *A History of Jewish Literature*, Vol. 1. Cleveland: Case Western Reserve University Press, 1972.

Index

Numbers in **_bold italics_** indicate pages with illustrations

Aaron 63, 68–70, **_68_**
Abel 56, **_56_**, 69, 85, 107
Abigail 45
Abraham 18, 24, 35–37, 38, 52, 53, 54, 55, 58–60, 61, 62, 65, 85, 93, 150, 165, 194
Abramovitz, Albert, *Wedding Dance* 25
Abravanel, Judah (Leone Ebreo) 95–96; *Dialoghi di Amore (Conversations of Love)* 96, **_96_**, 104–6; *Tlunot al Ha-Zman (Laments Against Time)* 96
Absalom 29, 47
abstinence 20, 21, 22, 41–42, **_41_**, 70, 116, 158
Abzug, Bella 157
Aciman, André: *Out of Egypt* 142
Adam 7, 31, 32–35, **_33_**, **_34_**, 55–56, 85, 93, 134, 150–51, 164–65, 180
Adler, Rachel: *Engendering Judaism* 138
adultery 30, 45, 50, 52, 87, 88, 116, 151
advice columns 136, 160–61
Aggadot 81
Agnon, Samuel Josef: *HaRofe Ugerushato (The Doctor and Divorce)* 146, 147
Agrippa, Cornelius 138
Aguilar, Grace: *The Escape: A Tale of 1755* 123–24
Ahasuerus 48, **_48_**, 49
ahavah 21
Akiva, Rabbi 21, **_22_**, 49, 53
Alami, Solomon: *Iggeret Mussar (Ethical Epistles)* 183
Allen, Woody 195
Allston, Washington 82
Amman, Jost 105
Amnon 47, 52
Anissimov, Myriam: *Comment va Rachel (How Is Rachel?)* 141
Ansky, S. 101, **_102_**; *The Dybbuk* 102

aphrodisiacs and love spells 84, 111
Appelfeld, Aharon: *Suddenly, Love* 148
Armistead, Samuel: *Folklore Literature of the Sephardic Jews* 79
arranged marriages *see* matchmakers
art, depictions of Jews in 104–14, 127; *see also* specific artists
artifacts, examples of 186–92
arts in the Bible 180–81
Asch, Sholem: *God of Vengeance (Gott fun Nekoma)* 145
Asher, Judas: *Anecdotes, Pranks, and Notions of the Children of Israel* 193
Aubier, Dominique: *Don Quixote, Prophet of Israel?* 106
Ausubel, Nathan: *Treasury of Jewish Folklore* 91–92
Avodat Kokhavim 83
Avram, Ben: *The Wedding* 28

Baal Shem Tov (Master of the Good Name) 11, 116–17
Bak, Israel 14, 142–43
Balfour, Arthur 14, **_133_**
Ballin, Joel: *Mother and Child* **29**
Balzac, Honoré de: *Comédie Humaine* 120
Baron, Salo W. 1, 9
barrenness 30, 36, 38, 39, 44, 52, 58–59
Bathsheba **_46_**, 47–48
Baum, Devorah: *The Jewish Joke* 194
Bava Bathra 199
Beham, Hans Sebald: *Moses and Aaron* **68**
Bellow, Saul 136
Ben-Amos, Dan: *Folktales of the Jews from the Sephardic Dispersion* 96–98
ben Eliezer, Israel *see* Baal Shem Tov

ben Gamliel, Rabbi Shimon 62
ben Halafta, Jose 18
ben Isaac, Solomon *see* Rashi
Benjamin of Tudela 76
ben Maimon, Rabbi Moses *see* Maimonides; Rambam
Benny, Jack 195
Benveniste, Vidal 94; *Efer ve-Dinah* 79–80
Ben-Yehuda, Eliezer: *Complete Dictionary of Ancient and Modern Hebrew* 15, 143
Ben Yohai, Rabbi Shimon 88, 179
Berakhot 82
Bereshit Rabbah 18, 21, 22, 58
Bernstein, Moshe: *The Exiles in Cyprus* 28
betrothal gifts 22, 32, 38, 45, 53, 86
Bezalel 180
Bialik, Hayim Nahman 15; *Sefer Ha'Aggadah (Book of Legends)* 88
Biblical use of "love" 51, 62
Bin Gorian, Mischa Yosef: *Mimekor Yisroel* 87–88
Bintel Brief (Bundle of Letters) 136
birth control 31, 151, 158
Blady, Ken: *Jewish Communities in Exotic Places* 76, 175
Bloch, Ivan: *Die Prostitution* 152
Blume, Judy: *Wifey* 160
Boaz 43–44, **_44_**
Boccaccio 78
Book of Esther 49
Botticelli 49, 50
Breishit Rabba 54
bride price 22, 32, 38, 45, 53, 86
Briss, Samy: *Flight of the Beloved* 28
Broeck, Crispijn van den: Delilah shearing the hair off Samson **_43_**
Bruce, Lenny 195

205

Index

Buschenthal, Lippmann Moses 193

Cahan, Abraham: *The Rise of David Levinsky* 135–36
Cain 56, **56**, 69, 85, 107, 151, 180
Calvino, Italo: *Italian Folktales* 97–98
Caro, Joseph: *Shulchan Aruch (Prepared Table)* 79, 89
Cervantes, Miguel de: *Don Quixote* 106
Chagall, Marc 28, 50; *Expulsion from Eden* 35; *Paradise* 35
Chaucer 50
Choson Kale Mazel Tove (Joy to the Groom and Bride) 25
circumcision 36, 40, 53, 59, 62, 134, 196
concubines 35, 38, 45, 47, 49, 52
conjugal relations 20, 21, 22, 111, 134, 151, 155
Conservative Judaism 12
consummation of marriage 21, 23, 151
Cranach, Lucas the Elder 42
Curiel, D.: *Venetian Ghetto* **9**

Dante 41, 50, 78
Darwin, Charles 129
Daubner, Jeremy *Jewish Comedy* 194
Daudet, Alphonse: *Les Rois en Exil* 120
David, King 10, 21, 29, 44, 45–48, **46**, 52, 65, 106, 152, 180
Davin de Caderousse 182
Deborah 51
de Bray, Salomon 50
Delacroix, Eugène: *Algerian Jewess* 24; *The Jewish Wedding in Morocco* 24–25, 127
del Buono, Mariano 179
Delilah 42, **43**
Deuteronomy 6–7, 20, 21, 24, 30–31, 40, 44, 52–53, 55, 60, 81–82, 86, 109, 152, 164, 166, 189, 190
Dickens, Charles: *Oliver Twist* 123; *Our Mutual Friend* 123
Dinah, molestation of 39–40, 47, 62
Disraeli, Benjamin 124–25; *Tancred; Or, The New Crusade* 125
divorce 12, 23, 30, 31, 52, 53, 89, 96, 102, **121**, 146, 155, 156, 199: *see also* get
Donatello 50, 106
Doré, Gustave: *Joseph Makes Himself Known to His Brethren* **64**
dowry 22, 32, 38, 45, 53, 86
Dreyfus, Alfred 13, **13**, **14**, 122, 139, 143

du Maurier, George: *Trilby* 120
Dürer, Albrecht: *Adam and Eve* **33**, 35

Ecclesiastes 21, 24, 30, 83, 118, 148, 166, 180
Ecclesiasticus (Wisdom of Sirach; Ben Sira) 181
Edelshtat, David 131
"Egyptian" Bedroom **41**
Eleazer of Mainz, Rabbi 55
Eliezer (servant of Abraham) 37–38, 53, 165
Eliezer (son of Moses) 67, 70
Elijah 55, 86, 91, 96–97, 100
Eliot, George (Mary Anne Evans): *Daniel Deronda* 125–26
Elkanah 44–45
Englander, Nathan 154–55
Esau 18, 38, 39, 53, 55, 61, 62, 65, 69, 86, 165, 170
Esther 48–49, **48**, 166
Eve 7, 31, 32 -35, **33**, **34**, 55–56, 85, 93, 134, 164–65, 180
Exodus 6–7, 20, 41, 52, 54, 55, 66–69, **67**, 106, 151, 165–66, 180, 189
Ezekiel 44, 106, 181
Ezra 44, 53, 76, 93, 180

family, functions within 52, 53–56, 65–66
family purity 18, 19, 21, 24, 53, 70, 151, 154
Farissol, Abraham 95
feminism 138–39, 157–58, 161; *see also* wife's rights in marriage
Firestone, Shulamith 157
Foa, Eugénie: *Rachel, ou L'heritage (Rachel, or the Inheritance)* 120–21
folklore 74, 76–79, 81–92, 94–95, 96, 98, 101, 126, 145; *see also* humor
food as expression of love 164
food in the Bible 38, 164–67, 170
food rules 20, 165, 166, 167, 175
food traditions 164–78, 187, 188, 189, 196; holidays 167, 173–74; international 167, 168, 170, 174–78
Forverts (Jewish Daily Forward) 136
Frank, Anne 148–49
Frankel, Rabbi Zacharias 12
Freud, Sigmund 2; *Interpretation of Dreams* 132; *Jokes and Their Relation to the Unconscious* 195
Friedan, Betty 157
Fust, Johann 182

Gaster, Moses: *Ma'Aseh Book* 90–91

Geiger, Rabbi Abraham 12
Genesis 6, 18, 21, 24, 29, 32, 34–39, 41, 52, 54, 55, 56–65, 84–86, 93, 150–52, 155, 165, 180
Genesis Rabbah 18, 20, 33, 62, 86, 134
Gentileschi, Artemesia 50
Gerber, Jane: *Jews of Spain: A History of the Sephardic Experience* 72
Gershom 67, 70
get 30, 31, 52, 155
ghetto, Venice 8, **9**, 107
Ginsberg, Asher 15, 143
Ginzberg, Louis: *Legends of the Jews* 56–57, 89
Giorgione 50
Gittin 21, 30
Glueckel of Hameln 114–15, **115**
God: and human language 93; as matchmaker 18–19; and sex 150–61
God's love for: Abraham 35–37; David 45–47; humankind 3, 6, 7, 34–35, 49, 66, 72, 84–85; Isaac 38; Israel 50, 51, 53, 66; Jacob 62; Moses 42; Noah 57–58; Samson 42
Golden Calf 54, **67**, 68
Goldin, Farideh: *Wedding Song* 102–3
Goldin, Hyman: *The Magic Ring* 89
Goldman, Emma 138, 157
Gomer 50, 152
Goncourt, Edmond: *Manette Salomon* 120
Goncourt, Jules: *Manette Salomon* 120
Gordon, Samuel: *Shem: A Study of Sisters* 128–29
Gottlieb, Maurycy: *Jews at Prayer on the Day of Atonement* 25
Graetz, Heinrich 1, 71–72; *History of the Jews* 71–72
Greenberg, Blu: *On Women and Judaism* 138
Grégoire, Abbé Henri 101, **101**
Guggenheim, Sara Hirsch: *Aurelie Werner* 128
Gutenberg, Johann 182

Ha-am, Ahad 15, 143
Hagar 18, 29, 36, 37, 59
Haggadah 173, **173**, 179; Prague 24, 35, 50, 106; Venetian 41–42, **41**
Halachah 20, 21, 31, 81, 138, 152, 154
Halevi, Judah 49, 72–73, **73**
Haman 48, 49, 167, 187
ha-Nadi, Yehudah 81
ha-Nagid, Samuel 71

Index

Hannah 44–45
Haredi 1–2, 12, 153–56
Harizi, Judah al- 76
Hasidism 11, 12, 116–17, 144, 154, 198
Heine, Heinrich 49–50, 73, 126–27, 166
Herzl, Theodor 13, 14, 122, 143, *143*; *Altneuland (The Old-New-Land)* 144–45; *Der Judenstaat (The Jewish State)* 13, 122
Herzog, Emil *see* Maurois, André
Hilkot Ishut 155
Hillel 30, 181
Hiram 180
Hirsch, Rabbi Samson Raphael 12, 25
history: arts, artists, and craftspeople 25, 35, 179–86; early Renaissance Europe 93–101; food traditions 167, 168, 170, 171, 174–75, 176–78; Jewish (general) 7–17; Jewish Golden Age (Spain) 71–80, 93–94; late Renaissance through 18th century 104–18; 19th century America 130–31, 157; 19th century England 122–27; 19th century Europe 119–22; 19th century Germany and Austria 126–28; 20th century 132–34, 149, 156; 20th century France 141, 156–57; 20th century Middle East 142
Hogarth, William: *The Quarrel with Her Jewish Protector* 113
Holocaust Survivor Cookbook 176–78
Holofernes 50
Hosea 20, 23, 47, 50, 53, 111, 152
Hullin 53
humor, traditions of 193–200
husband's responsibilities in marriage 20, 21, 22, 23, 24, 54, 74, 155

Ibn Adret, Rabbi Solomon, of Barcelona 186
Ibn Daud, Abraham 71
Ibn Ezra, Abraham 73
Ibn Ezra, Moses 72
Ibn Gabirol, Solomon: *Keter Malkuth (Royal Crown)* 72
Ibn Yarchi, Abraham: *Ha-Manhig* 24
Immanuel of Rome (Immanuel Giudeo) 78–79; *Machberoth* 79
incest and inbreeding 29, 47, 52, 56, 151
infertility 30, 36, 38, 39, 44, 52, 58–59
intermarriage 23, 40, 42, 44, 52–53, 62, 65, 113, 123, 125,
126, 127, 128, 129, 136, 148, 149, 154, 199
Isaac 18, 36, 37–38, 53, 55, 59–61, 62, 65, 165, 194
Isaiah 6, 20, 54, 57, 109, 137, 156, 182, 189
Ishmael 18, 29, 36, 37, 38, 55, 59, 60
Israels, Jozef 25, 35; *A Jewish Wedding* 25
Isserles, Moses 24

Jacob 18–19, 38–41, 47, 53, 55, 61–63, 65, 69, 85–86, 150, 165, 170
Jacobson, Howard: *The Finkler Question* 141–42
Jeremiah 21, 39, 91
Jewish entertainers 198; *see also* specific names
Jewish languages 14, 93–103
Jewish life, maintenance in diaspora 94–95
Jewish recipes 164, 167–78
Jhabvala, Ruth Prawer 156
Jonathan 21, 29, 45
Jong, Erica: *Fear of Flying* 159
Joseph 39, *40*, 41, 47, 62–65, *64*, 69, 165
Joshua 42, 70, 152–53
Jud Suss 115, *116*
Judah 7, 53, 64, 65, 152, *153*
Judges 42, 152
Judith 50

Kabbalah 83–84, 110, 146, 198
Kaplan, Anatoli: *Golden Wedding* 29
kashrut 20, 165, 166, 167, 175
Kaufmann, Isidor: *Child with Lulav* **188**
Keats, John: *Ode to a Nightingale* 43
ketubbah (marriage contract) 23–24, 30, 54, 74, 79–80, **188**
Ketubbot 30, 129
kiddushin 23; *see also* marriage ceremony
Kiddushin (Talmud/Midrash) 20, 23, 53, 54, 55, 199
Kirchner, Paul: *The Wedding* 25
Klimt, Gustav 50
Koheleth 180–81
Kompert, Leopold: *Der Dorfgeher (The Village Peddler)* 127
Kops, Bernard 141
Kranz, Rabbi Jacob (Dubner Maggid) 77
Krasny, Michael: *Let There Be Laughter* 194

Laban 18, 37–38, 39, 53, 61, 86, 165
Landers, Ann (Esther Lederer) 161

languages, Jewish 14, 93–103; *see also* Yiddish
Leah 19, 39, 61, 62, 86
Lemlich Shavelson, Clara 138
Levenson, Sam 199
LeVine, Jay 92
Levita, Elia: *Bovo-Bukh* 99–101
Leviticus 7, 19, 52, 59, 81–82, 102, 151, 152, 166, 175
Leviticus Rabbah 134
Levy, Alphonse 119; *Hozen (Bridegroom)* **120**; *Matzah Gnebflich (Matzo Balls)* **167**
Levy, Mrs. Esther 166
Levy, Uriah Phillips 130
Lewis, Mary Anne (Mrs. Benjamin Disraeli) 125
Leyden, Lucas van: *The Expulsion from Paradise* 34
libido 33, 42, 47, 85, 87, 95, 105, 134, 150–61
Lilith 82, 85
literature: Jewish Golden Age (Spain) 71–80, 95–96; late Renaissance through 18th century 104–18; Midrash 81–92; 19th century England 122–27; 19th century Europe 119–26; 19th century Germany and Austria 126–28; 19th century Hebrew 135; 19th century Russia 128–30; 20th century 134–45; 20th century England 141–42; 20th century France 139–41; 20th century Palestine and Israel 144–45, 146–48; Yiddish 84, 90, 99–102, 144, 145–46
Lot and his family 35, 58, 59, 151
love: between husband and wife 18, 20, 21, 23, 24, 30, 36, 37, 38, 39, 48, 54, 77, 86, 88, 93, 117, 122, 137–38; between siblings 29, 69–70, 74–75, 79–80, 107; of children for parents 55, 62, 63, 65, 87; of country 130, 145; definitions of 21; friendship-love 21, 29, 45, 104; humankind's for God 3, 6, 21, 49, 60, 96, 104, 148; of Jews for Israel 145; of parents for children 29, 36, 53, 55, 59, 87, 90, 107, 108, 114–15; romantic 19, 38, 45, 74, 77, 86, 112–13, 127, 134, 155, 157, 160; same-sex 52, 72, 145, 151; spiritual 49; unequal, of parents for children 38, 55, 61, 62, 165; *see also* God's love
Luna, Beatrice de 106–7

Maimon, Rabbi Solomon ben Joshua: *Autobiography (Lebengeschichte)* 117–18

Index

Maimonides, Moses 19–20, *19*, 24, 30, 54, 83, 170, 179, 182; *Essay on Intercourse* 73–74; *Guide for the Perplexed* 9–10, 21–22; *Mishneh Torah (Hilchot Mamrim)* 53, 180; *see also* Rambam
Malachi 30, 53, 55
Malamud, Bernard 136; *The Magic Barrel* 137
Manasseh ben Israel 109–10, *109*, 184; *Hope of Israel* 109
Mapu, Abraham, *Ahavat Tsiyon (Love of Zion)* 135
Marlowe, Christopher: *The Jew of Malta* 107
marriage: ceremony and rituals 22–28, 32; husband's responsibilities 20, 21, 22, 23, 24, 54, 74, 155; levirate 30–31, 44, 152; preparations for 19, 22, 25; purposes of 20; wife's rights in 21–22, 23, 24, 30, 31, 54, 85, 138, 155
Marx, Groucho 199
Masaccio: *Expulsion of Adam and Eve from Eden* 35
Master E.S. 42
Master of the Barbo Missal 179–80
masturbation 151, 160
matchmakers 19, 38, 91, 95, 107, 135, 137, ; *see also* Eliezer (servant of Abraham); God
Maupassant, Guy de: *Mont Oriol* 120
Maurois, André: *Climates* 140
McPartland, John: *Sex in Our Changing World* 158
Megillah 49, 61, 187
Meir, Rabbi 90
Mekhilta 20
Menachos 21, 152
Mendele the Bookseller *see* Sforim, Mendele Mokher
Mendelssohn, Felix 112
Mendelssohn, Fromet Guggenheim 112
Mendelssohn, Moses 11, *12*, 111–12
Meyer, Henri: *The Traitor: The Degradation of Alfred Dreyfus* 14
Micah 130
Michal 45, 46
Michelangelo 35, 50, 106
Midrash 81–92
mikvah 19, 25
Milton, John 49; *Samson Agonistes* 42
Miriam 66, 68, 70, 180
Mishneh Torah 19, 21, 22, 23, 53, 81, 106, *106*, 155, 180
Modena, Leone da 108, 109;

Hayye Yehuda (Life of Judah) 109; *Historia de'ritti hebraici (History of Jewish Rites)* 31, 109
Modern (Neo-Orthodox) Judaism 12, 25
monogamy 18, 22, 32, 38, 160; *see also* polygamy
Montefiore, Judith Cohen ("A Lady"): *The Jewish Manual* 166
Mordechai 48, 49
Moses 7, 21, 41, 42, 53, 54, 66–70, 66, 68, 151, 165, 173, 181
Mozart, Wolfgang 50
Muchnik, Michael: *The Ring and the Rose* 28
musical traditions 180

Nachmanides (Ramban) 36, 65
Naomi 29, 43, 44, *44*
Nathan 46, 47, 48
Nathan, Joan 174–75
Nedarim 54, 179
Nehemiah 44, 181
niddah (laws on family purity) 18, 19, 21, 24, 53, 70, 151, 154
Niddah (tractate) 151
Noah 57–58, *57*, 93, 151, 165, 196
Noah, Mordechai Manuel 130
Numbers 69–70, 88, 165, 180, 181, 190
Nuremberg Chronicle 57

Oholiab 180
Oppenheim, Moritz Daniel 25, 127; *Scenes of Traditional Jewish Life: The Wedding* 25
Oppenheimer, Joseph 115, *116*
oral Torah *see* Mishneh Torah
Oring, Elliott: *The First Book of Jewish Jokes* 193
Orthodox Judaism 12, 19–20, 28, 31, 138, 149, 153–56, 157, 158, 180, 189; Haredim 2, 12, 154, 155
Oz, Amos 147, 148; *My Michael* 147; *A Tale of Love and Darkness* 146–47
Ozick, Cynthia 136

Paley, Grace: *Disturbances of Men* 138–39
Pann, Abel 35
Parenzo, Meir 106
Parsons, Charles: Turkish couple getting married *26*
Peninnah 44–45
Peretz, Isaac Leib 144, 145
Pesachim 193
Pesikta da Rab Kahana 88
Petachia of Ratisbon 76
Petrarch 78
Phillips, Jonas 130
Pinter, Harold 141

Pirkei Avot 54
Plaskow, Judith: *Standing Against Sinai: Judaism from a Feminist Perspective* 138
Pogrebin, Lettie Cottin 157
Pollak, Jacob: *Ma'aseh Buch (Book of Stories)* 84, 86
polygamy 10, 18, 19, 38–38, 44–45, 55; *see also* specific names
Pomerantz, Rachel: *Peeto Alta Hashemesh (Suddenly the Sun Rose)* 155
pornography 113, 158, 159
Potiphar's wife *40*, 41, 47
Prenner, Anton Joseph von: *Tower of Babel 94*
printing 10, 94, 98, 104, *105*, 109, 142–43, 182, 184
prohibition on graven images 6–7, 35, 106
prohibitions on sex 52, 53, 151–52
promiscuity 111, 151
prostitutes and prostitution 10, 42, 62, 95, 111, 113, 145, 152–53, 155
Proust, Marcel: *À la recherche du temps perdu (Remembrance of Things Past)* 139–40
Proverbs 6, 21, 24, 53, 54, 55, 59, 63, 151
Pyne, Anne Forer 157

Rabban Gamaliel 88
Rabban Ze'ev 50
The Rabbi Presides Over a Divorce 121
Rabinovich, Solomon Naumovich *see* Shalom Aleichem
Rabinyan, Dorit: *All the Rivers* 148
Rachel 18–19, 38–39, 44, 53, 61, 62, 85–86, 96, 165
Rahab 152–53
Rambam (Rabbi Moses ben Maimon) 83, 116
Ramban (Nachmanides) 36, 65
rape 40, 41, 47, 52, 59, 65, 158
Rappaport, Shloyme Zanvi *see* Anski, S.
Rashi 21, 36–37, 54, 69, 70, 82, *82*, *83*, 179; *Commentary on the Tractates of the Babylonian Talmud* 9
Raskin, Saul 50
Rav or Rava (Rabbi Abba Areka) 20, 55, 193
Ravad (Rabbi Avrohom ben David of Provencal) 20
Ravnitky, Yehoshua 88
Rebecca (character in Ivanhoe) 123
Rebecca (Matriarch) 18, 23, 37–38, *37*, 39, 53, 55, 61, 62, 165

recipes: Armenian Chicken with Applesauce 175; Asparagus Tart Remembered from South Africa 177; Babka 168; Bagel 169; Carrot Tsimmes (A Fuss Over Carrots) 171; Charoseth 173; Cheese Puffs 169; Cheese Spread Remembered from Kolosvar, Hungary 178; Chicken Soup 170; Corn Meal Pudding 171; Easy Honey Cake Cookies 174; Flanken 172; Fruit Cake Remembered from Occupied Paris 177; Gefilte Fish 170; German Cookies 176; Great Brisket 172; Helzl 169; Herring and Apple Salad 168; Kreplach Dough Remembered from Smooch, Poland 177; Mandel Broit Remembered from Lebow, Latvia 177; Matzah Apple Kugel 174; Moroccan Moufleta 176; Neshe's Halishkes (Sweet and Sour Stuffed Cabbage) 164; Noodle Pudding (Lukshen Kugel) 171; Pitchah 169; Potato Latkes 167; Red Lentil Soup 170; Rose Michaels' Borsht 170; Ruggaleh Dough Remembered from Sighet, Romania 176; Russian Galushki 175; Sally Feldman's Stuffing 172; Shakshuka (Egg Mishmash) 169; Yemenite Locusts 175
Reform Judaism 12, 27, 180
religious and symbolic arts and crafts 179–92
Rembrandt van Rijn 35, 42, 48, 49, 184; etching of Rabbi Manasseh ben Israel *109*; *Joseph and Potiphar's Wife* ***40***, 41
Reni, Guido 41
Reuwich, Erhard: *Jewish Moneylender **185***
Rojas, Fernando de: *Tragicomedia de Calisto y Melibea (Celestina)* 95, ***95***
roles of family members 52, 53–56, 65–66
Rose, Ernestine 157, ***157***
Rosten, Leo: *Giant Book of Laughter* 194
Roth, Henry 136; *Call It Sleep* 136–37
Roth, Philip 136, 159; *Portnoy's Complaint* 158–59
Rothschild, Leopold, marriage to Marie Peruga 26, ***27***
Rowlandson, Thomas: *Ladies Trading on Their Own Bottom **114***; *The Jew Rabbi Turn'd to a Christian* 113–14

Rubens, Peter Paul 42, 49; *Bathsheba at the Fountain* 48
Rubin, Reuven 48; *The God Seekers* 35
Ruth 24, 29, 43, 44, ***44***
Ryback, Issachar Ber: *Wedding in a Village* 25

Saadiah Gaon 20
Sabar, Yona: *The Folk Literature of the Kurdistani Jew* 76
Samson 42–43, ***43***
Samuel 45, 83
1 Samuel 21, 29, 45, 55, 82–83, 91
2 Samuel 29, 45, 46, 47, 52, 180
Sand, George: *Chateau de Desertes* 120
Sanhedrin 30, 58, 61, 81
Sarah (Matriarch) 18, 35–37, 38, 44, 52, 54, 55, 58, 59, 60, 85, 96, 150, 165, 194
Sarah (wife of Shabbtai Zvi) 10, 111
Saul, King 45, ***82***, 83
Schaps, Malka *see* Pomerantz, Rachel
Schatz, Boris 15, 143
Schechter, Solomon 182
Scheits, Halma: *David Admiring Bathsheba **46***
Schneiderman, Rose 157
Schneuer, David: *First Meeting* 28
Schnorr von Carolsfeld, Julian: *Fleeing from Gomorrah **60***; *Joseph Being Sold by His Brothers into Slavery **63***; *Moses Killing an Egyptian **66***
Schoffer, Peter 182
Schwartz, Howard: *Jewish Tales of the Supernatural* 74–76
Schwartz-Bart, André: *Le Dernier des Justes (The Last of the Just)* 140
Scott, Sir Walter: *Ivanhoe* 123
Second Commandment 6–7, 35, 106
seduction 33, 41, 52, 59, 152
Sefer Ha'Aggadah (Book of Legends) 88–91
Sefer ha-Zohar (Book of Splendor) 83–84
Seixas, Gershom Mendes 130
sexuality 33, 42, 47, 85, 87, 95, 105, 134, 150–61
Sforim, Mendele Mokher: *Fishke der Krumer (Fishke the Lame)* 143–44
Shabbat (Tractate) 21, 52, 62, 101, 117
Shahor, Chaim (Hayyim) 35, 50, 106
Shakespeare, William 104, 107; *The Merchant of Venice* 107–8

Shalom Aleichem 143; *Tevye the Dairyman* 129
sibling rivalry 38, 39, 56, 61, 62–65, 85, 86
Sidgwick, Mrs. Alfred *see* Ullmann, Cecily
Silverman, Joseph H.: *Folklore Literature of the Sephardic Jews* 79
Singer, Isaac Bashevis 145–46
Socrates 77
Solomon, King 24, 47, 48, 49, 76, 118, 180, 181; *Shir haShirim (Song of Songs/Song of Solomon)* 49–50, 72–73
Solomon, Simeon 50
Sotah 20, 33, 54, 74
Spark, Muriel 156
Spenser, Edmund: *Marriage Ode—Epithalamium* 49
Spinoza, Baruch 110–11, 146
Steinem, Gloria 157
Stern, Steve: *The Wedding Jester* 137–38
Stoppard, Tom 141
Strange, Robert, after Guercino, Esther beseeching Ahasuerus ***48***
Struck, Hermann: *Havdalah **188***
The Sword of Moses 84

Taanit 19
Talmud Bavli 47
Tamar (daughter of King David) 29, 47, 52
Tamar (daughter-in-law of Judah) 152, ***153***
Telushkin, Josepy: *Jewish Humor* 198
Tintoretto, Jacopo 41
Titian 35
Torah *see* Mishneh Torah; specific books
traditions: food 164–78, 187, 188, 189, 196; humor 193–200; music 180
Tubal-Cain 180
Tzvi, Shabbtai *see* Zvi, Shabbtai

Ullmann, Cecily: *Scenes of Jewish Life* 141
ultra–Orthodox Judaism 1–2, 12, 153–56
Uriah 47

Van Buren, Abigail (Pauline Philips) 161
Veit, Philip 112
Veronese 49
Vilna Gaon 11, 21
Vivaldi 50
Vogelweide, Walther von der: *My Brother Man* 76
Voltaire 124

Wajsbrot, Cecile: *La Trahison (Betrayal)* 156–57
Warshavski, Mark 29–30
Weill, Alexandre: *Braendel* 121–22
Weill, Shraga 50
wife's rights in marriage 21–22, 23, 24, 30, 31, 54, 85, 138, 155
William of Paris 82
Wischnitzer, Mark 179; *A History of Jewish Crafts and Guilds* 183
The Wisdom of the Chaldeans 84

Wissenschafft des Judentums 126
Witch of Endor **82**, 83

Yad Ishut 54
Yebamoth 20
Yehoshua, A.B.: *Molkho (Five Seasons)* 147, 148
yichud 21
Yiddish: in America 131, 136; curses in 98–99; in Europe 93, 101–2, 103, 119, 129, 134, 141, 184; literature in 84, 90, 99–102, 144, 145–146; opposition to 101, 143; origins of 98, 101
Yossei 54
Youngman, Henny 199

Zalman, Rabbi Elijah ben Shlomo 11, 21
Zangwill, Israel: *The Melting Pot* 135, 156
Zipporah 53, 70
Zunz, Leopold: *Zur Geschichte und Literatur (On History and Literature)* 126
Zvi, Shabbtai 10–11, **11**, 111, 114